The Economics of Retailing and Distribution

To Joe:

In appreciation

of our shared interests

The Economics of Retailing and Distribution

Roger R. Betancourt

Professor of Economics, University of Maryland, College Park, USA

Edward Elgar

Cheltenham, UK • Northampton, MA, USA

Published by
Edward Elgar Publishing Limited
Glensanda House
Montpellier Parade
Cheltenham
Glos GL50 1UA
UK

Edward Elgar Publishing, Inc.
136 West Street
Suite 202
Northampton
Massachusetts 01060
USA

A catalogue record for this book
is available from the British Library

Library of Congress Cataloguing in Publication Data

Betancourt, Roger R.
　　The economics of retailing and distribution/Roger R. Betancourt.
　　　　p. cm.
　　Includes bibliographical references and index.
　　1. Retail trade. 2. Marketing. I. Title.
　　HF5429.B467　　2005
　　381'.1—dc22

2004050640

ISBN 1 84376 925 5 (cased)

Typeset by Cambrian Typesetters, Frimley, Surrey
Printed and bound in Great Britain by MPG Books Ltd, Bodmin, Cornwall

Contents

Tables

Preface

The idea for this book arose as a result of my long-term collaboration with David Gautschi. While on sabbatical from the University of Maryland in 1996, I held the Kermit O. Hanson Chair at the Graduate School of Business of the University of Washington. There, David and I co-taught a Ph.D. Seminar on 'The Economics of Retail Systems'. It became clear to us that the ideas we had developed on the role of distribution services in retail systems needed to be systematically integrated with a broad range of literature in marketing and economics in order to reach their full potential. We thought it made sense to write a book designed to accomplish this task.

Unfortunately for the book project, David made a permanent move from academia to a full-time job in industry with Deloitte and Touche in 1998. Thus, I faced the choice of scrapping the book altogether or going ahead with the project by myself. Towards the end of 1999, and after many months of indecision, I decided to write the book alone for two reasons. First, the original idea for the book seemed as sound in 1999 as in 1996. Second, since the Spring of 1997, I have taught a graduate seminar on 'The Economics of Retail Systems' once a year at Maryland. This seminar facilitated progress on my chapters in the early going and made the task of writing the book alone less onerous in various ways. Perhaps most importantly, it generated a setting that elicited comments by several cohorts of Ph.D. students in economics, and recently one in marketing, for which I am thankful.

I am indebted to Menglin Cao for careful reading of several chapters (2–4, and 6). Jeff Perloff commented on Chapter 3, Mike Smith and Dave Malueg on Chapter 5, Nuno Limão on Chapter 7, Chuck Ingene and Debbie Minehart on Chapter 8 and Arturs Kalnins on Chapter 9. To all of them my sincere thanks without incrimination.

Also, it was my good fortune that Brian Ratchford moved to Maryland's R.H. Smith School of Business in the Fall of 1999. His interests in the intersection of marketing and economics overlap with my own and his presence nearby has facilitated and encouraged completion of this project. Similarly, it has been my good fortune that our earlier ideas have been adopted by others, ranging from Ph.D. students and assistant professors to senior scholars. I have tried to acknowledge these efforts by bringing in their contributions at the relevant points in the book. I offer my apologies to anyone whom I have neglected in so doing.

I must acknowledge the support of Jose Miguel Mugica, who invited me to present the book's ideas at various forums in Spain during critical stages in their development. Earlier versions of the work in the book have also been presented at seminars, workshops and conferences in the US and abroad. While these are too numerous to mention individually, I would like to thank participants for their comments, and organizers for their invitations.

Underlying the writing of the book are three guiding principles. First, earlier material on the economic role of distribution services has been integrated with new material. Second, whenever possible an attempt is made to develop novel material as a result of investigating systematically the economic role of distribution services in settings not subjected to this scrutiny before. Last but not least, an effort is made to cover particular topics intensely rather than all potential topics superficially. Thus, the book aims to provide a basis for future extensions and applications as well as an integration of previous findings and insights with strands of literature in marketing and economics.

Last but not least my wife, Alicia, has supported all the activities associated with this endeavor without complaints and often with enthusiasm. This has made my life very pleasant.

Abbreviations

ARCO	Atlantic Richfield Company
ATM	Automatic teller machine
BC	Betty Crocker
BLS	Bureau of Labor Statistics
CES	Constant elasticity of substitution
CKR	Chevalier, Kashyap and Rossi
COL	Cost of living index
CP	Channel profit
CPI	Consumer Price Index
C(Capital)	Cost of capital
C(GS)	Cost of goods sold to retailers
C(M)	Cost of manufacturing
C(R)	Costs of retailing (excludes cost of goods sold)
DH	Duncan Hines
DVD	Digital video disk
EDI	Electronic data interchange
EDLP	Everyday low pricing strategy
EVA	Economic value added
FF	Franchise fee
FS	Feenstra and Shapiro
FTC	Federal Trade Commission
GDP	Gross domestic product
GLA	Gross leasable area
GM	General Motors
HKMR	Hoch, Kim, Montgomery and Rossi
IFA	International Franchise Association
KCV	Kadiyali, Chintagunta and Vilcassim
LHS	Left-hand side
LS	Large sample
M	Profit margin
MCBE	Mixed commodity bundling equilibrium; or mixed commodity bundling equilibria
MOM	Manufacturers' operating margin as a proportion of sales
MVA	Market value added
NADA	National Automobile Dealers Association

NAICS	North American Industrial Classification System
OE	Operating expenditures
OECD	Organization for European Cooperation and Development
OLS	Ordinary least squares
P	Pillsbury
PCBE	Pure commodity bundling equilibrium; or pure commodity bundling equilibria
PLMA	Private Label Manufacturers Association
PROMO	Promotional pricing strategy
R	Retail gross margin per unit as a proportion of price; also, retail gross margin as proportion of sales
RHS	Right-hand side
ROM	Retailers' operating margin as a proportion of sales
RP	Retailers' profit
RPM	Resale price maintenance
RSP	Retailers' share of channel profits
RTS	Returns to scale
S	Sales
SB	Store brand
SHR	Sayman, Hoch and Raju
SIC	Standard Industrial Classification
SII	Structural Impediments Initiative
SKU	Stock keeping unit
SMSA	Standard Metropolitan Statistical Area
SS	Small sample
TV	Television
UFOC	Uniform franchise offering circular
UK	United Kingdom
UPC	Uniform product code
US	United States
USDA	United States Department of Agriculture
VHS	Video home system
WAC	Washington Apple Commission

1. Introduction

Many of the ideas as well as the approach presented below are as applicable to the wholesale sector as they are to the retail sector. In order to emphasize this applicability the more general term 'distribution sector' is often used in what follows whenever the issues or arguments are essentially the same in the context of retail or wholesale. Nevertheless, the analysis here focuses explicitly on the retail sector and this is stressed by the choice of title for many of the chapters.[1]

Defining and understanding a distribution system is a difficult task for at least three reasons. First, the distribution activity encompasses any mechanism for making available goods and services to consumers. Hence, it includes the activities of the department store, the supermarket and auction companies on the Internet as well as those of the travel agent, the telephone company and the local branch of a bank. An important difference between the first three activities and the last three activities is that in the first three what are being distributed to consumers are usually outputs of the manufacturing and agricultural sectors and in the last three what are being distributed are outputs of the service sector. Output measurement in the service sector is notoriously difficult and the distribution activity itself is part of the service sector.

Measurement difficulties in the case of services have begun to attract the attention of economists. Initial steps in addressing this issue, especially at the conceptual level, can be found in a conference volume edited by Griliches (1992). Since measuring the output of distribution activities is a major task in any analysis of services, it is not surprising that one of the chapters in this conference volume is devoted to the distributive trades (Oi, 1992). Along the same lines earlier empirical work on the role of services in the economy, Syrquin and Chenery (1989), has been recently disaggregated to focus on the distribution sector, Anderson and Betancourt (2002). The latter authors find different patterns of evolution with respect to income for the distribution sector than had been found by the former authors for services: namely, it follows an inverted-U pattern rather than a rising pattern.

Second, since the retailing activity provides a link between consumers and producers or wholesalers, it is going to be affected by the characteristics of both the consumers and the producers or wholesalers. Thus, long-term demographic and technological changes that affect consumers and producers will have an indirect impact on retailers. For instance when refrigeration becomes

1

widely available to households at low cost, the range of products that the retail system can make available to them is different from when no such refrigeration is available. Similarly when a society is populated increasingly by households with two income earners, the demands of consumers for some retail services, extended hours for example, become very different from when a society has an insignificant fraction of such households. Understanding the indirect impact of long-term demographic and technological processes is not an easy task.

Third, since distribution is an economic activity it will be directly affected by all the factors that affect any economic activity. For instance technological change will also have a direct impact on the retail or wholesale system. The by now ubiquitous presence of optical scanners in supermarkets and the rapid spread of retailing and wholesaling through the Internet are two well-known examples. Similarly, the regulatory environment that prevails in a society will have a direct impact on the distribution system. For example, restrictive zoning laws in France during the 1950s (Loi Royer) provided powerful incentives for the development of hypermarkets there before they were introduced elsewhere. In general, variations in the prices of major inputs and outputs of this sector, for example rents and interest rates, would be expected to generate significant adjustments in the variables controlled by economic agents operating in this sector.

Substantial variations in so many different possible characteristics create difficulties for understanding the distribution system. They come to the fore when one attempts to make international comparisons. To illustrate, in the early 1990s the OECD commissioned a study of the distribution systems in seven advanced countries to seven different researchers (Japan: Maruyama, 1993; UK: Dawson, 1993; France: Messerlin, 1993, Germany: Lachner, Tager and Weitzel, 1993; Sweden: Wibe, 1993; Italy: Pellegrini and Cardani, 1993; and the US: Betancourt, 1993). Each study was carried out in a different manner and no attempt was made to synthesize the results.

The rest of the introduction is devoted to two tasks. Despite its difficulty, it is important to understand the distribution system from a variety of perspectives and in the next section arguments are put forth that justify this assertion. In the subsequent section, the approach taken here to this difficult and important topic is presented together with an overview of the progress made in the chapters that follow.

1.1   IMPORTANCE OF THE TOPIC

One reason for the importance of the topic is the economic size of this sector and, consequently, the substantial amount of resources devoted to it in any economy. A good measure of the economic importance of this sector in terms of size is its contribution to GDP relative to other sectors. For the US, for example, the wholesale and retail trade accounted for 16.5 per cent of GDP in 1996, measured in constant dollars (1992).[2] The magnitude of this percentage is not unique to the US. For instance, Anderson and Betancourt (2002) find that the average contribution to GDP of the retail and wholesale trade for a group of 74 countries during the period 1950–1983 is 13.5 per cent.[3] The wholesale and retail trade together rank second only to manufacturing in their contribution to GDP in the US, and the retail trade constitutes between 50 and 60 per cent of the distribution sector's contribution to GDP in any one year.

It has to be noted that the above figures are a lower bound to the importance of retailing's contribution to GDP, or its economic importance, from the following perspective. Many retailing activities are attributed to sectors other than the retail sector in the national income accounts for a variety of reasons. This is especially so in the retailing of services. In the case of eating and drinking establishments, for example, difficulties in separating production activities from distribution activities have led to changes in classifications such as the ones just discussed (see note 2). A similar phenomenon manifests itself in other industries. For instance, what part of the contribution of the banking activity to GDP is due to retail banking? Similarly, what part of the contribution of communications or transportation to GDP is due to the retailing of communication services or transportation services? The arguments throughout the book are also applicable to the retailing of these services,[4] but the explicit measurement of the retailing of these services at the level of the national income accounts is not practically feasible with current methodology.[5] On these grounds, the national income accounts statistics substantially understate the economic importance of retail activities.

Dramatic changes in the economy have led to major changes in our measurement of economic activity and these changes will accentuate the understatement of the economic importance of retail activities when the latter are defined to correspond solely with the census definition of the distribution sector. For instance, one can access an Internet service and acquire most of the information necessary to purchase a car from a dealer, including a fixed amount to be paid above dealer cost for the specific car one wants and the name of a salesman that handles Internet sales at the dealership nearest one's home. The dealer must pay this specialized Internet service provider a fee to be part of the list of dealers to which users of the Internet service are directed. This specialized service will be classified as part of the activities of the information sector under NAICS.[6] Before the Internet most of this information would have been provided by the auto dealer and would have been viewed as part of the activities of the retail sector. While the retailing function performed is quite similar in both cases, namely the provision of information, our recorded measurement of the contribution to economic activity of the retail sector is different.

Notwithstanding these issues of underestimation, the contribution to output of the distribution sector as measured in the national income accounts has been, is and will remain quite large. In the past, two issues have dominated the discussion of the evolution of this sector over time: its contribution to employment and to labor productivity. For instance, two of the main findings of an early classic on the topic, Barger (1955), are: 1) the fraction of the US labor force engaged in the retail and wholesale trade increased between 1930 and 1950, whereas that in manufacturing decreased; and 2) output per man-hour in this US economic sector rose considerably less during this period than output per man-hour in manufacturing. More recent work by Oi (1992, Table 4.2) for the period 1950–87 shows that these two trends have continued.

The more recent data, however, provides two additional insights. First, it allows a split of the distribution sector between wholesale and retail. This split shows that the above two trends are more pronounced for the retail trade than for the wholesale trade. Moreover, it also shows that the retail trade share of employment in 1987 was 22 per cent, compared to 6.8 per cent in wholesale and 21.4 per cent in manufacturing. Hence, the economic importance of the retail sector measured in terms of the number of persons who earn their living in this sector is considerably larger than in terms of its contribution to output. Second, it allows a direct comparison between employment and hours, which shows for 1987 a share of hours worked in retailing equal to 19 per cent compared to 7.2 per cent in wholesale and 23.4 per cent in manufacturing. The difference between employment and hours is due to the greater use of part-time workers in retailing, which also contributes to the finding that average hourly earnings of retail workers are substantially lower than those in wholesale or manufacturing. Therefore the nature of work in the retail trade raises issues relevant for current social policy, since the availability of pensions and health benefits for part-time workers is less than for full-time ones.

One result of the imbalance in trade between the US and Japan is that the importance of the distribution sector in facilitating or hindering trade has arisen as a policy issue. Indeed, a new acronym has been added to our vocabulary, Structural Impediments Initiative or SII, and differences in the efficiency of the distribution sector across countries have become a potential culprit for the existence of structural impediments to trade. While the theoretical basis for attributing this imbalance to an inefficient distribution system is ambiguous, there is a positive empirical association between the level of trade and the level of services available to the distribution sector in terms of communication and transportation facilities.[7]

Similarly, the importance of the distribution sector in understanding macroeconomic phenomena has been highlighted recently by Burstein, Neves and

Rebelo (2003). The authors find the standard model used to analyse the behavior of the real exchange rate in exchange rate based stabilization programs unable to explain, among other things, the behavior of the real exchange rate after the introduction of these programs. They introduce into the standard model a distribution sector in which tradable goods must be combined with distribution services before they can be consumed. With this feature they are able to explain variations in the real exchange rate after the introduction of the 1991 Convertibility plan in Argentina far better than the standard model. They also suggest, in their conclusion, that other puzzles in international macroeconomics might be better understood by explicitly including the distribution sector in the analysis.

Ongoing work by MacGee (2002) develops a complete markets two-country multi-sector general equilibrium model that includes the provision of distribution services. In his model any traded good used for final consumption is produced by combining traded intermediate goods and distribution services specific to that good. With this modification to the standard complete markets two-country multi-sector general equilibrium model MacGee resolves one existing puzzle in this literature. That is, the data shows consumption to be correlated across countries, for example, 0.36 for the US versus the rest of the world. While the standard model without the modification predicts a correlation of 1 across countries for consumption, MacGee's modification of the standard model generates correlations of 0.37, 0.45 and 0.33 for three different assumptions on investment adjustment costs.

Is there evidence on the nature of differences in retail systems across countries, especially productivity or efficiency differences? In a widely cited study Smith and Hitchens (1985) compared the distribution sector in the US, the UK and Germany. First, they showed (Table 1.1) that in 1980 the contribution of the distribution sector to GDP was 17 per cent for the US, 12.5 per cent for the UK and 9.4 per cent for Germany. In all three countries, however, the contribution of the sector to employment was considerably larger than to output (21.5 per cent in the US, 17.3 per cent in the United Kingdom and 14.4 per cent in Germany). In the same year (Table 1.3) the share of retailing in distribution (in terms of GDP contribution) was 55 per cent for the US, 54 per cent for the UK and 52 per cent for Germany. The relative labor productivity of the US in retailing compared to the UK was 2.39 and compared to Germany it was 2.49 (Table 2.6). This comparison was based on sales per capita for the 1971–72 period for the US and the UK and for the 1972–67 period for the US and Germany.

Ito and Maruyama (1991) compared several advanced countries using value added per person engaged in retailing (Table 3.1). Value added was measured as sales times the proportionate gross margin. They find that relative to total value added per person engaged in industry, Japan's productivity in

1985 was 0.76, the US was 0.70, Germany 0.68 and the UK 0.58. On the other hand, Baily (1993) found that in general merchandise retailing US labor productivity was 2.5 times that of Japan, 1.04 times that of Germany and 1.21 that of the UK during the period 1987–88. Baily used value added per full-time equivalent employee as his measure of labor productivity.

What do we learn from these dramatically different results? In the US, UK and Germany comparisons of Baily and Smith and Hitchens there are three sources of differences. First, the measure of output of retailing in the former is value added while in the latter it is sales; second, the former study refers to a branch of retailing whereas the latter refers to the whole sector; third, the time period of the comparison in Baily is 15 to 20 years later than in Smith and Hitchens. All three sources of differences identify important issues that need to be and will be addressed in subsequent chapters: namely, the appropriate definition of retail output and the potentially different performance of different branches of retailing across space and time.

In the US–Japan comparison an important part of the explanation may be measurement problems. Part-time employment is far more prevalent in US retailing than in Japanese retailing; the Ito and Maruyama measure does not adjust for this while the Baily measure does. Hence, the former measure over-states labor productivity in Japan relative to the US. In addition, Japanese manufacturers detail workers to the retailers of their products but keep them on their own payrolls. Their contribution to output is captured in the Ito and Maruyama measure of the output of retailing but their contribution to employment is not. It is captured in the level of employment by the manufacturers. This does not affect the Baily measure. On this account the Ito and Maruyama measure also overstates labor productivity in Japanese retailing relative to the US and to other countries.

Understanding the distribution system is of direct importance to the field of industrial organization. All of the issues that arise in this field with respect to other industries arise as well with respect to the retail or wholesale sector, but they often take different forms in retailing. For instance, in evaluating the degree of concentration in an industry and what it may imply for merger policy, for example, it becomes necessary to take into account that retailing is in some sense a local or at best regional activity in a way that manufacturing is not. Furthermore retail firms are intrinsically multiproduct, offering a variety of explicit goods or services and implicit distribution services. The provision of distribution services plays a fundamental role in retailing that is not necessarily shared by other industries. For instance, variations in distribution services are a main factor generating different types of retail organizations.

Price comparisons or analyses of competition across different retail establishments that ignore these features are likely to be misleading. For instance, one of the sources of bias in the recent controversy about the CPI is explicitly identified as outlet substitution bias (Boskin et al., 1996). The multiproduct nature of price setting at the retail level has been found to be important at the macroeconomic level as well (Lach and Tsiddon, 1996). Finally intertype competition is more important in retailing than in other industries; one can even argue that it is a unique feature, because of its intrinsically local nature and the role of distribution services in creating different types.[8] Thus, in evaluating the competitive impact of the Staples and Office Depot merger, one of the factors that both sides tried to control for was the possibility of intertype competition. That is, they controlled for the presence in a local market of other types of stores, besides office supplies superstores, that sell office supplies such as computer superstores and warehouse clubs (Gleason and Hosken, 1998).

To conclude, understanding the retail system is also important for the study of marketing. Marketing researchers operate at lower levels of aggregation than industrial organization researchers and focus on issues that impact firm decisions in operational settings, for example heterogeneity of customers. Nevertheless, many of the economic issues addressed by marketing researchers are similar to or the same as those addressed by economists. Furthermore, in some settings the interests of researchers in both fields coincide. For instance, Wernerfelt (1994) has argued that in evaluating marketing designs it is necessary to take into account the payoff functions of all members adjacent to a channel, including the consumer. A basic feature of the approach taken to the analysis of retail systems in this work is the provision of an explicit mechanism for linking the benefits received by the consumer from the retail system to the activities of the retailers.

Ironically, many issues of interest to economists have been analysed by marketing scholars with substantial training in economics, or economists working in marketing departments, and published in marketing or business journals. Part of the reason may have been that mainstream economists often ignored the role of the distribution sector in the economic system during the 1970s and the early 1980s. Whatever the reason for this phenomenon, however, the trend of significant analyses of economic issues by marketing scholars continues unabated to this day. Indeed, perhaps one of the best illustrations of the trend can be seen in the numerous items in marketing and business journals in this book's references.

1.2 APPROACH AND SCOPE

Our approach is anchored in the following definition of the function of retail systems: the provision of goods and services to consumers together or jointly with a set of distribution services.[9] In general it can be viewed as part of the New Institutional Economics in the sense of applying the tools of economics to explain the workings and evolution of institutional arrangements (for example Furubotn and Richter, 1997). More specifically, it identifies distribution costs, which are transaction costs, and the distribution services into which these costs map as key determinants of the functioning of retail systems. It also pays serious attention to characteristics of retail systems that enhance the importance of the analysis of property rights, for example the bundling of distribution services with the explicit products or services sold at retail. The analysis of property rights lies at the core of the New Institutional Economics.

In the first part of the book (General considerations) I develop the main implications of adopting this view of the function of retail systems for standard models of competition in retail markets and for the empirical analysis of retail gross margins (Chapter 2), for the analysis of retail demand (Chapter 3), and for understanding the nature of retail supply (Chapter 4).

Chapter 2 contains a detailed description of the costs consumers incur in patronizing retail organizations and we map these costs into a set of five broad categories of distribution services that retailers provide. These categories are: assortment, assurance of product delivery (at the desired time or in the desired form), information, accessibility of location, and ambiance. Each one of these distribution services can be viewed as an output of any retail organization. At the same time, each of these distribution services can be viewed as a fixed input into the (household) production functions of consumers. This view of distribution services as outputs of retail firms and fixed inputs to consumers provides the mechanism for analysing an essential characteristic of retail markets: *cost shifting*. We document the implicit recognition of this issue in the economics and marketing literature of the last 30 years and illustrate the benefits of our particular formalization of the idea for the explanation of retail price dispersion and the existence of different types of retail firms in equilibrium under monopolistic competition.

A second essential characteristic of retail markets is that the distribution services implicitly provided with the goods or services explicitly provided by any part of the retail system are usually not priced independently of these explicit outputs, that is, there is *bundling* of explicit output and distribution services. We also show in Chapter 2 some of the benefits of a particular formalization of this idea in terms of a simple model with one explicit output and one distribution service. This model, which is an adaptation of the models of Bliss (1988) and Betancourt and Gautschi (1993a) put forth by Betancourt and Malanoski (1999), allows us to analyse competition and welfare issues in a straightforward fashion. Furthermore it generalizes the full-price model of services (Ehrlich and Fisher, 1982), which is used to analyse retailing under the assumption of perfect competition, and it brings out one of its limitations. The full-price model breaks down when there are increasing returns to scale in the provision of distribution services.

Since Chapter 2 introduces the approach employed throughout the book, it concludes by discussing two alternative validation processes. First, there is a thorough discussion of measurement issues and empirical evidence in the context of explaining variations in retail gross margins across retail branches. The retail gross margin has been a center of attention in this industry for many years but empirical progress in its explanation has been slow.[10] We show how the emphasis on distribution services leads to an empirical framework for explaining retail gross margins that is supported by the empirical results available across branches of the retail sectors in the US, Germany, France, Holland and Spain. Second, there is a detailed discussion of a case study that illustrates how to measure and employ these concepts in a strategic setting.

Chapter 3 contains a methodological foundation for the analysis of retail demand by formally incorporating distribution services as fixed inputs into a general version of the household production model. This provides a rigorous basis for the analysis of retail demand with data on purchases rather than consumption, for example scanner data. Even without distribution services the household production model has important and little-known implications for the substitutability and complementarity that arises in retail demand as a result of price changes. This chapter derives them formally and illustrates them in practice, with a detailed analysis of two empirical studies drawn from the marketing literature.

Subsequently, the formal implications of the existence of distribution services for the substitutability and complementarity that arises in retail demand are derived. The main implications of this approach to retail demand for the nature of retail competition and for the creation of retail agglomerations are also explicitly drawn here. Finally, this analysis is related to several strands of literature on retailing. In particular I discuss in detail here two recent studies, one in agricultural economics and the other in marketing, which implement this approach to retail demand empirically.

What is the appropriate definition of retail output or supply? Simple as the question seems, it has generated a variety of answers in the literature: for instance, sales, value added, the retail or gross margin and a measure that includes the consumer! Retail firms produce two different kinds of outputs: the goods and services explicitly sold and a set of distribution services that implicitly accompany any retail exchange. In Chapter 4 modern production theory is used to show the conditions under which the latter set of outputs collapses to the value added or gross margin measures and the former to the sales measure. This formulation brings out that the existing evidence on economies of scale in retailing implies that there are economies of scale with respect to distribution services, not necessarily with respect to the explicit output of retailing. Furthermore, these tools and the accompanying econometric techniques are used to show that the role of the consumer in retail supply is incorporated by accounting for the endogeneity of certain variables. Recognition of these issues provides a sound basis for productivity measurement in retailing and this topic concludes the text of this chapter. Since the provision of assortment, however, is a most important and distinctive characteristic of retailing, an appendix to this chapter presents a formal specification of a production function for assortment that is consistent with modern production theory.

In the second part of the book (Interactions between consumers and retailers) I apply the previous ideas to establish the multiproduct nature of retailing and its pricing implications (Chapter 5), to highlight important and neglected aspects of the packaging decision by retailers (Chapter 6), and to understand familiar institutional forms that provide the context for the interactions between retailers and consumers (Chapter 7).

What should the focus of interest be for analysis: item prices or item prices at particular points of purchase? This question becomes interesting because retailing is essentially a multiproduct activity. And, most pricing issues in retailing need to be examined taking into account this feature. In Chapter 5 I undertake this task. First, the basic result in the literature on multiproduct pricing is presented here: namely, its connection to the cross price elasticity of demand. Furthermore, its implications are illustrated with two studies from the marketing literature. Second, the main extensions of this result to a situation where distribution services are variable and subject to the choice of retailers are presented here. These services play a critical role in explaining why gross complementarity prevails among most items offered by retailers. Moreover, they are also essential in understanding pricing in the Internet and this is one of the implications of the extended analysis discussed in detail in this chapter.

Another important topic addressed in this chapter is the practice of loss leading. The strict interpretation of the latter concept (pricing below marginal cost) is meaningless in a single-product, single-period world. Furthermore, the most insightful explanation of this practice in the literature, Lal and Matutes (1994), uses the provision of a distribution service (information) as a key to the explanation. In this context, I discuss two recent empirical studies that show how the gross complementarity implied by this model (and, more importantly, by the existence of distribution services in general) is consistent with persistent empirical phenomena. This consistency is shown to be absent from alternative models. Finally, an appendix addresses a somewhat related but specialized topic in the context of multiproduct retailing: namely, the construction of cost of living indexes on the basis of scanner data.

The next chapter examines the literature on a specialized business practice in terms of the framework developed here. Namely, in Chapter 6 we consider a business practice that shifts storage costs and, thus, implies the provision of different levels of assurance of product delivery by the retailer: packaging. In economics, packaging is treated as a form of commodity bundling and the literature emphasizes the welfare losses to consumers from this practice. Marketing scholars have followed this lead at lower levels of aggregation. By allowing for intertype competition in the provision of distribution services, however, one can explain the empirical evidence available in both types of literature and show that the welfare losses associated with the commodity bundling involved in packaging can be substantially ameliorated by intertype competition in retailing.

The last chapter in this part brings out the importance of distribution services, especially assortment, in determining the main retail forms that we actually observe in the market place. Looking at food store trends in the last century brings out the importance of expanding assortments in the development of the modern supermarket. A model of assortment based on Messinger and Narasimhan (1997) is developed and used to frame a discussion of the econometric evidence on the choice of assortment levels by supermarkets. Subsequently, the analysis is extended in the spirit of Bhatnagar and Ratchford (2000) by allowing explicitly for spatial competition in the choice of assortment and prices. Consumer heterogeneity is introduced to help differentiate between breadth and depth of assortment and identify the retail forms that stress these different dimensions. While this distinction facilitates a rudimentary classification of retail forms, it still leaves out two important retail forms: non-store retailers and shopping centers and shopping malls. I discuss both of them explicitly.

Non-store retailers are a retail form that includes, among others, two institutions providing similar distribution services – mail order catalogues and the Internet. Since the former has been around for a while, a detailed study of their evolution by Michael (1994) is used to frame and complete the discussion of the Internet as an institution started in Chapter 5. Chapter 7 concludes with a discussion of shopping centers and shopping malls. These retail forms have been expanding in the US over the last 50 years. While the demand for increasing assortments is an important feature in this expansion, especially for shopping centers, other issues acquire importance in this setting. For example, the ability to enforce contracts and internalize externalities by a single authority and the increasing demand for entertainment activities associated with regional and super-regional shopping centers.

In the third and last part of the book (Interactions between retailers and other agents) I consider the role of distribution services in the interactions between retailers and economic agents other than customers. While in the previous part of the book distribution services are viewed as an essential, indispensable factor for understanding the nature of interactions between consumers and retailers, in this part a change in perspective takes place. Distribution services remain important and the focus of our attention, but no claim is made here that all channel issues (Chapter 8) or all aspects of franchises (Chapter 9) have to be looked at through the lenses of distribution services. The claim is merely that in some important aspects of these two topics it is useful, insightful and perhaps even necessary to do so. Finally the book concludes with an explicit discussion (Chapter 10) on the retailing of services, which is a topic where distribution services usually play a critical role.

An important economic role of distribution services lies in the ability it confers to those who control these services for affecting outcome variables of interest such as profits, prices and output in the form of turnover. In the setting of interactions between retail firms and consumers, it is automatically or implicitly assumed that retail firms rather than consumers will decide on the levels of these services. In a channel context, however, it is no longer automatically assumed that the 'upstream' firm has to control the distribution service and the question of what advantages follow from the power of control acquires greater importance and relevance.

Chapter 8 shows that control of a distribution service by a retailer in a bilateral monopoly setting where the manufacturer is a Stackelberg leader shifts economic power, measured in terms of the price–cost margin, towards the retailer. It also tends to increase prices and distribution services relative to the integrated solution. Control by the manufacturer, on the other hand, has no effect on the relative economic power of the two agents in the channel. This last result, however, is not robust to relaxing the assumption of a single-product distribution channel. This conceptual basis provides the framework for looking at the empirical evidence on whether economic power has shifted from manufacturers to retailers. A detailed review of the few existing studies suggests the need for incorporating distribution services more systematically into the empirical analysis. While the empirical evidence does not suggest major shifts in power between retailers and manufacturers, it does suggest that retailers have substantial economic power.[11]

More generally, retailers have incentives to become complex organizations through backward integration, moves into new markets and the addition of new product categories or varieties. Distribution services affect these incentives. Both the evolution of Wal-Mart and the introduction of private labels are used to illustrate these processes. Finally, a somewhat selective review of the marketing and economics literature on channel issues highlights the treatment of distribution services in this context, relates some of the results to the previous analysis in the chapter and in the book, and sets the stage for the analysis of franchises in Chapter 9.

Franchises are a form of vertical contractual relations, which are reviewed in Chapter 8. Nonetheless, franchises are so pervasive as an organizational form in retailing that they deserve and get more detailed treatment in this chapter. I start by presenting as much relevant information as possible from all sources on this organizational form and its contract provisions. This leads to a separate discussion of each of the two main examples of product trade name franchises: gas stations and automobiles. This type of franchise system is characterized by being an institutional device focused on the distribution of goods and by relying on a very limited set of provisions from the universe available in franchise contracts. By contrast business format franchises, the other type of franchise system, are primarily but not exclusively institutional devices for the distribution of services, and they tend to rely on most and sometimes on all of the distinct provisions available to a franchise contract.

A particularly interesting finding in this chapter is the variety of arrangements with respect to the role of initial investment in the franchise by the franchisee. It is the critical contract feature in automobile franchises. It plays no role in the lessee–dealer franchise arrangements of gas stations. And, it is an important feature of the contract arrangements in business format franchises. This feature is driven by, among other things, the need to provide assurance of product delivery in the desired form beyond minimum levels. The implications of endogeneity for the choice of organizational form embedded in this characteristic have been ignored by existing empirical literature.

Finally, the book concludes in Chapter 10 with an explicit consideration of the retailing of services and a brief discussion of main accomplishments. The chapter starts with a discussion of characteristics of services viewed as fundamental in the literature and it goes on to draw their main implications for the retailing of services. Some of these implications are illustrated in a detailed discussion of two applications of our approach to the financial services industry. Our main accomplishments are indicated in terms of providing foundations for further research, drawing novel results and guiding future research possibilities especially in the retailing of services.

NOTES

1. An explicit discussion of how the approach applies to the wholesale sector is available in Betancourt (1993).
2. These figures are taken from the US Statistical Abstract, 1998 (Table No 1274). With the adoption of the North American Industrial Classification System (NAICS) in 1997 by the US Census Bureau, the retail sector is redefined to exclude eating and drinking establishments. This brings US practice in line with the rest of the world and it lowers the contribution of the distribution sector to GDP in the US reported in the text by about 1 per cent. Discussion of this issue as well as other ones underlying the development of NAICS is available at http://www.census.gov/naics.
3. This average excludes hotels and restaurants in every country from the distribution sector. It corresponds exactly to the NAICS classification in excluding eating and drinking establishments from the distribution sector.
4. For a detailed illustration of how these arguments apply to the case of retail banking see Hanak (1992a).
5. While it is not feasible to pursue issues related to the measurement of retailing activities in

some of these service industries at this aggregate level, it is feasible to address them at lower levels of data aggregation.

6. This is a new sector created as a result of the switch from the standard industrial classification (SIC) to NAICS in 1997.

7. At the analytical level Bandyopadhyay (1998) found, using the continuum of goods model and the approach to retail systems presented here, that an increase in the efficiency of the distribution sector could raise or lower the trade balance depending on the size of distribution costs and on preferences for distribution services. On the other hand, at the empirical level (1999) one of her most robust results was that the higher the level of infrastructure variables associated with the development of the distribution sector, for example communications and transportation, the higher the level of gross bilateral trade flows among countries.

8. Industrial organization textbooks, for example Pepall, Richards and Norman (1999, p.468), associate retail competition with intrabrand competition because they take the point of view of the manufacturer implicitly. But intertype competition among retailers is consistent with both inter- and intrabrand competition from the point of view of the manufacturer, and so is intratype competition in retailing.

9. Whether one is discussing the retailing of goods or services, the basic function to be performed by the system is conceptually the same.

10. At one point one contributor to the retail literature asserted 'economic theory does not yield much that can readily be used.' (Nooteboom, 1985).

11. In addition an interesting case study by Goldsmith (2002, Chapter 3) reveals how the choice of assortment by retailers could have led to the elimination of Betamax video rentals.

PART I

General considerations

2. The economic function of retail organizations

A main theme of this work is that the economic function of any retail organization is to provide consumers with a set of distribution services together with the explicit items or services bought at retail. Section 2.1 discusses six types of distribution or transaction costs incurred by consumers and how they map into five distribution services or outputs provided by retail organizations. One implication of this discussion is that the shifting of distribution or transaction costs between retailers and consumers is an essential characteristic of retail markets. This characteristic is discussed in section 2.2, where we also explain the two formal economic concepts used to capture cost shifting: namely, distribution services as outputs of retail institutions and as fixed inputs into the purchase or consumption activities of consumers. Subsequently, section 2.3 discusses a second essential characteristic of retail markets: the bundling of these distribution services among themselves and with the items or explicit services provided at retail. I also present here basic implications of these characteristics for the specification of demand and cost functions.

Characteristics such as the above two are elementary yet powerful in helping us understand the functioning of retail markets. For instance, they are sufficient to generate price dispersion and product variety with respect to distribution services in these markets, which is illustrated with a simple model of monopolistic competition in section 2.4. Furthermore, they have profound implications for competition and welfare in these markets. Some of these are derived in section 2.5 by means of a model that provides a basis for analysis in various parts of the book. In section 2.6 I demonstrate how this model generates the so-called full price model of services as a special case, which also brings out limitations of the full price model. Section 2.7 discusses the measurement of distribution services and empirical evidence on their role in explaining retail margins at the sectoral level. Finally, section 2.8 illustrates the measurement of distribution services at the store level and a strategic application of these concepts.

2.1 DISTRIBUTION COSTS AND SERVICES[1]

In order to carry out their purchase or consumption activities consumers incur a variety of costs that can be characterized as distribution or transaction costs. We begin by identifying six types of distribution costs that consumers can incur when interacting with any part of the retail system. Among the most easily identifiable ones there are, of course, direct time and transportation costs. The former include the opportunity costs of travel time to and from a retail establishment, waiting time inside or outside the establishment and time spent in planning purchase activities. The latter include the monetary costs of transport to and from the purchase site. These costs are obvious enough that they require no further elaboration.

Purchasing or consumption activities also generate distribution costs in the form of adjustment costs as a result of the unavailability of products or services at the desired time of (or in the desired amount for) consumption or purchase. These adjustment costs arise as a result of additional time and transportation costs incurred due to forced search or due to the increased expenditure or lower utility associated with altering the consumption or purchase bundle of goods and services. Economists would also characterize these costs as the costs of rationing through unavailability. While not as obvious as the previous ones, they are ubiquitous and play an important role, for example, in the development of one-stop shopping institutions and in the success of technological innovations such as ATMs.

One type of distribution costs stressed in the retailing literature (Ingene, 1984a) is psychic costs. These are costs inflicted on the consumer utilizing the retail system by undesirable characteristics of the retail environment. Examples of these characteristics would be drudgery, anxiety or disagreeable social interactions.

Another type of distribution costs is storage costs. These would arise, for instance, in the purchase of household products in bulk. An example would be purchasing wine in cases rather than in bottles. Storage costs feature prominently in the development of a particular retail form, warehouse stores. The last type of costs to be considered explicitly is information costs. Information may be desired with respect to price, availability, physical attributes or performance characteristics of the goods and services provided at the retail level as well as with respect to similar characteristics of the retail establishment. The acquisition of this information entails costs through the use of time, transport and other resources. Economists often characterize these costs as search costs.

Having considered the demand or end-use side of the market, it is useful to switch perspective and consider the supply or retail system side. Any particular configuration of a retail system imposes a particular level of these six types of distribution or transaction costs on consumers. Furthermore, different retail forms entail different levels of these costs for consumers. In order to make these points more easily, it is convenient to think in terms of five broad categories of distribution services that are provided by any retail organization, albeit at different levels. There is some degree of arbitrariness in the level of detail at which one chooses to describe these services. My particular choice here of five categories and the implied level of aggregation has three aims: providing a framework in which any particular type of retail establishment can be included, establishing the link between these services and the costs just described for the consumer and leaving no doubt that the production of these services requires resources. At various points in the arguments throughout the book, however, I will disaggregate some of these five services and at other points I will aggregate them into a single service.

Distribution services are difficult to define and measure with precision. Perhaps the most difficult one to define and measure is what may be labelled *ambiance*. It determines the level of psychic costs imposed on the consumer by the nature of the retail environment. While this service is difficult to define and measure, it is clear that some types of retail establishment specialize in providing low and others high levels of this service. Discount stores are examples of the former where the associated lower prices of the goods sold in these establishments are due, at least in part, to the resources saved by providing low levels of ambiance. By contrast, high scale stores such as Nieman Marcus are examples of the latter type of establishment. The higher prices associated with the products sold there are due, at least in part, to the cost of the resources used in providing high levels of ambiance, including part of the costs of operating sites in high-rent districts.

A second category of distribution services provided by a retail system is the level of product *assortment*, which for some purposes can be subdivided into breadth (different product lines) and depth (different varieties within a product line). This service affects the levels of several types of distribution costs experienced by consumers who patronize retail institutions. For example, it affects direct time and transportation costs associated with multiple shopping trips. It also affects adjustment costs associated with forgoing an item for purchase or consumption. Examples of retail activities stressing product breadth are supermarkets, department stores and hypermarkets. Examples of retail activities stressing product depth are specialty stores of various kinds. For a given number of goods sold, higher levels of assortment will entail higher costs for the retailer, for instance the costs of labeling and layout.

Our next category of distribution services is *accessibility of location*. It is the easiest one to define and measure in many situations. At the most elementary level it is the distance to the retail establishment. It affects the direct time and transportation costs experienced by consumers in their purchasing or consumption activities. For a given number of goods sold, a retail system may provide greater accessibility to consumers by having several retail sites in a given market area, and this configuration would entail higher costs than operating a single retail site.

A fourth type of output provided by the retail system is *assurance* of product delivery, which can be disaggregated into delivery at the desired time and in the desired form. The former is accomplished through the extension of opening hours as well as through the provision of credit,[2] for example. The latter includes functions such as breaking bulk as well as risk-bearing through the acquisition of ownership or the provision of warranties. This service affects several types of distribution costs: the direct time costs of waiting inside or outside the establishment, adjustment costs due to unavailability, and storage costs forced upon the consumer by the lack of availability at the desired time in the desired quantities. The provision of higher levels of this service leads to higher costs for the providers in the retail system in the form of costs of extended opening hours, credit provision, storage and risk-bearing.

Last but not least among the distribution services provided by the retail system is the amount of *information* with respect to prices, availability and other characteristics of the goods and services provided as well as of the retail establishment. The provision of higher levels of this service through advertising and sales personnel, for example, leads to higher costs for the retail system. On the other hand, it lowers consumers' costs of information, adjustment and storage.

Several implications of the previous discussion of distribution costs and services are worth emphasizing at this point. First, there is no necessary one-to-one mapping between the six types of distribution costs and the five types of distribution services. Since we concentrate on distribution services in what follows, we will not try to provide an exhaustive account of the possible mappings here. Second, there is jointness in the provision of distribution services. For instance, by providing information on store hours a retailer increases assurance of product delivery at the desired time as well; similarly, by providing deeper assortments a retailer increases assurance of product delivery in the desired form. Finally, some distribution services are *specific* to a product or line of products whereas others are *common* to the entire assortment. For example, by having two identical stores instead of one, a retailer is providing higher levels of accessibility of location to the entire assortment. Similarly by adding a new product line, the retailer is expanding the breadth of assortment for all the items that he or she carries. Hence, these two services are examples of common distribution services. By contrast, other services such as information on the nature of a specific item are of value only to the item at issue. For example, how well a suit or a shoe fits or the operating properties of an appliance are examples of information specific to the item or the product line.

2.2 COST SHIFTING

One implication of the previous discussion is that cost shifting is an essential characteristic of retail markets. Thus, it will be the focus of this section and it will play an important role throughout the book. In each of the five categories of distribution services identified above, we have illustrated how providing higher levels of any of these distribution services entails higher costs for the retailers. We have also illustrated how higher levels of these services lower different types of distribution costs incurred by consumers. That is we have illustrated the shifting of costs that takes place in retail markets between retailers and consumers.

The idea of cost shifting is not novel either in the economics or in the marketing literature. For instance, in economics Fuchs (1968) attributes the productivity gains of supermarkets to putting the consumers to work; in marketing Ingene (1984a) discusses productivity in terms of the shifting of functions between consumers and retailers. What the previous discussion makes clear, however, is that this is not a limited phenomenon but a pervasive one that takes place in all the possible dimensions of distribution services that a retail system provides. Hence, it can be misleading to discuss productivity by looking at only one of these dimensions.

Considering the pervasiveness of cost shifting in retail markets, it is useful to be as rigorous and precise as possible in capturing this notion. On the side of the retail system this can be made precise by identifying each of these distribution services as an output of any retail organization. The fundamental economic characteristic of any output is that providing higher levels of the output entails higher levels of cost. This criterion is clearly satisfied by each of the distribution services identified above. Once again thinking about the functions of marketing systems in terms of outputs is not new. For instance, Bucklin (1973) identifies four indexes of output for the distribution sector as a whole. These collapse to accessibility, assortment and a more limited definition of assurance of product delivery. While the identification of the five categories of distribution services in the previous section as outputs of the retail system is somewhat recent (Betancourt and Gautschi, 1986, 1988), it can be viewed as an application and extension of Bucklin's basic idea. This approach of treating distribution services explicitly as outputs has also been adopted by Oi (1992), who creates a list that overlaps with the one above.

A decision to treat each of these services as output implies that any retail organization that provides a higher (lower) level of any of these services is shifting distribution costs onto (away from) itself and away from (onto) its customers. Thus, it is desirable to have an equally fundamental concept as output on the demand side that can allow us to capture the shifting of costs between consumers and retailers. This concept is that of a fixed input.

Each of these distribution services that are outputs of retail organizations will be viewed as a fixed input into the production functions of end users, especially into the household production functions of consumers. The fundamental economic characteristic of a fixed input is that higher levels of this input lower or at least do not increase the costs of producing any given level of output.[3] Hence, this concept captures the description of how each of the distribution services identified in the previous section affects the various types of distribution costs experienced by consumers. Thus, these two concepts provide us with a precise mechanism to capture the shifting of costs between consumers and retailers that permeates retail markets. An increase in a distribution service by a retailer increases the retailer's costs in its role as an output and it usually decreases the distribution costs of any consumer who chooses to patronize the retailer in its role as a fixed input into the (household) production function of the consumer.[4]

An advantage of this conceptualization is that it brings out the role played by both participants in the retail market. The consumer chooses a level of each of these distribution services when she chooses to patronize a particular retailer. The retailer chooses the levels of each distribution service that he provides by its choice of mode of operation and the characteristics of the market will determine the equilibrium configuration that is actually observed. Another advantage of this conceptualization is that it brings out the role of a retailer as a multiproduct producer with respect to distribution services. This makes it immediately clear that statements about productivity require controlling for the level or the mix of each of these outputs in some fashion. To illustrate, saying that the increase in productivity of supermarkets is due to making the consumer work more (shifting distribution costs to the consumers) ignores the considerable lowering of distribution costs to the consumers from the larger and deeper assortments of supermarkets as well as from their convenient parking facilities. The fact that these retail forms have not only succeeded but seem to be expanding along these dimensions would suggest that the net result is a lowering of the overall distribution costs experienced by the consumer.

2.3   BUNDLING

All five of the distribution services discussed above are bundled together in any retail setting, which generates one type of bundling. A second type of bundling, however, is generated by the bundling of these distribution services with an additional indispensable output of the retail system omitted from the previous discussion – the explicit goods or services distributed by the retailer. This type of bundling generates another essential feature of retail markets: namely, the consumer explicitly pays for these items or services and only implicitly for the outputs of distribution services that are bundled with them.[5] One should also note that there can be jointness in the provision of a distribution service and in the provision of explicit outputs. For instance, an increase in assortment usually entails an increase in the number of items to be distributed by the retailer. To sum up, in viewing the retailer as a multiproduct producer we have one more dimension of output and this dimension is different from the others in that it is the one that is explicitly priced.[6]

For purposes of analysis this dimension of output must be treated differently from the others. There are two ways of specifying the demand for the explicit output of a retailer depending on the assumptions one makes about the retailer's decision variables. One can assume that the retailer chooses the quantities of the items for sale. In that case the demand function faced by the retailer is specified as an inverse demand function. For instance,

$$p = f(Q, D, W, p')$$ (2.1)

where p is the retailer's price, Q is the quantity of explicit items for sale, D is a vector of outputs representing the five distribution services identified previously, W is the full income of a representative consumer and p' is a set of other prices that can potentially affect the consumer's demand. This demand function has the following properties: it is a non-increasing function of the quantity of items distributed ($f_Q \leq 0$), a non-decreasing function of each of the distribution services provided ($f_D \geq 0$, for all elements of D), and a non-decreasing function of full income ($f_W \geq 0$).[7] Thus, consumers are willing to pay the same or a higher price for a given set of items (Q) that come in a bundle with at least one distribution service at a higher level and all the others the same as another bundle. The other two properties are standard ones for inverse demand functions.

In some instances we want to specify the retailer as choosing prices rather than quantities. In these cases the demand function faced by the retailer would be specified in standard form as

$$Q = g(p, D, W, p')$$ (2.2)

The variables are the same as before. This demand function would have the following properties: it is a non-increasing function of the retail price ($g_p \leq 0$), a non-decreasing function of each of the distribution services provided ($g_D \geq 0$, for all elements of D), and a non-decreasing function of full income ($g_W \geq 0$). In this case consumers are willing to buy the same or more explicit items at a given price when they come in a bundle with at least one distribution service at a higher level and all the others the same as in another bundle. The other two properties are standard ones for ordinary demand functions.[8]

The above two specifications capture the consequences of the bundling of explicit outputs with distribution services on the demand side. With respect to the supply side, this bundling merely implies that a retailer is a multiproduct producer and any special features of the bundling can be captured through the properties of a multiproduct cost function, which can be specified in general as follows:

$$C = C(Q, D, v) \qquad (2.3)$$

where C are the costs of retailing, v is a vector of input prices[9] and Q and D are as defined previously. The main property of interest of this function presently is that it is increasing in outputs. That is, $C_Q > 0$ and $C_D > 0$, for all elements of D.[10]

2.4 PRICE DISPERSION AND PRODUCT VARIETY IN DISTRIBUTION SERVICES

In this section we illustrate two important consequences of bundling in terms of a simple model of monopolistic competition. First, the bundling of distribution services with the explicit output sold at retail is a fundamental source of equilibria with price dispersion and differential cost shifting in retail markets. Second, the bundling of distribution services among themselves is a fundamental source of equilibria with product variety in distribution services and differential cost shifting in retail markets.

Consider a representative profit-maximizing retailer who faces the demand function in (2.1), that is, a quantity setter, and who is subject to the cost function in (2.3). Her objective is to maximize the profits (π) of retailing activities. Thus,

$$\pi = pQ - C(Q, D, v) - wQ, \qquad (2.4)$$

where w is the price of the items acquired from suppliers. Hence, wQ is the cost of goods sold. To keep matters simple we will assume that there is only one distribution service subject to the retailer's control, D.

The first-order conditions for profit maximization can be written, after some manipulation, as

$$(p - w)Q/C - S_Q = p \in Q/C \qquad (2.5)$$

$$S_D \, C/Q = p\delta \qquad (2.6)$$

where S_Q is the proportionate increase in costs from distributing an additional item ($C_Q Q/C$) and S_D is the proportionate increase in costs from providing an additional unit of the distribution service ($C_D D/C$). $\in$ is the absolute value of the reciprocal of the price elasticity of demand ($-f_Q Q/p$) and δ is the reciprocal of the distribution services elasticity of demand ($f_D D/p$).

If the market is to be in long-run equilibrium, profits must be zero. Therefore, this condition implies from (2.4) that $(p - w) = C/Q$. In other words the retail gross margin obtained from selling an additional item must equal the average costs of retailing this additional item. Imposing this condition on the short-run equilibrium ones leads to

$$(p - w)/p = \delta/S_D = \in/\ (1 - S_Q). \tag{2.7}$$

The left-hand side of this equation is the retail gross margin per unit expressed as a proportion of the retail price, R, and it moves in the same direction as the retail price.

Equation (2.7) can be used to establish the following proposition:

Proposition 2.1: Heterogeneity among consumers with respect to price sensitivity or the demand for distribution services is sufficient to yield equilibria with price dispersion and differential cost shifting even if firms are identical.

To illustrate the validity of this proposition consider first two market segments, A and B, where consumers differ with respect to their price sensitivity by having different values of a constant price elasticity of demand: $\in(A) > \in(B)$.[11] We will assume the cost function for firms to be such that $S_D = (1 - S_Q) = k$, where k is a constant.[12] Long-run equilibrium in segments A and B requires, by (2.7), that the 'retail gross margins', R, be such that $R(A) = [\delta\ (A) = \in(A)]/k > R(B) = [\delta\ (B) = \in(B)]/k$. If the inverse demand function has the following form, $p = h\ (D)Q^{-\in}W$, then $\delta = (h_D\ D)/h(D)$. Note that $h_D = \partial h(D)/\partial D$. The retail price will always be higher in A than in B. If the reciprocal of the distribution services elasticity is decreasing (increasing) in D, however, the level of distribution services will be lower (higher) in A than in B. In either case there will be price dispersion and a different level of distribution costs (differential cost shifting) borne by consumers in long-run equilibrium.

When consumer heterogeneity is generated by differences in the valuation of distribution services, we can establish a similar conclusion. For this purpose, let the inverse demand function have the following form, $p = D^\delta m(Q)W$. The price elasticity of demand is now variable, that is, $\in = -[\ m_Q\ Q/m(Q)]$, and the distribution services elasticity of demand is now constant. If in segment A consumers value distribution services more than in segment B, $\delta(A) > \delta(B)$. This situation can arise because the opportunity cost of their time, for example, is different.[13] It follows from (2.7), under the same assumptions on k as before, that $R(A) = [\delta(A) = \in(A)]/k > R(B) = [\delta(B) = \in(B)]/k$. Thus, the retail price will be higher in the segment with the higher valuation of distribution services. Moreover, there is a wide array of combinations of distribution services, D, and output, Q, that are consistent with this equilibrium, including many which entail differential cost shifting in the two markets.

Consumer heterogeneity as a source of equilibrium price dispersion in retail markets is quite pervasive. Many of the models in the literature that seek to explain price dispersion can be recast in these terms, despite their seemingly different approaches.[14] What has not been noticed is that these equilibria usually imply differential cost shifting as well. For instance, Salop and Stiglitz's (1977) seminal analysis of imperfect information requires low and high search costs types of consumers to generate different price equilibria; and the implied cost shifting of information between consumers and retailers differs across these equilibria.

Generalization of the previous model to more than one distribution service is straightforward (Betancourt and Gautschi, 1988). Suppose that there are two distribution services, D_1 and D_2. The long-run equilibrium condition becomes

$$R = (p - w)/p = \delta_1 / S_1 = \delta_2 / S_2 = \in/(1 - S_Q), \tag{2.8}$$

where the subscripts 1 and 2 indicate the respective distribution service.

Equation (2.8) can be used to establish the following proposition:

Proposition 2.2: Consumer heterogeneity with respect to the valuation of different distribution services is sufficient to generate equilibria with product variety in distribution services and differential cost shifting at the same retail price, even if firms' cost functions are identical.

To illustrate the validity of this proposition, assume that consumers in both markets have the same constant price elasticity of demand and firms in both markets have the same cost function, given by $C = c(v, D_1, D_2) Q^\beta$. These assumptions ensure that the retail gross margin and the prices in both markets will be the same, since $R = \in/(1 - \beta)$ in both cases. What differs between the two markets is at least one of the two distribution services elasticities, let us say $\delta_1 (A) > \delta_1 (B)$ and $\delta_2 = k$ in both markets. If S_1 is an increasing function of D_1, for example, both markets can be in long-run equilibrium at the same retail price. If D_2 is the same in both markets, this merely requires Q to be larger in market A than in market B. In any event, this generates equilibria with product variety in distribution services and differential cost shifting with respect to at least the first distribution service.

Consumer heterogeneity with respect to distribution services is an important source of equilibria with product variety in distribution services. These equilibria imply a different degree of cost shifting of distribution services. While this phenomenon has received far less attention than price dispersion in the literature, there are analyses employing different approaches that generate the same result.[15] For instance, Oi's (1992) location and store choice model (section 4.4.2) requires consumer heterogeneity with respect to location and other shopping costs, which correspond to assurance of product delivery in the desired form in our terminology, to generate equilibria with product variety in distribution services and differential cost shifting for each consumer at the same full price at competing stores for the marginal consumer. The full price model is a perfectly competitive model, in contrast to the one considered here.

Extensions of the analysis to richer environments, that is, allowing for different cost functions and more than one explicit product, would expand the opportunities for retail price dispersion and product variety in distribution services to arise as characteristics of equilibria. These two consequences of the bundling of distribution services among themselves and with the explicit products sold at retail lead to the coexistence of different retail forms that we observe in the market place, which is a topic that will reoccur throughout the book, for example, in chapters 6 and 7.

2.5   COMPETITION AND WELFARE IN RETAIL MARKETS

In this section I explore the consequences of cost shifting and bundling for competition and welfare in retail markets. This will be done in the context of a simple model which is an adaptation of several contributions in the literature. Bliss (1988) points out that a major problem for any retailer is to offer a consumer good enough value in the store to keep her at the store. He captures this idea in terms of an indirect utility function. Betancourt and Gautschi (1993a) reformulate Bliss's idea in terms of an expenditure function and extend it by incorporating distribution services into the analysis. Betancourt and Malanoski (1999)[16] adapt the model for empirical analysis and note how it generates the full price model as a special case.

Consider a representative retailer who faces the demand function in (2.2), that is, a price setting retailer, and the cost function in (2.3). This retailer wants to choose prices and distribution services to maximize profits subject to the constraint of keeping a representative consumer patronizing the store. To keep matters simple we will focus on the single price, single distribution service situation. The problem can be specified as maximizing profits, defined as in (2.4), subject to the constraint that the choice of price and distribution service affects the expenditure function, $E(p, p', D, Z^0)$, of the representative consumer in the following way: it keeps her patronizing the retailer because her level of expenditures will be less than or equal to the minimum cost of attaining the same level of satisfaction at another establishment, E'. Z^0 represents the optimal level of the consumption activities of the consumer.[17]

Formally, this is captured as follows:

$$L = pQ - C(v, Q, D) - wQ + \mu[E' - E(p, p', D, Z^0)] \qquad (2.9)$$

where μ is a Lagrange multiplier that measures the degree of competition in a sense to be explained below. Optimal choices of retail prices and distribution services by the retailer in this setting must satisfy the following first-order conditions:

$$p[\, 1 - (1/\in)(1 - \mu)] = C_Q + w \qquad (2.10)$$
$$p(\partial Q/\partial D) + \mu r = C_D + (C_Q + w)(\partial Q/\partial D) \qquad (2.11)$$
$$E' - E(p, p', D, Z^0) = 0, \qquad (2.12)$$

where $r = -(\partial E/\partial D)$ is the shadow price of distribution services or what the consumer would be willing to pay for an additional unit of distribution services if it were available in the market at an explicit price. $\in$ is the absolute value of the price elasticity of demand for the explicit output.[18]

A lowering of the competitive standard faced by the optimizing retailer by one unit means a $1 increase in the lowest cost to a representative consumer of attaining her optimal level of consumption activities at an alternative establishment. μ measures the marginal contribution to the profits of the retailer of such a lowering of the competitive standard. When μ is zero we have the standard monopoly situation; the retailer gains no sales. When μ is unity we have the standard competitive situation; the retailer gains all sales.[19] If μ is 0.5, the benefit to a retailer of keeping a representative customer is half of the sales.[20] Thus, the value of μ can be thought of as a direct measure of the degree of competition from similar establishments faced by the retailer.

The power of competition from other similar establishments in retail markets can be illustrated by a special case that eliminates the economic consequences of bundling and leads to what one may label the Pareto efficient degree of cost shifting from the point of view of welfare. It leads to the following proposition:

Proposition 2.3: If the marginal cost functions are independent in outputs $(C_{DQ} = 0)$, perfectly competitive behavior ($\mu = 1$) eliminates the consequences of bundling of distribution services with the explicit items sold at retail and leads to Pareto efficient cost shifting in retail markets.

When μ equals unity (2.10) implies that retail prices are set to equal the marginal cost of producing plus retailing the explicit items sold. This result implies for (2.11) that the level of distribution services will be set solely by the condition that the shadow price of the distribution service equals the marginal cost of producing the service. Thus, bundling becomes irrelevant to the market outcome and the degree of cost shifting that prevails between consumers and retailers is Pareto efficient. This special case also brings out the importance of imperfectly competitive behavior in imparting to retailing its special characteristics.

When μ departs from unity, the choice of prices by the retailer is going to be affected in general by the choice of distribution services, which is a direct consequence of the bundling of explicit items with distribution services. This observation follows directly from (2.10) and (2.11). Moreover, it also follows from these equations that the degree of cost shifting between the consumer and the retailer will in general be affected by the degree of competition from other similar establishments (μ) as well as the general competition for the consumer's dollar, which is measured by the price elasticity ($\in$).

To ascertain the consequences for welfare of retail competition, however, it is useful to look at two special cases: first, suppose that prices are given, perhaps due to government regulation. Then, we have

Proposition 2.4: When the marginal costs with respect to explicit output are constant or increasing ($C_{QQ} \geq 0$) and there is cost shifting, an increase in competition from similar establishments (μ) increases welfare.

When prices are given, (2.10) is irrelevant. Consider the case of constant marginal costs with respect to Q, (2.11) can then be rewritten as $M(\partial Q/\partial D) + \mu r = C_D$, where M is a positive and constant profit margin per unit. An increase in μ requires an increase in distribution services if C_D is increasing in D because r, the shadow price, is decreasing in distribution services due to the convexity of the expenditure function in the fixed input.[21] Moreover, $(\partial Q/\partial D)$ must be decreasing in D or else demand would increase without bound as a result of increasing distribution services. By (2.12) an increase in D increases the welfare of the representative consumer, who can now attain the same level of utility as before at a lower cost, since the expenditure function is decreasing in D, or a higher level of utility at the same cost as before. A similar argument holds if C_D is decreasing in D, because second-order conditions in this case require marginal revenues (the LHS of 2.11) to cut marginal costs (the RHS of 2.11) from above. The importance of this result is that it contradicts the conventional wisdom stemming from Hotelling's (1929) model. The reason is that Hotelling assumed that the marginal costs of providing distribution services (location in his case) were constant at the zero level.[22]

Consider now a situation where the price elasticity of demand is constant but prices are not given. It allows us to establish the following proposition:

Proposition 2.5: When the marginal costs with respect to explicit output are constant or increasing ($C_{QQ} \geq 0$) and there is cost shifting, an increase in competition for the consumer's dollar ($\in$) generates ambiguous welfare results if the marginal costs of distribution services are increasing in distribution services.

Equations (2.10) and (2.11) can be rewritten as

$$(p - C_Q - w) = (p/\in)(1 - \mu) \qquad (2.10)'$$
$$(p/\in)(1 - \mu)(\partial Q/\partial D) + \mu r = C_D \qquad (2.11)'$$

An increase in $\in$ requires a lowering of p in (2.10)$'$ under our assumptions. This increase leads to a decrease in distribution services by (2.11)$'$ when the marginal costs of distribution services are increasing in D, since we saw above that both terms on the LHS are decreasing functions of D. From the expenditure function of the consumer in (2.12) this implies that welfare goes up due to the decrease in p and down due to the decrease in D. Hence, a quantitative evaluation is necessary to determine the net effect on welfare. A similar argument can be made for increases in competition through changes in (μ).

From the point of view of economics, the existence of cost shifting in retail markets necessitates accounting for what happens to distribution services in welfare evaluations of changes in these markets. From the point of view of marketing, the existence of cost shifting supports including distribution services in consumers' payoff functions, as proposed by Wernerfelt (1994), to evaluate marketing designs in retail markets. The model presented in this section provides one mechanism for implementing both welfare evaluations in economics and efficiency comparisons in marketing that account for the role of distribution services in retail markets.

2.6   FULL PRICE MODEL OF RETAIL SERVICES

In this section I show how the model of the previous section generates as a special case a standard model in the literature on retailing. It is a model developed by Ehrlich and Fisher (1982) to analyse the demand for advertising. They argue that if retailing is competitive, consumers must face the same full price at all stores. Stores can compete by cutting prices or supplying more services but they are always subject to the constraint of the constant full price.

We can generate their model in the previous framework as follows: interpret the distribution service (D) as the amount of information provided by the retailer. As we saw in the analysis of Proposition 2.3, perfectly competitive behavior results in the first-order conditions, (2.10) and (2.11), collapsing to the following ones

$$p = C_Q + w \tag{2.13}$$

$$r = C_D. \tag{2.14}$$

The constraint that the full price is constant implies in our model that

$$p + r = C_Q + w + C_D = K \tag{2.15}$$

The full price is nothing other than the sum of the retail price and the shadow price paid by the consumer for the distribution service. K is just a constant. Our analysis brings out two restrictive features of this model. First, there is only one value of the constraint that is consistent with perfect competition in Ehrlich and Fisher's model: namely, that value of the full price that exactly covers both marginal costs. If the firm provides so much information that the shadow price of information becomes zero to the consumer,[23] then the full price coincides with the retail price. As the firm lowers the amount of information provided, the value of information to the consumer increases and the retail price decreases. But, this must happen in such a way that their sum equals the retail price when the value of information is zero.

Second, and perhaps more economically relevant, the marginal cost function for information must be increasing in the amount of information or the retail market is not feasible in Ehrlich and Fisher's model. Suppose C_D is decreasing in D. When the constraint is imposed at the maximum level of distribution services, so that p is the full price because r is zero, equilibrium is possible because the constraint is not really binding. Attempts to depart from this level, however, are impossible. If the retailer decreases the level of information, p decreases, r increases and the marginal cost of increasing the output of explicit items increases (under the usual assumption that C_Q is increasing in Q). The marginal cost of providing information, however, increases as you provide less information and equilibrium can not be restored. Increasing returns in the provision of information by the retailer or advertising pricing schemes incorporating quantity discounts generate decreasing marginal costs of information.

Ehrlich and Fisher's model can be useful in capturing cost shifting between consumers and retailers under decreasing returns to information. The model developed earlier, however, allows us to capture the same phenomenon without imposing this restriction.[24] Ehrlich and Fisher's model has been the basis for an important strand of work in the retailing literature, for example Ratchford and Stoops (1992). Furthermore, the same assumption that all consumers face a given identical full price characterizes other related contributions, for example Deacon and Sonstelie (1991). Hence, the relevance of the model in section 2.5 is wider than the present context.

2.7   MEASUREMENT AND EVIDENCE

Discussions of measurement and evidence will take place throughout the book for two reasons. First, measurement is dependent on the level of aggregation, the purpose of the analysis and the availability of data corresponding to theoretical concepts. Measurement can take place at the level of the store, firm, sector, region or nation. In this section we will focus on measurement at the sectoral level. Second, in dealing with evidence, account must be taken of the fact that distribution services, as indicated earlier in this chapter, have been acknowledged in the economics and marketing literature for many years although they have been given different names and interpretations by different authors. Evidence can also be presented at each of the levels mentioned above. At any level, however, statements in the literature referring to the service level, the marketing mix, promotion effort, and so on, usually map into one or more of the five distribution services identified in section 2.1. In this section we will focus on evidence specifically aimed at identifying these five distribution services at the sectoral level.

By sectoral level data I mean disaggregation of the retail sector of a country into its various components at some level. For instance, in the case of the US, the 1982 Census of Retail Trade allows disaggregation into 49 different retail sectors, 14 of which are at the four-digit SIC level and the remainder at the three-digit SIC level. In France and Germany one can obtain data for the same year that allows disaggregation into 50 and 52 retail sub-sectors, respectively. Unfortunately, the categories are not identical.[25] For example, the most striking difference is that in France the food sector has 14 categories while in the US it has four and in Germany it has five. In any event, in working with sectoral level data the choice of categories is determined, largely, by the statistical agencies collecting the data.

The analytical objective that we will consider is understanding the determinants of retail gross margins across different retail sub-sectors. The definition of profits in (2.4) allows the retail gross margin as a proportion of sales, R, to be expressed as follows:

$$R = (pQ - wQ)/pQ = C(Q, D,v)/pQ + \pi/pQ. \qquad (2.16)$$

The expression on the right-hand side of the first equality is unproblematic from the point of view of measurement. pQ is measured as the sales of the retail sub-sector; wQ is measured as the cost of goods sold by the retail sub-sector; and the ratio of their difference to sales can be used to calculate the retail gross margin as a proportion of sales. Availability of data on sales and the cost of goods sold for each sub-sector allows the calculation of this basic concept.

Matters get complicated, however, when we consider the expression on the right-hand side of the second equality. First, the concept of profits in the definition is economic profits, not accounting profits. The former are not directly observable. Second, the specification of the first term on the right-hand side of the second equality depends, in general, on whether we assume quantity setting behavior, (2.1), or price setting behavior, (2.2). At this level of aggregation it is difficult to make much progress on either issue. Hence, one procedure to deal with the first difficulty is to assume that in each retail sub-sector monopolistic competition leads to zero economic profits.[26] To deal with the second difficulty we view the denominator in (2.16) as a revenue function.[27]

Equilibrium in each sub-sector is characterized by the representative retailer choosing the level of distribution services and output or price that satisfies the demand of the representative consumer. The latter patronizes each sub-sector at different times throughout the year and demands, in general, a different combination of distribution services and output or price. In essence, this uses the time dimension to separate these retail sub-sector markets in the same way that the hedonic approach uses the space dimension to separate, for example, housing markets.

A semi-reduced form specification which captures the previous discussion is:

$$R = h(Q, D; v, W) + u, \qquad (2.17)$$

where $h = C(Q, D; v)/S(Q, D; W)$.[28] Since h is the ratio of a cost function (C) to a revenue function (S), its functional form must be non-linear. Furthermore, the impact of a variable that appears in both numerator and denominator on the 'retail gross margin', R, measures the relative effect of the variable on costs and revenues. u is a stochastic error term which is assumed to be independent and identically distributed across the retail sub-sectors.

Conceptually Q is the explicit output of the retail sub-sector. The sales of each sub-sector deflated by a price index for each sub-sector is an appropriate measurement. Since these price indexes are usually not available,[29] standard practice is to measure Q as sales per establishment or shop. D is a vector of distribution services. In this context a conceptually appropriate measure of accessibility of location (D_1) is the number of establishments in each retail sub-sector. Fortunately, these data are usually available for each sub-sector.

With respect to assortment (D_2), it is possible to construct two conceptually appropriate measures on the basis of information provided, for example, by the US Census of Retail Trade. For each retail sub-sector one can obtain the number of establishments carrying a product line and the sales of each product line for a universe of 30 product lines.[30] This information allows the construction of two different indexes of assortment for each sub-sector. The first one is a weighted average of the number of product lines carried by a sub-sector, using the number of establishments in a sub-sector carrying a product line relative to the total number of establishments in the sub-sector as weights. The second one is the entropy of the distribution of sales across product lines in each sub-sector, that is, $D_{2i} = -\sum_j (S_{ji}/S_i)\ln(S_{ji}/S_i)$. j identifies the product line and it runs from 1 to 30, whereas i identifies the sub-sector. Either index measures the breadth of assortment in a retail sub-sector.

The remaining three distribution services identified in section 2.1 are more difficult to measure at the sectoral level. Assurance of product delivery (D_3) and information (D_4) have several dimensions. Furthermore some of these dimensions are common to all items in an assortment and others are specific to a subset of items. In practice, assurance of product delivery is measured as the average of inventory holdings per establishment at the beginning of the year and at the end of the year, and information is measured as advertising expenditures per establishment. Since the first measure fails to capture the provision of extended hours, for example, and the second fails to capture the provision of information at the store, for example through in-store promotions or selling effort, another empirical construct can be added to these two to capture, at least partially, these dimensions: namely, the payroll per establishment of each sub-sector (D_6). Finally, ambiance (D_5) can be measured in the US data by the gross value of assets in building and structures per establishment for each sub-sector.[31] It is a weak measure.

In the three references cited in this section, alternative versions and extensions of (2.17) have been estimated with sectoral data for the US, France and Germany using a logistic functional form and alternative estimation techniques. One of two main regularities in the results is the rejection, in every country, of the linear specification in favor of this non-linear one by a non-nested test. The other one is rejection in every country, by a classical F-test, of the hypothesis that the measures identified in this section, taken together, are not important determinants of retail margins. Finally, we reproduce in Table 2.1 the results for one set of estimates of (2.17) employing a logistic functional form and using non-linear least squares as the estimation method.

Table 2.1   Estimated coefficients

	Q	D_1	D_2	D_3	D_4	D_5	D_6
US	−9.22*	−0.94*	0.12	−5.55*	82.81*	−5.66	36.41*
France	−3.12*	−0.96*	0.04	−0.21	n.a.	47.22*	19.72*
Germany	−1.67*	−1.22*	−0.41$^\nabla$	1.43$^\nabla$	n.a.	−9.49	10.22*

Notes:
n.a.= not available; * = t-ratio >2.5; $^\nabla$ = t-ratio > 1.75.

Retail sub-sectors that provide greater levels of output and accessibility of location in equilibrium increase revenues by more than they increase costs and, thereby, experience lower 'retail gross margins' in all three countries. Retail sub-sectors that provide greater levels of specific distribution services increase costs by more than they increase revenues and, thereby, experience higher 'retail gross margins' in all three countries. These individual results are not only robust across the three countries, which can be seen from Table 2.1, but they are also robust to alternative versions and extensions of (2.17), which can be seen by consulting the references. They are consistent with the observed variations in these variables between, for example, supermarkets and department stores. The results on information are also robust to alternative specifications, but no data is available for France and Germany. Finally, the results on assurance and ambiance are sensitive to both country and specification. This is not surprising since these variables are poor measures of the theoretical constructs. With respect to assortment, however, the results may simply mean that its impact on costs cancels out its impact on revenues.[32]

By the way of a conclusion to this section, we consider briefly the main alternative explanation of 'retail gross margins': namely a mark-up model (for example Nooteboom, 1985).

$$R = (OE/S)[1 + m(Q, D, X)], \qquad (2.18)$$

where OE are operating expenses excluding the shopkeeper's labor, S is sales, Q is sales per shop, D is referred to as the service bundle or product service package in the mark-up literature, and X are other variables said to affect the mark-up in various circumstances. The discussion of the service bundle in this literature refers to a subset of the same concepts that we are calling distribution services. For instance, one particular application of this model to 16 Dutch retail sub-sectors over the period 1976–83 (Nooteboom, Kleijweg and Thurik 1988) implements the model by including the reciprocal of Q, average inventory holdings relative to sales (D_3/Q in the notation of this section), (OE/S), and time series variables in a linear regression. The coefficient of

$(1/ Q)$ is estimated to be positive with a t-ratio greater than 2.5, which is what one would expect from the results in Table 2.1 for Q in all three countries. A positive coefficient estimate with a t-ratio greater than 2.5 is also obtained for (D_3 /Q). This result is what one would expect for Holland from the result in Table 2.1 for Germany.

Summing up: the conceptualization of distribution services as outputs of retail firms and fixed inputs into the household production functions of consumers provides an attractive framework for the empirical analysis of retail gross margins; it is not rejected by the data at the sectoral level for four different countries; and it generates results that can be used to explain those of the main alternative approach to the analysis of retail gross margins employed in the literature.

2.8   DISTRIBUTION SERVICES AS STRATEGIC TOOLS: AN ILLUSTRATION

It is fitting to conclude this chapter by reporting on a unique study that illustrates two practical aspects of the issues stressed in this chapter: how to measure distribution services at the store level, and how their role in creating price dispersion and product variety in equilibrium allows them to act as strategic instruments for survival in the presence of category killers. Barber and Tietje (2004) investigate what happens to the retail market for home improvements or hardware stores in a California community as a result of the entry of a Home Depot store. Prior to this entry, there were two stores that could be viewed solely as hardware stores in this community: one with the profile of a local hardware store and another with the profile of a regional hardware store.

Barber and Tietje (2004) identify six strategic variables for each store type, namely pricing and the five distribution services identified in section 2.1. They measured these variables in two different ways. The first was an 'objective' way through in-store visits by six 'mystery shoppers' that were given detailed instructions on how to measure these concepts. For instance, the authors developed a typical shopping basket of 24 items relevant for the hardware retail industry with the help of a pricing analyst from a national trade name franchise, and used this basket to measure: pricing, as a weighted average of ten of these items available at all three stores in all the visits; assortment, as the percentage of the 24 items in the shopping basket that were carried by the store (regardless of whether or not they were in stock) during any one visit; assurance, as the percentage of these items that were in stock during any one visit. The first two concepts were measured with just one variable and the same was true of accessibility of location, which was measured as distance from the town center for each store. The third concept, however, was also measured in terms of the total weekly hours the store was opened and how much time it took to purchase a single item during a visit. Information was also measured in two different ways: recording how much in-store product information was available and how much time it took to obtain unsolicited assistance. Finally, ambiance was measured by rating each of six dimensions on a scale of 1 to 7, for example, pleasant atmosphere and well dressed employees were two of the dimensions. Nevertheless the scores on the six dimensions were averaged to obtain a single measure of store ambiance.

To complement this first 'objective' measure the authors conducted two surveys of community members: one two months before and another six months after the Home Depot store opened. The surveys had two key questions for our present purposes. The first one asked respondents to indicate the most important reason for their selection of the hardware store at which they shopped most often. Consumers had a list of 20 aspects from which to select the most important. These 20 aspects were in turn reduced to 14 aspects and the latter were grouped into the six dimensions of strategy mentioned above through the use of principal components.

Pricing policy was evaluated in terms of two dimensions, everyday low pricing and sale prices; assortment was evaluated in terms of three dimensions, overall product selection, number of different product categories and range of selection within each category; accessibility was rated in terms of one dimension, store location and convenience; assurance was rated in terms of two dimensions, having merchandise in stock and quality of merchandise; information was assessed in terms of three dimensions, overall service level, knowledgeable and friendly employees; similarly, ambiance was assessed in terms of store layout, atmosphere and speedy checkouts.

A second question asked respondents to rate the importance of each of the 20 items on a scale of 1–5. These scores were averaged for each of the six strategic variables after eliminating the aspects found to be weak or irrelevant by the principal components analysis. Two results stand out. First, there was no statistically significant difference between the first and the second survey on the average score given to each strategic variable. Thus, preferences over these variables seem stable.

Since the survey also identified where the consumer shopped most often, it was also possible to calculate these average scores for consumers loyal to each of the three types of stores. Table 2.2 presents the combined (over the two surveys) importance ratings for all respondents and for those who shop most often at each of the three stores. The second result stands out from this table. Namely, importance ratings vary dramatically across consumers. Thus, there is considerable consumer heterogeneity with respect to these strategic variables.

Table 2.2 Importance ratings[33]

Variable	All consumers		Home depot		Regional loyalist		Local loyalist	
Assurance	4.40	(5.8)	4.54	(3.5)	4.40	(6.3)	4.41	(7.1)
Information	4.17	(15.8)	4.00	(3.5)	4.15	(13.6)	4.31	(25.3)
Assortment	4.01	(27.8)	4.38	(49.3)	4.00	(28.2)	4.00	(20.1)
Accessibility	4.01	(29.8)	3.86	(9.0)	4.08	(37.5)	4.04	(17.5)
Price	3.76	(14.1)	4.08	(33.3)	3.74	(9.7)	3.68	(11.0)
Ambiance	3.19	(1.3)	3.09	(0.00)	3.18	(1.5)	3.27	(1.3)

While all consumers and the patrons of each type of store rate assurance first and ambiance last in importance, the similarities stop there. Regional and local loyalists rate information second in importance while Home Depot customers rate assortment second in importance. Similarly regional and local loyalists rate price next to last in importance while Home Depot customers rate price third in importance.

A third result is also evident from Table 2.2. The numbers in parentheses represent the percentage of consumers indicating the variable as the primary determinant of store choice. Over 80 per cent of Home Depot's clients choose the store on the basis of assortment or price, which are ranked, respectively, second and third in importance by these customers. Over 65 per cent of the regional store customers choose the store on the basis of assortment and accessibility, which are ranked, respectively, fourth and third in importance by these customers. Over 45 per cent of the local store customers choose the store on the basis of assortment and information, which are ranked, respectively, fourth and second by these customers.

One of the authors' findings is a close but not perfect correspondence between the 'objective' measures of the strategic variables and consumers' perceptions of these variables across the stores. For instance, they find that their 'objective' price index shows Home Depot to have the lowest price among the three stores and this is in accord with the perceptions on pricing reported in Table 2.2. Similarly, they also found that Home Depot had the highest percentage of the 24-item basket carried by the store or available in stock and this agrees with their importance as reflected in the perceptions on assortment and assurance shown in Table 2.2. On the other hand, the 'objective' measure of accessibility, distance to the center of town, is inconsistent with the importance it has for customers choosing the regional center. Barber and Tietje suggest as a possible explanation that the survey question definitely included location as well as convenience, whereas the objective measure ignores the convenience dimension.

With respect to ambiance, the mystery shoppers rate the local store as the best performer and the patrons of the local store give it a higher score in terms of importance than the patrons of the other two stores. Finally, information has two very different dimensions in the 'objective' assessment. The provision of in-store information can be accomplished on a self-service basis, but the amount of time that it takes to get assistance requires availability of personnel dedicated to the task. Home Depot does very well on the former and very poorly on the latter and the opposite is the case for the local retailer. The survey measure reported in Table 2.2 is primarily picking up the second dimension and it is reflected on how well the local store performs on this variable.

What is the final result of all this effort? The authors also gathered information on the sales and profitability of the incumbent stores before, immediately after and six months after the opening of the Home Depot store. They also discussed the strategy pursued by the local store with its managers. Both incumbent stores lost significant market share as a result of the new entrant; yet the local store was able to maintain its profitability while the regional one was experiencing losses immediately after the opening and six months later. The explanation was that the local store increased the prices of some items to retain profitability and it also emphasized the provision of some services especially valued by its customers such as prompt in-store assistance and friendly and knowledgeable employees. In terms of the model of section 2.4, a new equilibrium with greater price dispersion and product variety in distribution services is generated by the new entrant and the use of these variables strategically by the local incumbent.

NOTES

1. This section draws heavily from earlier work (Betancourt and Gautschi, 1988).
2. Providing credit allows a consumer to acquire products without either waiting to have the cash in hand or making an additional trip to a bank or ATM to secure the cash.
3. This characteristic is one of the defining properties of any restricted cost function (Fuss and McFadden, 1978).
4. In some situations a consumer may not take advantage of the fixed input provided by a retailer. For instance, a consumer may not avail herself of the information provided by a sales assistant. This is perfectly consistent with the definition of the distribution service as a fixed input as it does not directly increase the costs to the consumer of ignoring this information. All we are assuming is that there is free disposal of the distribution service by the consumer. In so far as the prices of the items sold by a retailer increase because of the availability of assistance, the costs to the consumer will be affected indirectly and one would expect this particular form of service to be eliminated if many consumers find it irrelevant. Nevertheless, this set of circumstances is logically consistent with the definition of a fixed input.
5. There can be exceptions, of course, as in the cases where delivery services are explicitly charged for when a customer employs them or when a gas station charges differentially for self-service and full-service.
6. Incidentally, retailers sometimes engage in production as well as distribution of the explicit

items sold. In these cases it is frequently impossible to separate the distribution activity from the production activity. This happens frequently in the case of services. For example in the case of restaurants, production and distribution of a meal are usually inseparable. Hence, the explicit output of the restaurant would be the meals. The five categories of distribution services would continue to be relevant. The main practical consequence of inseparability between the explicit output of distribution and its production would be that the value added generated by a restaurant would be greater than that of a typical retail form that did not engage in production activities. This would be so precisely because of the contribution of production activities to value added in the case of restaurants.

7. These properties are derived in Betancourt and Gautschi (1988).

8. In the next chapter we discuss in greater detail the derivation of this demand function.

9. These input prices correspond to the inputs used by the retailer other than the goods or items acquired from suppliers for resale, namely the capital, labor and intermediate products used in the retailing activity.

10. In Chapter 4 we discuss the underpinnings of the cost function and its properties in greater detail.

11. Note that we have an inverse demand function; hence $\in(A) > \in(B)$ implies a greater price sensitivity in B than in A when measured in the usual way, that is, in terms of the reciprocals.

12. This can be generated by the following function: $C = c(v)D^{\alpha}Q^{\beta}$, where v are input prices and $\alpha = (1 - \beta)$.

13. Chapter 3 argues that one of the main effects of distribution services on household activities is to economize on the household's use of time in purchasing tasks.

14. For an illustration in terms of rich and poor consumers with different search costs, see Lal and Matutes (1989). For an illustration in which consumer heterogeneity makes it impossible to attain a first best outcome without middlemen, see Biglaiser and Friedman (1999).

15. In this context we should note that the desire to allow for the role of several distribution services and the analytical difficulties in doing so lead De Palma et al. (1994) to develop a simulation model.

16. The model that follows borrows heavily from this last reference.

17. The expenditure function of the consumer will be discussed in greater detail in the next chapter.

18. Notice that this elasticity is the reciprocal of the one in the previous section, since here we are using the ordinary demand function instead of the inverse demand function used there.

19. This case encompasses two different situations: Bertrand behavior where a firm behaves as if it were a perfect competitor, and perfect competition proper. Note that the degree of competition in this model is exogenously determined.

20. Values greater than unity violate second-order conditions. Thus, the unit interval is the relevant range.

21. See Chapter 3 for elaboration.

22. See Betancourt and Gautschi (1993a) for elaboration.

23. Recall from the previous section that r is decreasing in distribution services.

24. It is shown in Chapter 4 that, in general, there are compelling arguments in favor of the assumption of increasing returns or declining marginal costs in distribution services.

25. For a discussion of the measurement issues that arise in international comparisons of retail sub-sectors see Betancourt and Gautschi (1996).

26. An alternative is to specify a function of market structure variables for the second term on the RHS of (2.16). For an example of this alternative see Betancourt and Gautschi (1993b).

27. Betancourt and Gautschi (1992a), for example, pursue the implications of quantity setting and price setting in this empirical context.

28. Estimation of (2.17) with a cross-section of sectoral data for a particular country is facilitated because W, full income, and v, input prices, can be assumed to be the same across the retail sub-sectors.

29. This situation is changing. For instance, at this time BLS has implicit price deflators that are publishable for 40 of the 64 retail sub-sectors identified at the four-digit level (Foster, Haltiwanger and Krizan 2002).

30. The number of product lines in the universe varies over time for the US Census and it also differs for other countries.
31. In France and Germany it can be measured as the value of new construction per establishment.
32. This framework has been applied to Spanish sectoral retail data for 1992 by Santos-Requejo (1996). In the case of Spain there were 25 identifiable retail sectors, mainly at the four-digit level. The variables were defined and measured as indicated above whenever possible, for example, just as in the case of France and Germany advertising expenditure data were not available for Spain. The results of the analysis are essentially the same as those for the other three countries. For example, sales per establishment and payroll per establishment are both statistically significant at the 1 per cent level and have the same sign as reported above. While accessibility of location also has the same sign as reported above, it is not statistically significant at the 1 per cent level. None of the other individual coefficients are statistically significant at the 1 per cent level, which is the same result obtained above for Germany.
33. All the information in this table comes from Tables 6, 7 and 8 in Barber and Tietje (2004).

3. Retail demand

An intrinsic feature of retail demand, stressed in the development of the approach in the previous chapter, is that it depends on distribution services. Another intrinsic feature of retail demand, which was not stressed in the previous chapter, is its multiproduct nature. Section 3.1 is an introduction to the household production model. This model provides a natural and rigorous basis for capturing these two fundamental features of retail demand and it is a well established framework in both the economics and marketing literature. Section 3.2 contains the implications of the household production model for the substitutability and complementarity that arises in retail demand as a result of price changes. How these concepts apply to recent empirical marketing literature is shown in section 3.3. The two studies discussed in detail reflect best practice in the marketing literature and allow us to illustrate important implications of this approach to retail demand. More generally, they illustrate how this approach provides a conceptual foundation for the use of scanner data.

Section 3.4 details the immediate implications of the household production model for the substitutability and complementarity that arises in retail demand as a result of changes in distribution services. The analysis of these changes relies on the distribution services' elasticity of demand, which is a concept intrinsic to the approach to retail demand emphasized in this book. Section 3.5 discusses more general and subtle implications of our approach to retail demand, namely implications for retail competition and agglomeration effects. Section 3.6 concludes by explicitly relating the concept of distribution services to several strands of retailing literature. Parenthetically, an Appendix to the chapter includes a derivation of Cournot's aggregation condition in this model and proofs of three of the main results stated in the text.

3.1   THE HOUSEHOLD PRODUCTION MODEL AND RETAIL DEMAND[1]

Various contributions to the literature in the 1960s led to the development of the household production model. One strand, Becker (1965), emphasizes the model as a mechanism to incorporate time explicitly into the analysis of consumption, whereas the other strand, Muth (1966) and Lancaster (1966), emphasizes accommodation of the reality that many items purchased by consumers, for example electricity, yield no direct satisfaction but are used to produce the commodities that actually generate satisfaction, for example temperature comfort. A clear and concise formulation of the model is available in Deaton and Muellbauer (1980) and it has become the standard point of departure in the literature. It can incorporate either strand of literature, and it is the basis for earlier work on retail demand by Betancourt and Gautschi (1990, 1992b). Their two-stage formulation provides a useful starting point.

The first stage can be described as follows:

$$\text{Min } pQ \text{ s.t. } h(Q, D, Z; A) = 0, \tag{3.1}$$

where Q, the vector of choice variables, represents all the goods and services employed by the household in production, including the goods and services purchased from different retailers as well as the time employed by the household in production activities. p is a corresponding vector of given prices, including the opportunity cost of the household's time. D is a vector of distribution services provided by the retailers which the household patronizes during its purchasing activities. They act as fixed inputs in the household's production activities.[2] Z is the vector of commodities produced by the household, which are the ones that produced satisfaction or utility directly. A is the household's endowment of capital, including human capital. While it is included here for completeness, it will be dropped from the subsequent discussion since we make no explicit use of this feature of the model in what follows. h is a quasi-convex transformation function.[3]

A choice of Q that satisfies the optimization problem in (3.1) generates the following cost or expenditure function for the household,

$$E(p, D, Z). \tag{3.2}$$

This function has the following properties, familiar from duality theory: 1) Non-decreasing, concave and linear homogeneous in prices (the elements of p); 2) increasing in outputs (the elements of Z) or the commodities that yield satisfaction; 3) non-increasing and convex in distribution services (the elements of D); and 4) it satisfies Shepard's Lemma or the derivative of the expenditure function with respect to price is the Hicksian demand function.

The third property follows from assuming the distribution services provided by a retailer act as fixed inputs into the household production activities. Just as noted in Chapter 2, this property allows the shifting of distribution costs between consumers and retailers to be captured formally on the demand side. It has two useful implications for a concept already employed in the previous chapter. First, it shows that by defining the shadow price of a distribution service as the negative of the contribution to expenditures of increasing a distribution service by one unit, that is, $r = -(\partial E/\partial D) = -E_D$, the shadow price will always be non-negative. Second convexity implies that $E_{DD} > 0$, which in turn implies that the shadow price is decreasing in the distribution service. Namely, $r_D = -E_{DD} < 0$. In addition, the fourth property generates the conditional or Hicksian demand function for a good or item purchased from a particular retailer as

$$Q_k = E_k = (\partial E/\partial p_k) = g_k(p, D, Z), \qquad k = 1, \ldots, K. \tag{3.3}$$

In the second stage the household maximizes utility by choosing the optimal levels of the commodities that yield satisfaction (Z), subject to the constraint that the household's full income (W) be sufficient to cover the costs of producing the commodities, that is,

$$\text{Max } U(Z) \text{ s.t. } W \geq E(p, D, Z), \tag{3.4}$$

where $U(Z)$ is an increasing, strictly quasi-concave utility function. The first-order conditions for an interior solution are given by

$$U_i(Z) = \lambda E_i(p, D, Z), i = 1, \ldots, I, \text{ and} \tag{3.5}$$
$$W = E(p, D, Z), \tag{3.6}$$

where $\partial U/\partial Z_i = U_i(Z)$, $\partial E/\partial Z_i = E_i(p, D, Z)$ and λ is a Lagrange multiplier. The solution of (3.5) and (3.6) yields the demand functions for the commodities that yield satisfaction,

$$Z_i = f_i(p, D, W), \qquad i = 1, \ldots, I. \tag{3.7}$$

Finally, substitution of (3.7) into (3.3) yields the Marshallian or uncompensated demand functions for any item purchased from a retailer,

$$Q_k = E_k = (\partial E/\partial p_k) = g_k(p, D, f_i(p, D, W)), \quad k = 1, \ldots, K. \tag{3.8}$$

This system of demand functions is a multiproduct generalization of the ordinary demand function (2.2) specified in Chapter 2. It arises from a standard specification of the household production model adapted to capture the role of distribution services. And, it provides a rigorous and general foundation for the discussion of retail demand.

3.2 SUBSTITUTABILITY AND COMPLEMENTARITY IN RETAIL DEMAND: PRICES

For any demand equation in system (3.8) one can decompose the effect of a change in a price on the quantity demanded in terms of elasticities as follows:

$$\in_{kl} = \in_{kl}^{*} + \Sigma_i \, \omega_{ki} \, \eta_{il} \qquad k, l = 1, \ldots, K, \qquad (3.9)$$

where $\in_{kl} = (\partial Q_k/\partial p_l)(p_l/Q_k)$, $\in_{kl}^{*} = [(\partial Q_k/\partial p_l \mid Z)](p_l/Q_k)$, $\omega_{ki} = (\partial Q_k/\partial Z_i)$ (Z_i/Q_k), and $\eta_{il} = (\partial Z_i/\partial p_l)(p_l/Z_i)$.

The first term on the RHS of equation (3.9) captures the production effect of a change in the price of a retail item. It represents an adjustment to the change in the context of the optimization in the first stage when the levels of the commodities that yield satisfaction (Z) are given and the household minimizes the costs of producing these given levels of the commodities. If $k = l$, one has the production effect of a change in the own-price of a retail item. It will always be negative due to the concavity in prices of the expenditure function, that is, $E_{kk} < 0$. If $k \neq l$, one has the production effect of a change in the price of another retail item and it leads to

Definition 1: Two retail items (*k, l*) are *net* substitutes, independent or complements as the production effect ($\in_{kl}^{*}$) is positive, zero or negative, respectively.

One important technical feature of the household production model is that it forces one to think about the role of retail items as inputs in the production of a set of commodities that yield satisfaction. It immediately leads to three possibilities when the price of an item changes: the item may be an input into the production of only one commodity produced by the household; or it may be an input into the production of every commodity produced by the household; or it may be an input into the production of some commodities but not others. This feature has important economic consequences. When retail items are used exclusively in the production of different commodities (Z_i), for example, they will be net independents.[4] In the extreme if only one item is used to produce every commodity there is a negative own production effect and a zero cross production effect so all items are net independents.[5] If an item is used in the production of every commodity, then this item can in principle have relationships of net substitutability or complementarity with any other item.

Relations of net substitutability in production tend to arise in settings where the analysis is conducted at low levels of time aggregation. For instance, steak and fish are likely to be substitutes in the production of nutrition at any given meal but are likely to be complements in the production of nutrition during a weekly period. In other words for most analytical purposes retail items are likely to be net complements or net independents.

The second term in (3.9) represents the consumption effect of a change in the price of a retail item. It captures the adjustment to the change in the context of the optimization problem in the second stage. When the price of an item used in the production of a commodity changes, the effective price of consuming that commodity changes and the household responds by adjusting its consumption of these commodities in the manner predicted by standard consumer demand theory. Notice that the only analytical difference between the optimization in the second stage and standard consumer theory is that, since the budget constraint of the household (3.6) is non-linear, the consumption prices of these commodities are the marginal costs of producing them (which in general are not constant). There is an important substantive difference, however, which is best brought out by looking at the nature of the individual elements in the sum making up the consumption effect.

One of the two terms in the multiplication, ω_{ki} [$= (\partial Q_k/\partial Z_i)(Z_i/Q_k)$], represents the proportionate change in the usage of the kth item in the production of commodity i as a result of a change in the production of this commodity. This term is zero if the kth retail item is not used in the production of commodity i and positive otherwise (assuming no regressive inputs). The other term in the multiplication, η_{il} [$= (\partial Z_i/\partial p_l)(p_l/Z_i)$], is the proportionate change in the demand for commodity i as a result of a change in the price of the lth retail item. The same technical characteristic of the household production model emphasized above also plays a role here. Namely, if a retail item l is used in the production of only one commodity, the consumption effect will have only one element in the sum; if this retail item is used in the production of every commodity there will be I terms in the sum; and if this item is used in the production of some commodities but not others, there will be as many terms in the sum as commodities in which this item is used in production.

In both extreme cases, however, it can be shown that the consumption effect will be negative.[6] This result is derived for the case where the item is used in the production of every commodity in the technical appendix. In the text below I provide an intuition for the result in the case where the item is used solely in the production of a single commodity. For the in-between cases, one could find situations with a positive consumption effect, but they would be rare for they would require at least two retail items used in the production of two different commodities, these two commodities would have to be substitutes in consumption and the substitution effect between these commodities would have to dominate the income effect.[7]

Since the marginal costs of producing a commodity always increase as a result of an increase in the price of an item used in its production, the household's response to this price increase, if the commodity is a normal good, will be to decrease its consumption. That is, a negative substitution effect in consumption will be reinforced by a negative income effect in this case. If $l = k$, this merely says that the own uncompensated price elasticity, which is the sum of the production effect and the consumption effect, will be negative. If $l \neq k$, this leads to

Definition 2: Two retail items are *gross* substitutes, independent or complements as the sum of the production effect and the consumption effect, $\in_{kl}$, is positive, zero or negative, respectively.

Consequently, all items used in the production of the same commodity that are net independent or complements with each other will be gross complements. Even those items that are substitutes with each other in the production of the same commodity, that is, net substitutes, will be gross complements if the consumption effect dominates the production effect.[8]

Summing up, there is a strong tendency toward gross complementarity among all retail items. The existence of a negative consumption effect in most situations is one powerful reason for this conclusion. The exclusive use of many retail items in the production of different commodities by a household and its consequent implication of net independence among these items is a second powerful reason for this conclusion. Finally, the use of some retail items in the production of different commodities and the use of others exclusively in the production of a single commodity implies an asymmetry in the consumption effects of these two types of items and, consequently, in the degree of gross complementarity that they generate.

3.3 APPLICATIONS

Mulhern and Leone (1991) have done an empirical study of the demand for four brands of the product category cake mix and the same four brands of the product category cake frosting (Betty Crocker (BC), Pillsbury (P), Duncan-Hines (DH), and the store brand (SB)). The choice of the product categories reflects items that are 'use' complements and have few brands. 'Use' complements is a term used in the marketing literature to capture what we have defined as net complements in the context of the household production model. Their study allows the illustration of two things: a practical way of estimating the concepts of the previous section; and, more importantly, how these concepts allow for an explanation of results that would be difficult, if not impossible, to explain without them. In particular the low level of aggregation at the product category permits a clear illustration of the asymmetry of gross complementarity relationships and its source in the consumption effect.

One characteristic of this study is that it is based on scanner data for two stores over a two-year period. Each store is analysed separately. The study obtains weekly prices, and sales quantities (and unit cost data)[9] matched to the promotional activities of the stores. Any week the brand is promoted or is on special offer a dummy variable is used to capture this phenomenon. This dummy variable controls for changes in specific distribution services that enhance visibility such as features or displays associated with the promotions. One aim of the study is to estimate the effects on demand of regular prices as well as promotions using a consistent framework. The authors estimate separately two sets of seemingly unrelated regressions: one for each product category after correcting each equation for first-order serial correlation.

The functional form of the ith demand equation in each of the two four-equation systems (one equation for each brand in a system) would be the following semi-log:

$$Ln\ Q_{it} = \alpha_{1i} + [\beta_{1i}\ (1/p_{it}) + \Sigma\gamma_{1k}\ (1/p_{kt})](1 - X_{it}) + [\beta_{2i}\ (1/p_{it})$$
$$+ \Sigma\gamma_{2k}\ (1/p_{kt})](X_{it}) + \alpha_{2i}\ X_{it} \tag{3.10}$$

where t is the week, the 1 identifies the regular price parameters and the 2 the offer or promotion price parameters. X_i is a dummy variable that takes the value of 1 if a promotion is on for brand i during the week and 0 otherwise. The index k varies across brands and categories. Thus, each equation generates eight estimates of regular price parameters and eight estimates of special offer or promotion price parameters in their study.[10] For each of the two estimated systems, Table 3.1 presents the estimates of the price elasticities associated with the regular prices (four diagonal elements for each system and 28 off-diagonal elements for each system).[11] Note that

$$\in_{1ii} = (-\beta_{1i}/p_i)\ \text{and}\ \in_{1ik} = (-\gamma_{1ik}/p_k),\ i, = 1,\dots 4;\ k=1,\dots,8,\ i \neq k. \tag{3.11}$$

Prior to discussing the results in Table 3.1 it is useful to set the stage for relating the elasticities in (3.11) to our earlier discussion. Let the household production processes be making of a cake with frosting, C, and making of a pound cake (with no frosting), P. M is cake mix and F is frosting. There are two categories of elasticities: namely cross-category relationships where $M \neq F$, and within-category relationships where $M = M$ and $F = F$. Notice that in the within-category case $i = k$ implies own-brand effects and $i \neq k$ implies cross-brand effects.

Only parameters significantly different from zero at least at the 10 per cent level were reported and used in the calculations. Consider first the cross-category effects (off diagonal blocks). Most of the results indicate gross independence and the non-zero results all indicate, as expected, gross complementarity.

Table 3.1 Regular price elasticities for cake mix and frosting (store 2)

Cake Mix		$(\in_{MM})$				$(\in_{MF})$			
		BC	DH	P	SB	BC*	DH*	P*	SB*
	BC	-2.35	0	0	0	0	0	0	0
	DH	0	-1.62	2.36	0	0	-0.30	0	0
	P	0	0	-3.48	0	0	0	0	0
	SB	0	0	0	-3.86	0	0	0	0
Frosting		$(\in_{FM})$				$(\in_{FF})$			
	BC*	0	-0.66	-0.91	0	-1.15	0	0	0
	DH*	0	-1.44	0	-0.58	0	-5.37	0	0
	P*	0	-0.97	-2.06	0	0	0	-2.64	0
	SB*	0	0	0	0	0	0	0	-1.02

There are, however, strong asymmetries in the results. The price of frosting has no effect on the demand for cake mix except for one case (Duncan Hines frosting is a gross complement with Duncan Hines cake mix). On the other hand, the price of cake mix does affect the demand for frosting within brands and across brands for all frostings but the store brand. Moreover there is a pattern in these asymmetries, since in all comparisons we have $\in_{MF} \geq \in_{FM}$. Mulhern and Leone (1991) explain this finding by asserting (p.72) 'This result may be attributable to the primacy of cake mix over frosting.'

The results of the previous section help explain this pattern in a less arbitrary fashion. Equation (3.9) from the previous section can be written as

$$\in_{MF} = \in_{MF}{}^* + \omega_{MC}\eta_{CF} + \omega_{MP}\eta_{PF} \text{ and}$$
$$\in_{FM} = \in_{FM}{}^* + \omega_{FC}\eta_{CM} + \omega_{FP}\eta_{PM} = \in_{FM}{}^* + \omega_{FC}\eta_{CM}, \qquad (3.12)$$

because to make a pound cake (P) you need no frosting, so that $\omega_{FP} = 0$. First, the continuity of the expenditure function implies that the cross partials in the production effects are symmetric so that for any two items $\in_{MF}{}^* = \in_{FM}{}^*$ $[(P_F Q_F / P_M Q_M)]$. This term will be negative.[12] Second, the two terms in the consumption effect for $\in_{MF}$ will have opposite signs. An increase in the price of frosting will lead to a negative consumption effect through the first term, which captures a lower demand for cake mix to make cakes with frosting, and a positive consumption effect through the second term, which captures a higher demand for cake mix in consumption through the higher demand for pound cakes. Third, an increase in the price of cake mix will have only one negative consumption effect on the demand for frosting, which captures a lower demand for cakes with frosting, thus reinforcing the negative production

effect for $\in_{FM}$. Thus, $\in_{MF} \geq \in_{FM}$ implies $\in_{FM} * [(P_F \, Q_F \, /P_M \, Q_M) - 1] +$
$\omega_{MP}\eta_{PF} - \omega_{FC}\eta_{CM} \geq - \omega_{MC}\eta_{CF}$. The three terms on the left-hand side will be
positive and, therefore, their sum is likely to dominate the single term on the
right-hand side, which will also be positive.[13]

For the within-category relationships, the own-brand effects are given by

$$\in_{MM} (i = k) = \in_{MM} * + \omega_{MC}\eta_{CM} + \omega_{MP}\eta_{PM} \text{ and}$$
$$\in_{FF} (i = k) = \in_{FF} * + \omega_{FC}\eta_{CF} . \tag{3.13}$$

Both are expected to be negative and that is what we observe in Table 3.1. All
eight diagonal elements are negative. For the within-category relationships the
cross-brand effects are given by

$$\in_{MM} (i \neq k) = \in_{MM} * (i \neq k) + \omega_{MC}\eta_{CM} + \omega_{MP}\eta_{PM} \text{ and}$$
$$\in_{FF} (i \neq k) = \in_{FF} *(i \neq k) + \omega_{FC}\eta_{CF} , \tag{3.14}$$

and the production effects are expected to be positive, since within a category
all brands would be net substitutes, while the consumption effects are expected
to be negative. In all but one case the off-diagonal elements in the diagonal
blocks are zero, indicating that the consumption and the production effects
balanced out or that the data is not sufficient to identify whatever differences
may exist. The one exception indicates that Pillsbury's and Duncan Hines'
cake mix are gross substitutes.

The results for promotions exhibit a similar pattern and the same is true of the
results for the other store. When gross complementarity prevails among these
cross categories with respect to both prices and promotions, retailers can exploit
them to their advantage in their pricing decisions. Morever these gross complementarities introduce a potentially significant wedge between the objectives of
the retailers and the objectives of manufacturers in the use of special deals and
promotions. These two issues will be explored further in Chapter 5.

Next consider the related study by Hoch, Kim, Montgomery and Rossi
(1995), (HKMR). It illustrates an alternative way of implementing the model
empirically and one can use its results to illustrate two properties of demand
elasticities of retail items in the context of the household production model.
Namely, items used in the production of many household commodities tend to
have more elastic demands than those that are used in the production of a few
or only one household commodity. And, gross complementarity can exist even
within the same product category given the definitions of product categories
one can employ in practice. One should add that the focus in this chapter is not
the focus of the authors who state at one point (p.26) 'we seek only to explain
the variation in elasticities across stores. We do not attempt to identify factors
that could explain differences in mean elasticities across categories . . . under-

standing differences . . . is an interesting topic.' We will visit the aspect of the study stressed by the authors in Chapter 5.

HKMR obtain 160 weeks of scanner data by Uniform Product Code (UPC) for 83 stores from Dominick's Finer Foods, a supermarket chain in Chicago.[14] The data contains unit sales, retail price, profit margin, and a special deal code indicating shelf-tag reductions or in-store coupons for 18 categories which are reproduced in the first column of Table 3.2. In the first stage of their analysis, HKMR estimate store-specific price elasticities for each of the 18 product categories separately. In order to do so, however, the authors have to aggregate the 4636 individual retail items available by UPC into each of the 18 categories. They do so by constructing 265 aggregates of items (about 15 per category) on the basis of size, form, flavors and type that account for at least 50 per cent of sales in a category. The resulting number of items per category is presented in column 3 of Table 3.2.

Table 3.2   Category price elasticities

Food category	UPCs	Number of items	Own price	Sum of cross price
Soft drinks	619	10	–2.59	–0.59
Refrigerated juice	108	12	–2.24	1.5
Frozen juice	105	14	–1.95	1.4
Canned soup	89	18	–1.66	0.04
Frozen entrees	500	12	–1.65	0.88
Bottled juice	242	21	–1.49	1.4
Graham/saltines	230	10	–1.46	0.45
Dairy cheese	367	17	–1.44	0.72
Cereal	298	21	–1.14	0.94
Canned seafood	180	12	–0.96	–0.83
Cookies	637	13	–0.90	–0.70
Snack crackers	197	15	–0.79	–0.07
Non-food category				
Bath tissue	57	9	–2.28	–0.14
Toothpaste	296	11	–2.00	1.55
Laundry detergent	303	10	–1.99	0.31
Fabric softener	140	8	–1.77	0.98
Liquid dish detergent	178	13	–1.64	0.90
Paper towels	90	12	–1.21	1.26

For each of the categories a linear in the logs or double-log demand system is estimated separately. For instance, with ten items in a category as in soft drinks, for example, the equation for the ith item in the ten-equation system for soft drinks would look as follows:

$$q_{jti} = \alpha_i + \tau_j D_j + \Sigma_k \in_{jik} p_{jtk} + \delta_i \text{Deal}_{it} + B_i F_{it} + \Phi_{jt-1} q_{jit}$$
$$i, k = 1, \ldots, 10; t = 1, \ldots, 80. \tag{3.15}$$

where q's are logs of unit sales standardized by size and p's are logs of prices of items. The price of each item is constructed as a Divisia price index[15] of all the UPCs that make up that item. α_i is an item-specific intercept. D_j is a store dummy variable that generates a store-specific intercept (τ_j). The price elasticities are given by $\in_{jik} = \eta_{ik} + \lambda_{jik,}$ where $\lambda_{jik} = \lambda_{ji}$ if $i = k$ and zero otherwise. Hence, the own-price elasticities differ across stores but the cross-price elasticities are the same across stores. Among the other variables is information on a dummy variable (Deal) indicating the operation of temporary price reductions or store coupons and indicators of display features (F). Both are item-specific but not store-specific. Finally they included lagged sales, which are forced to have the same effect for all items in a category but can differ across stores.

With scanner data estimation can be conceptualized in terms of a representative consumer for each store, just as in the previous study. In contrast to that study, however, all cross-category effects are suppressed in this one. One reason for this approach is that HKMR focus on explaining variations in the elasticities across stores.

For each of 18 categories HKMR estimate the coefficients of the system in (3.15) using 80 weeks of data and reserving the other 80 weeks for validating the model. These estimates allow them to construct the following average own-price elasticity of demand for each category

$$\in_{ii} = \{ \Sigma_j \Sigma_i w_{ji} (\eta_{ii} + \lambda_{ji}) \}/J, \tag{3.16}$$

where w_{ji} is the share of the unit volume of item i in the volume of the category for store j. These estimates are presented in the fourth column of Table 3.2, where we have arranged the categories within the food and non-food groups in descending order in absolute value terms.

A striking feature of the results is the substantial differences in the own-price elasticities across categories. For instance, the soft drinks elasticity is more than twice as large as the cereal elasticity in absolute value. This is what one would expect from the analysis in the Appendix, that is, own-price elasticities are larger for items used in the production of many commodities. It is shown there that a sufficient condition for demand to be elastic is that a retail item be used in every household production activity and, more generally, that retail items used in many household production activities will tend to have a more elastic demand than those used in only a few or one, because there will be more negative terms in the consumption effect. Cereals are typically used only at breakfast whereas soft drinks can be consumed in the context of a greater variety of household production activities, ranging from all meals to snacks, parties and picnics. Not surprisingly, soft drinks and refrigerated juice are very elastic while cookies and snack crackers are inelastic.

In the non-food group a similar argument can be used, for example, to explain the difference in own-price elasticities between toothpaste and paper towels. For instance if every household member leaves home before breakfast and returns in time to go to sleep, the consumption of toothpaste need not be affected relative to a situation where every household member stays at home all day. The same is unlikely to be true for the consumption of paper towels.

HMKR also calculate a category level elasticity as follows

$$\in_c = \{\Sigma_j \Sigma_k w_{jk} (\eta_{ik} + \lambda_{ji})\}/J. \tag{3.17}$$

This elasticity answers the question in the following conceptual experiment: if all k item prices in a category are increased in the same proportion, by how much will volume sales in the category decrease? It also allows us to estimate the sum of the cross-price elasticities of demand in a category as follows:

$$\Sigma_k \in_{ik} = \in_c - \in_{ii}, \text{ for } i \neq k. \tag{3.18}$$

These estimates are presented in the fifth column of Table 3.2. The most interesting feature of the column is that even in a setting where one expects most items within a category to exhibit a relation of gross substitutability, one finds five categories in which a relation of gross complementarity across all items within the category prevails.

Part of the explanation is that items within each category that are used in many different household production activities will have a tendency toward gross complementarity due to the consumption effect (the same soft drink at various meals or other occasions). Part of the explanation is that for certain definitions of the consumption goals or household activities items within each category can be even complements in 'use' or net complements (for example providing different snack crackers or cookies for guests at a party). Part of the explanation is that these items are purchase complements. Since the study uses weekly scanner data, it captures indirectly the benefits of one-stop shopping during the week and over this period households can easily purchase together items that are substitutes at any one time (for example different types of canned seafood for different daily meals and different types of bathroom tissue for different bathrooms).

Summing up, interpretation of these two studies illustrates how the modifications of the traditional economic analysis of consumer behavior stressed in section 3.2 enhance our understanding of the estimation of price elasticities of demand. More generally, since both of these studies employed scanner data they illustrate the applicability of this view of retail demand to the analysis of purchases. This feature increases the relevance of our approach, because scanner data have become typical for estimation of price elasticities of demand in the marketing literature. Moreover, recently this type of data has attracted the attention of economists, for example Feenstra and Shapiro (2003). Finally, it is also noteworthy that these two studies illustrate the applicability of this approach to retail demand in the estimation of price elasticities based on regular prices or on both regular and promotional prices.

3.4   SUBSTITUTABILITY AND COMPLEMENTARITY IN RETAIL DEMAND: DISTRIBUTION SERVICES

A distinguishing feature of this analysis is the role that distribution services play in retail demand. Since analytically they play the role of quantities that are the dual of prices in their effects on quantity demanded, for any demand equation in system (3.8) one can obtain the distribution services elasticity of demand, $\in_{kj}$, and decompose the effect of a change in a distribution service on the quantity demanded as follows:

$$\in_{kj} = \in^*_{kj} + \Sigma_i \, \omega_{ki} \, \eta_{ij} \qquad [\, k = 1, \ldots, K, \text{ and } j = 1, \ldots, J], \qquad (3.19)$$

where $\in_{kj} = (\partial Q_k/\partial D_j)(D_j/Q_k)$, $\in_{kj}^* = [(\partial Q_k/\partial D_j \mid Z)](D_j/Q_k)$, $\omega_{ki} = (\partial Q_k/\partial Z_i)(Z_i/Q_k)$, and $\eta_{ij} = (\partial Z_i/\partial D_j)(D_j/Z_i)$.

The first term on the RHS of (3.19) captures the production effect of a change in the jth distribution service. That is, it represents the consumer's response in terms of the quantity demanded of the kth item or input given the levels of the commodities that yield satisfaction (Z). And, it leads to the following definition of substitutability and complementarity

Definition 3: An item or input k and a distribution service j are *net* complements, independents, or substitutes as the production effect, $\in^*_{kj}$, is positive, zero, or negative, respectively.[16]

In general the distribution services of a given retailer will be net independent or net complements with most if not all items in the assortment of that retailer. For instance, if the distribution service is specific and provides, for example, information on a particular item in a retailer's assortment, it will be a net complement to that item in whatever household production activity the item is employed. If the distribution service is common to all items in an assortment it will usually be a net complement or a net independent to all items in that assortment that are purchased by the consumer.[17] While the relation between the distribution services of a retailer and the items in that retailer's assortment is typically one of net complementarity, there is one important relation of net substitutability in this analysis. At the most fundamental level all distribution services, except for ambiance, are substitutes for the use of the household's own time in purchase activities. Since purchase activities can be viewed as an intrinsic component of the production by the household of any commodity that yields satisfaction, distribution services other than ambiance can be viewed as net substitutes with the household's time input in the consumption activities that yield satisfaction.

The second term in (3.19) represents the consumption effect of a change in a distribution service. One of the two terms in the multiplication, $\omega_{ki} = (\partial Q_k/\partial Z_i)(Z_i/Q_k)$, is exactly the same as in section 3.2 and it has the same interpretation: the proportionate change in the usage of the kth item or input as a result of a proportionate increase in the production of the ith commodity. The other term in the multiplication, $\eta_{ij} = (\partial Z_i/\partial D_j)(D_j/Z_i)$, is the proportionate change in the demand for commodity i as a result of a proportionate increase in the jth distribution service. Just as in the case of prices considered in section 3.2, the type of usage of the item or input in the household production activities has economic consequences. Namely if the retail item or input is used in the production of only one commodity, the consumption effect will have only one term in the summation and it can be shown that this term will be positive if the commodity is a normal good.[18] If the retail item or input is used in the production of every commodity by the household, the consumption effect will have I terms in the summation and I show in the Appendix that it must be positive.

More generally, equation (3.19) leads to the following

Definition 4: An item or input k and a distribution service j are *gross* complements, independents or substitutes as the sum of the production and the consumption effect, $\in_{kj}$, is positive, zero, or negative, respectively.

Summing up, the analysis in this section leads to the conclusion that the main relationship between a retailer's distribution services and the items in that retailer's assortment is one of gross complementarity. First, the production effect normally leads to a relation of net independence or net complementarity between the distribution services of a retailer and any of the items in that retailer's assortment. Second, since the consumption effect of a change in distribution services is almost always positive, the relation between the distribution services of a retailer and any of the items in that retailer's assortment is one of gross complementarity.

3.5   RETAIL COMPETITION AND AGGLOMERATION EFFECTS[19]

Implicit in the discussion of the price elasticities (section 3.2) was the assumption that the item experiencing the change in price and the one experiencing the change in quantity were in the assortment of the same retailer. Similarly, in the discussion of distribution services elasticities (section 3.4) the change in the distribution service was assumed to impact the quantities of items in that retailer's assortment. Fortunately, there is nothing in the analysis that restricts one to that case. Furthermore, there is considerable value in explicitly considering how a change in price or distribution service by one retailer (*B*) affects the quantities demanded from another retailer (*A*). For, it is through these interactions that retail competition and agglomeration effects affect retail demand.

Consider first a rewrite of equation (3.9) that incorporates explicitly the effect on quantities demanded from retailer *A* induced by changes in prices controlled by retailer *B*.

$$\in_{kl}(A,B) = \in_{kl}{}^{*}(A,B) + \Sigma_{i}\, \omega_{ki}(A)\, \eta_{il}(B). \qquad k, l = 1, \ldots, K. \quad (3.9)'$$

If one lets item *k* be brand X in the assortment of retailer *A* and item *l* be the same brand X in *B*'s assortment, one has a situation where retail competition is likely to be most intense.[20] Clearly the production effect in (3.9)' $[\in_{kl}{}^{*}(A,B)]$ will be positive, since the two items would be net substitutes. While the consumption effect will be negative ($\eta_{il}(B) < 0$), it will only lead to a situation in which a price reduction by *B* of item *l* leads to an increase in the demand for item *k* of *A* when the positive production effect is dominated by the negative consumption effect. One would expect that most of the time the price reduction by *B* of brand X will result in a lowering of purchases of brand X from *A* by the representative consumer, and this is how a substantial amount of retail competition takes place.

Nevertheless for all those items in *A* that are net independent or net complements with the ones in *B*, any price reduction by *B* on these items leads to an increase in the demand for the items of retailer *A*, since the consumption effect is negative. This result provides an incentive for retailers to locate together, even in the absence of search costs, as long as there is not a substantial overlap between the two assortments. We shall see that these incentives are considerably stronger when we take distribution services into account.

Consider now a similar rewrite of (3.19) that explicitly incorporates the effects on the quantities purchased from A that are induced by changes in B's distribution services.

$$\in_{kj} (A, B) = \in^*_{kj} (A, B) + \Sigma_i \omega_{ki} (A)\eta_{ij} (B).$$
$$[\ k = 1, \ldots, K, \text{ and } j = 1, \ldots, J]. \tag{3.19}'$$

There are two important results that follow from (3.19)' and it is useful to highlight them by stating them as propositions. In Chapter 2 I stressed that some distribution services, referred to as common, made available by retailers affected all items in a retailer's assortment whereas others, referred to as specific, affected only a subset of the items. The results below apply to both but are especially relevant for common distributions services, for example expanded parking facilities which improve accessibility of location for all items in a retailer's assortment.

Proposition 3.1: A necessary condition for a common distribution service j from retailer B to be a gross substitute with items in the assortment of another retailer A [$\in_{kj} (A, B) < 0$] is that the items in the assortments of the two retailers be net substitutes in production [$\in_{kl}^* (A, B) > 0$].

If one looks at (3.19)' one finds that the consumption effect is positive, since usage, $\omega_{ki} (A)$, is always positive for at least one activity and zero otherwise and $\eta_{ij} (B)$ is positive due to the role of distributions services as fixed inputs in the representative consumer's activities. Hence, for gross substitutability to prevail, one needs $\in^*_{kj} (A, B) < 0$. Furthermore, for the jth distribution service in B to be a net substitute with the kth retail item in A's assortment one needs at least an item in B's assortment, for example l, to be a net substitute with the kth item in A's assortment. For instance, as the extended hours of retailer B increase (with A's constant) the consumer is drawn to buy more items of type l at retailer B and use them in production activities instead of items of type k available at retailer A only if k and l are net substitutes. An interesting implication of this result is that common distribution services are instruments of non-price competition that must work through the same channels through which price competition works. This feature of non-price competition is not widely known.

If retailers A and B have non-overlapping assortments then the net production effect of an increase in a common distribution service [$\in^*_{kj} (A, B)$] is more likely to be non-negative.[21] Since the consumption effect is always positive, it induces a relationship of gross complementarity between B's distribution services and the items in A's assortments in this situation. Similarly if a relation of net independence or complementarity prevails between items in A's assortment and items in B's assortment a relation of gross complementarity will exist between B's distribution services and these items in A's assortment. Finally, even for those items in A's assortment that are net substitutes with items in B's assortment, it is still possible that gross complementarity prevails between B's distribution services and A's items if the consumption effect dominates the production effect, which leads to

Proposition 3.2: When common distribution services of one retailer (j from B) are gross complements with the items in the assortment of another retailer (k from A), there is a demand side incentive for these two retailers to form a retail agglomeration.

When gross complementarity exists an increase in B's distribution services increases the demand for items in A's assortment by the representative consumer. This effect is powerful, for common distribution services affect every item in the retailer's assortment and, thus, create extensive possibilities for gross complementarity relationships to exist with items in another retailer's assortment. Both of these propositions have important economic implications.

For instance competition among specialists in the same product line is likely to be more intense than among general merchants in the same category, because specialists tend to stock more items that are net substitutes (relative to the total number of items) in their assortments. Hence, there are greater possibilities for gross substitutability to exist between the assortments of two specialists in the same product line than between the assortments of two general merchants or a general merchant and a specialist. Gross substitutability intensifies competition with both price and non-price instruments. In contrast, a lowering of price or an increase in a distribution service by a general merchant may increase demand for many of the items of another general merchant or a specialist that are net complements or independent with the item experiencing the price reduction or the increase in a distribution service.[22]

Finally, one should point out that the magnitude of the effect of distribution services as an instrument of non-price competition or as an incentive to agglomerate is also intimately affected by how much it reduces the marginal costs of the consumer's production activities. Namely, the magnitude of $\eta_{ij}(B)$ in $(3.19)'$ will be larger the greater the reduction in the marginal cost of producing Z_i as a result of an increase in the jth distribution service. These effects will vary considerably with a location or a society's circumstances, including for example variations in ease of transportation, communication facilities and the security of transactions.

3.6 DISTRIBUTION SERVICES AND THE RETAIL DEMAND LITERATURE

One of the themes of the book is that the literature has tried to grapple with some of the same issues emphasized here while using different names for the same concepts or doing so in an implicit manner. This point is well illustrated by the treatment of distribution services in the analysis of demand. Careful researchers account for these issues in their analyses either implicitly or explicitly.

Consider first the two studies reviewed in detail in section 3.3. Mulhern and Leone (1991) analyse each of two stores separately. HKMR (1995) introduce a store dummy for each of the stores in their analyses. In doing so, the former are, among other things, implicitly controlling for variations in distribution services that are common to all items in each of the two stores; similarly, the latter are, among other things, implicitly controlling for variations in common distribution services across the stores that remain constant over the time period of their analysis. Mulhern and Leone (1991) introduce a dummy variable that takes on the value of one when an item is being promoted (and zero otherwise) with the following justification (p.69) 'It can be interpreted as representing the nonprice activities such as special displays and shelftalkers that typically accompany price promotions.' [23] HKMR introduce a vector of feature indicator variables in their specification (p.21), which capture (item) specific distribution services in our terminology. Store dummies or feature dummies are effective practical ways of controlling for common and specific, respectively, distribution services at the estimation level.

Similarly, work by Bultez and Naert (1988) treats space devoted to product display as a specific distribution service in our terminology. Since they also review earlier literature along these lines, I will relate our discussion to theirs explicitly. They state (p.214) 'Direct effects are positive. . . . Cross effects . . . may either be negative or positive. . . . Substitute items yield negative cross elasticities, while complementary product classes generate positive ones.'. Going back to (3.19) one can rewrite it as follows to capture the nature of specific distribution services.

$$\in_{kl} = \in^*_{kl} + \Sigma_i \omega_{ki} \eta_{il} \qquad [\, k = 1, \ldots, K, \text{ and } l = 1, \ldots, K]. \qquad (3.19)''$$

If $l = k$, one has a direct effect. The impact of increasing a specific distribution service on the item to which it is specific is always non-negative because both the production effect, $\in^*_{kl}$, and the consumption effect are expected to be positive or at least non-negative in this case. The former is true by definition and the latter by the same reasoning as in section 3.4. If $l \neq k$, then the production effect will be negative if items k and l are net substitutes and non-negative if items k and l are net complements or net independents.[24] Hence, the assertions in Bultez and Naert are subject to the following qualification: net substitute items yield negative cross elasticities if the production effect dominates the consumption effect. Net complementary or net independent categories yield positive cross elasticities. More generally, the analysis here provides the theoretical underpinnings for the assumptions made in this strand of literature.

More recent literature has become cognizant of the approach to retail demand in this chapter and proceeds by extending or applying this approach. For instance, a careful analysis by Richards (1999) extends the model in this chapter to a dynamic setting. This extension allows the treatment of retail advertising and promotion expenditures as quasi-fixed inputs that generate different aspects of the distributions service information in a dynamic household production model. The resulting model is applied to the consumption of fresh fruit and empirically implemented with time series data for the United States.

This model yields a positive long-run distribution services elasticity of demand for Washington apples with respect to advertising expenditures by the Washington Apple Commission (WAC), which is essentially an estimate of the left-hand side of (3.19)″ when $k = l$. It also yields a positive long-run estimate of the distribution services elasticity of demand for apples from the rest of the United States with respect to advertising expenditures by WAC, which is essentially an estimate of the left-hand side of (3.19)″ when $k \neq l$.[25] Indeed, positive distribution services elasticities from WAC advertising are also found for bananas, oranges and other fruits. Moreover, advertising for bananas and for oranges has a similar positive effect on the other fruits (Richards, 1999, Table 4). Thus in this context advertising acts as a distribution service with positive spillovers to potentially competing products, which illustrates the complementarity emphasized here and in the two previous sections.

By contrast, while the distribution services elasticity of WAC promotion expenditures with respect to Washington apples is positive, the distribution services elasticity of WAC promotion expenditures with respect to apples from the rest of the United States is negative.[26] Furthermore, similar negative results also hold for this elasticity with respect to bananas, oranges and other fruits. This contrast is not surprising because advertising acts as a common distribution service and promotion expenditures act either as a specific distribution service or as a price reduction for Washington apples. That is, it is difficult to inform people of the value or benefits of Washington apples without appealing to the value or benefits of eating apples as well as all other fruits. Promotion expenditures by WAC (through price coupons, discounts or payments for displays), on the other hand, bring attention to or inform consumers about Washington apples in settings that are only applicable to these apples. Thus, they act as a specific distribution service or even as a price reduction that increases demand for this product at the expense of similar ones.

An innovative application emphasizing the role of distribution services in determining retail demand is undertaken by Koelemeijer and Oppewal (1999). These authors develop a choice experimental approach to analyse assortment depth (in terms of type and color) for cut flowers. They control for ambiance, price, and accessibility of location (of competing alternatives) in this experiment. Their analysis is based on estimating an extended logit model over a sample of 741 respondents that participate in the choice experiments. A number of interesting results are thereby obtained.

Some of these results are reported here to illustrate the power of their methodology. On the negative side two results are striking. First, the effect of prices on item choices is independent of assortment alternatives. Second, the effect of ambiance, another distribution service, on item choices is only an indirect one in that if store ambiance is poor and the competing store is not far, the consumer will leave to visit the competing store. Among the positive results, the following stand out. First, in predicting choices specifying color by variety dimensions is superior to specifying varieties first and color dimensions subsequently. Both dimensions of depth of an assortment are simultaneously relevant for the choice of cut flowers. Second, having deeper assortments by including additional colors within varieties affects the choice of assortment at the 5 per cent level of significance or lower for red and yellow tulips, blue irises on white ones and red dianthus on white but not vice versa. Third, the availability of a competing store affects the choice of assortment by affecting the inclusion of the following choices in an assortment: namely, large red and white roses, small red roses, red tulips, white irises and red lilies.

Assortment is a very basic and important distribution service but it is not easy to measure in many circumstances. The experimental choice procedure developed by these authors provides a way of confronting consumers with alternative choices of assortments. Furthermore, the authors also show how to extract economic implications of consumers' choices over these experimental alternatives for probabilities of purchase via the extended logit model. Finally, the econometric results of these analyses can be used as data inputs into algorithms designed to select optimal assortments. In light of this successful demonstration, one would expect further extensions of these procedures, for example to study quantities purchased rather than probabilities of purchase, as well as applications to settings other than the depth of assortment for in-store choice of cut flowers.

APPENDIX: COURNOT AGGREGATION AND THE CONSUMPTION EFFECT[27]

In this Appendix I derive a unique feature of the model, similar to Cournot aggregation in the standard consumer choice model, which is useful in proofs involving the consumption effect when an item is used in the production of every commodity. Consider the budget constraint, given by (3.6) in the text, and differentiate it with respect to the *l*th price. After manipulation, the Cournot aggregation condition in the household production model is given by

$$\Sigma_i \, \theta_i \, \eta_{il} = - S_l, \tag{3.A1}$$

where $\theta_i \, (= E_i \, Z_i/E)$ is the marginal budget share of the *i*th commodity in total expenditures, recall that $[\, E_i = (\partial E/\partial Z_i)]$, and $S_l \, (= p_l \, Q_l/E)$ is the budget share of the *l*th item in total expenditure.

Consider now the weights (ω_{ki}) of the consumption effect in the text (3.9). These weights can be written as

$$\omega_{ki} = [(\partial Q_k/\partial Z_i)p_k/E_i \,] \, \theta_i \, /S_k, \tag{3.A2}$$

which implies that $\theta_i = \omega_{ki} \, S_k$ whenever ω_{ki} is not equal to zero, that is, whenever the item is used in the production of the *i*th commodity. If the item is used in the production of the *i*th commodity, the term in square brackets in (3.A2) is unity because this term is simply the ratio of the marginal costs of increasing the output of the *i*th commodity measured in two different ways.

These two results have the following implication for consumption effects when items are used in the production of every commodity.

1) Own-price Effect

Suppose that $k = l$ in (3.9), the consumption effect becomes

$$\Sigma_i \, \omega_{ki} \, \eta_{ik} = \Sigma_i \, (\theta_i \, /S_k)\eta_{ik} = - \, S_k \, /S_k = - \, 1. \tag{3.A3}$$

That is, the demand for these items will always be elastic, since the own-production effect is always negative.

More generally, this result suggests that the own-price elasticity of demand will be more elastic (larger in absolute value) for retail items that are used in the production of many different household commodities relative to those that are used in the production of a single household commodity.

2) Cross-price Effects

Suppose that $k \neq l$ in (3.9), the consumption effect becomes

$$\Sigma_i \, \omega_{ki} \, \eta_{il} = \Sigma_i \, (\theta_i/S_k)\eta_{il} = - \, S_l/S_k < 0. \tag{3.A4}$$

The second equality follows from (3.A1), and the inequality shows that changes in the price of items used in the production of every commodity will always have a negative consumption effect. Thus, they will be gross complements with items that are net complements or net independent as well as with those that are net substitutes if the consumption effect dominates the production effect.

More generally, the analysis here also suggests a systematic way of characterizing what has been called product salience in the literature by Albion (1983). Namely, from (3.A4) it follows that the size of the consumption effect will be greater (in absolute value) the larger the share of the budget of the item that experienced the price change.

3) The Distribution Services Effect

Differentiation of the budget constraint (3.6) with respect to the *j*th distribution service leads to a condition similar to (3.A1), namely

$$\Sigma_i \, \theta_i \, \eta_{ij} = - \, S_j > 0. \tag{3.A5}$$

where $\theta_i \, (= E_i \, Z_i/E)$ is the marginal budget share of the *i*th commodity in total expenditures and $S_j \, (= E_j \, D_j/E)$ is the budget share of the *j*th distribution service in total expenditure. Since E_j is the negative of the shadow price of the *j*th distribution service, the inequality in (3.A5) follows.

From section 3.4 the consumption effect is given by the left-hand side of (3.A6)

$$\Sigma_i \, \omega_{ki} \, \eta_{ij} = \Sigma_i \, (\theta_i/S_k)\eta_{ij} = - \, S_j/S_k > 0. \tag{3.A6}$$

The first equality follows from (3.A2), and the second equality as well as the inequality from (3.A5). Hence, an increase in a distribution service generates a positive consumption effect for all items that are used in the production of every household commodity.

NOTES

1. This section and the next one draw heavily from Betancourt and Gautschi (1990, 1992b).

2. We are assuming that the set of retailers that the household patronizes is given. This in turn implies that the level of distribution services available to the household at each of these retailers is also given. Allowing the household to choose over the retailers is tantamount to allowing the household to choose over the available levels of distribution services at these retailers. One way to think of this choice is as a third stage decision.

3. We discuss various features of transformation functions in the next chapter.

4. For a proof that in the absence of joint production of commodities, two items used exclusively in the production of different commodities are net independents see Betancourt and Gautschi (1992b, Theorem 3).

5. Incidentally, this definition is general enough to encompass both items that are purchased from a single retailer's assortment or from the assortments of two different retailers. We will discuss the latter case explicitly in section 3.5.

6. See theorems 1 and 2 as well as 1' and 2' in Betancourt and Gautschi (1992b).

7. See theorem 4 in Betancourt and Gautschi (1992b).

8. If the items are used in the production of two different commodities by the household, they would be net independents and since the consumption effect is almost always negative, gross complementarity is likely to prevail in this setting.

9. The overall purpose of the study was to analyse store profitability and its relation to pricing and promotions. In order to do so, however, demand elasticities had to be estimated. These other issues will be discussed in Chapter 5.

10. Incidentally, this formulation captures the demand function of a fictitious representative consumer of the store whose income does not change over the period and who does not take into account the prices of items that are not 'use' complements in deciding the quantity demanded of these two product categories.

11. I took the estimates in Table 4 of Mulhern and Leone and obtained the elasticities at the mean by using (3.11) and the mean values given in Table 1.

12. The cross partial results from the sum of two production effects. The first one arises from the activity of making cakes with frosting, which is negative because cake mix and frosting are net complements in the production of cakes with frosting. The second one arises from the activity of making pound cakes, which is zero because cake mix and frosting are net independents in the production of pound cakes.

13. Parenthetically, primacy can be interpreted as frosting expected to be a much smaller share of the budget than cake mix, which increases the size of the first term on the LHS.

14. These data are now available at Rossi's website.

15. A Divisia price index for each item can be calculated on the basis of the underlying UPC products as follows: $p_{it} = \sum_m \beta_{imt} p_{imt}$, where m indexes the underlying UPC products and the prices are expressed in terms of logarithms. $\beta_{imt} = P_{imt} Q_{imt} / \sum P_{imt} Q_{imt}$ or the share of revenues of the mth UPC product in the total revenues of the ith item in the tth week.

16. This definition is similar to Definition 1 in section 3.2, except that the signs are reversed due to the duality between prices and quantities. That is, an increase in a distribution service, which is an increase in a quantity, operates as a decrease in the price of the distribution service in generating substitutability and complementarity with retail items or inputs.

17. One possible exception is an increase in the distribution service depth of assortment. Since by definition the latter entails stocking additional types of items that are net substitutes with the existing ones (Betancourt and Gautschi, 1990), a net substitutability relationship between this distribution service and some of the items in an existing assortment could arise.

18. See theorems 6 and 6' in Betancourt and Gautschi (1992b).

19. This section draws heavily from Betancourt and Gautschi (1990, Section 4D).

20. One might wonder if a representative consumer would patronize both retailers. That is the situation that exists at shopping centers. Furthermore, Dudey (1990) shows how the existence of consumer search can lead firms selling the same items to locate in the same shopping center as an equilibrium outcome.

21. The assumption of non-overlapping assortments eliminates the strongest case of net substitutability, namely both retailers carrying the same brand of an item for any item. It is still possible, however, that an item in A's assortment is a net substitute with an item in B's assortment.

22. Incidentally, this argument also brings out that the provision of distribution services at no explicit prices generates a free-rider problem in some cases. For instance, acquiring information about an item from one merchant and purchasing the item from another who provides it at a lower price due to the cost savings from, among other things, not providing the information.
23. Whenever this variable is statistically significant it has a positive value, which is what the analysis in section 3.4 predicts.
24. When l differs from k, (3.19)″ implies one is changing a specific distribution service associated with item l and observing its impact on the quantity demanded of item k. An increase in the specific distribution service associated with item l increases the demand for all the commodities (i) where item l is used as an input, which also increases the demand for the kth item through the consumption effect. Nonetheless, and herein lies the difference with the situation when k equals l, given the level of commodity production for all i this increase in the lth specific distribution service decreases the demand for the kth item in all the activities where the latter item is a substitute for the lth one.
25. Incidentally the elasticity estimates are 0.215 with a t-ratio of 7.839 and 0.029 with a t-ratio of 11.537, respectively.
26. These elasticity estimates are 0.211 with a t-ratio of 8.983 and −0.234 with a t-ratio of −12.837, respectively.
27. This Appendix draws heavily from the Appendix in Betancourt and Gautschi (1992b).

4. Retail supply

One of the points stressed in Chapter 2 is that retail firms produce two kinds of outputs: the goods and services explicitly sold and a set of distribution services that implicitly accompanies any retail exchange. In this chapter I first show the implications of this view for the characterization of retail production in the simplest possible setting (section 4.1). Furthermore, here this characterization is used to generate two special cases that underlie the main answers in the literature to the question: what is the appropriate measure of output in retailing? Section 4.2 contains a discussion of the nature of economies of scale in retailing and the implications of the previous section for the empirical evidence provided by the prior literature. This discussion leads to the conclusion that economies of scale in retailing arise mainly as a result of the existence of elements of fixed costs in the provision of distribution services. Incidentally, the Appendix to this chapter shows how a functional form fashionable in the increasing returns literature provides a suitable and rigorous basis for capturing economies of scale in the production of assortment.

Modern production theory relies heavily on the duality between transformation functions and cost functions. Section 4.3 uses the dual approach to generate cost functions corresponding to the production concepts employed in section 4.1 and derives the corresponding implications for the measurement of economies of scale on the cost side. This measurement on the cost side is illustrated with the results from a recent study that confirms the main implications of the earlier ones based on the production side. Section 4.4 addresses the issue of the role of the consumer in retail supply. It demonstrates that standard econometric procedures are sufficient to capture the role of the consumer in retail supply. That is, there is no need to introduce the consumer directly into the production or transformation function of retailers. Finally, section 4.5 draws the main implications of the previous discussion for productivity analysis in retailing and discusses briefly several recent empirical studies.

4.1 TRANSFORMATION FUNCTIONS AND PRODUCTION FUNCTIONS

Throughout we have emphasized that the output of retail activities must be conceived of in at least two dimensions: Q or the quantity of goods sold; and

D or the quantity of distribution services provided, which for simplicity will be assumed here to be an aggregate of the five distribution services identified earlier in the book. This means that in describing the technological restrictions facing the retail producer, we must work with the transformation function or the generalization of the production function for the multiple output case. In general it can be specified as follows:

$$H(Q, D, X) = 0, \tag{4.1}$$

where *X* represents a vector of inputs. The function *H* is assumed to be quasi-convex in its arguments (for example, Varian, 1984). This simply means that with a given level of inputs the function describes the maximum combination of the outputs to be obtained or with a given level of outputs the function describes the minimum combination of inputs necessary to obtain these outputs.

It will be useful to consider a simple specification of this function to deal with two questions that keep reoccurring in the literature on retailing: when is value added a measure of the (distribution) services provided by the retail sector?; and, when are sales an exact representation of the gross output of this sector?[1] Consider the following special case of (4.1),

$$[Q - F(X_1)] + [D - G(X_2)] = 0, \tag{4.2}$$

where the input vector *X* has been partitioned into those that are used exclusively in the production of commodities and those that are used exclusively in the production of distribution services. If *D* and *Q* are not malleable each bracketed expression in (4.2) must also equal zero and each function in the bracketed expressions corresponds to a standard production function for the single output case, that is, $Q = F(X_1)$ and $D = G(X_2)$.

What assumptions have to be made in order to be able to go from (4.1) to (4.2)? First, the output function must be separable from the input function so that they can be written as follows:

$$H'(Q, D) - H''(X_1, X_2) = 0. \tag{4.3}$$

Second, the output function must be linear and additive in the outputs and the input function must be additive in the partitioned inputs so that they can be written as follows:

$$[Q + D] - [F(X_1) + G(X_2)] = 0. \tag{4.4}$$

In economic terms this requires no joint production of outputs and no common inputs in the transformation process. Clearly one would not expect (4.2) to be a reasonable specification of the actual transformation process in retailing. Nevertheless, it provides a useful conceptual basis for reviewing the discussion in the literature of arguments about the output of retailing.

Some writers have argued that value added is the appropriate measure of output in retailing, because it measures the output of distribution services. For instance, Ofer (1973, p.366) states 'If one could assume perfect competition in the entire retail industry a store's value added would be the exact measure of its service output.'. Let us assume that the quantities of goods sold, Q_s, equal the quantities of goods purchased by the retailer, Q_p, and that no other inputs are used in the production of Q_s, then (4.2) becomes

$$[Q_s - Q_p] + [D - G(X_2)] = 0. \qquad (4.5)$$

Perfect competition is not enough to write a value added production function where value added equals the distribution service output. In addition one needs the assumptions collapsing the transformation function from (4.1) to (4.2) and the ones leading to (4.5). Value added is fine as a measure of net output but it will depend in general on both Q and D. It will only be a one-to-one measure of D under the very restrictive assumptions identified here, which to our knowledge has not been noted in the literature.[2]

Other writers have argued that sales is the appropriate measure of gross output in retailing. One interpretation of 'appropriate' in this context is that variation in sales captures exactly variations in Q. Since, by definition, sales is the product of the retail price, p, and Q, this interpretation requires the retail price to be constant. Some writers, for example Smith and Hitchens (1985) or Ingene (1984b), have indicated three assumptions required for p to be constant. First, perfect competition so that all agents are experiencing zero profits. Second, the same type of merchandise being retailed so that the price of goods bought from suppliers, w, be the same across agents. Third, a constant level of distribution services across agents so that the retail price does not vary as a result of different levels of service provision. Our analysis here can be used to show that a fourth assumption is necessary for the retail price to be constant across agents. Under perfect competition we have, $p = w + C(v, D, Q)/Q$. Even if input prices, v, and distribution services are constant, the average costs of retailing will vary with Q unless the cost function takes the special form $C = C^*(v, D)Q$.

The analysis here generates the conditions under which this will happen. Let the output function be multiplicatively additive in the outputs and let the input function be multiplicatively additive in the partitioned inputs,[3] then we can write (4.1) as

$$Qg(D) - F(X_1)G(X_2) = 0. \tag{4.6}$$

If (4.6) is homogeneous of degree zero in Q and its corresponding inputs, (X_1), it can be shown that the cost function will take a functional form that allows the retail price to be independent of the output of commodities, Q. The single output production function can be written as $Q = F(X_1)(G/g)$, but F must be of the constant returns to scale form.[4] Once again sales is fine as a measure of gross output[5] but it will depend in general on Q and D; its separation into a price component that does not depend on Q and Q itself requires a fourth assumption not noted in the literature: namely, restrictions on the transformation function such as the ones just indicated.

To sum up, the general formulation in (4.1) is the proper specification of the transformation function for the analysis of retail activities. It allows one to capture, for instance, that there is jointness in increasing assortments and increasing the quantities of retail items sold or made available for sale or, similarly, that there is jointness in the provision of information through advertising and the quantities of goods sold.[6] The use of special cases of this function can eliminate economically relevant aspects of the transformation process in retailing such as the existence of joint production and common inputs. While these special cases can be useful, as we illustrate in the next section, one must keep in mind that they are special cases.

4.2   ECONOMIES OF SCALE IN RETAILING

The literature on retailing has identified three broad sources of economies of scale in retailing. For example, both Ofer (1973) and Shaw, Nisbet and Dawson (1989)[7] discuss the following ones: those that are due to some element of fixed cost; those that are due to demand uncertainty, which were termed by Robinson (1958) economies of massed reserves and are emphasized by Oi (1992); and those that are due to the association between average transaction size and store size. In practice, however, it is difficult to separate these different sources due to the jointness in production among distribution services and between distribution services and the quantities of goods sold.

In particular, the distinction we have made earlier between common and specific distribution services can be associated with the existence of some element of fixed cost and will be used to illustrate the difficulty of separation of these sources of scale economies. Consider a situation with two levels of a common distribution service, for example assortment: a high one and a low one. The high level requires more space and the costs of this additional space go up in proportion to the area of this space. The number of items that can be shelved, however, will increase in proportion with the volume generated by this space. Hence costs due to the additional assortment increase proportionally to the area; but, the turnover dimension of output and the costs of specific distribution services associated with each item go up in proportion to the increased volume associated with the area. Thus, an increase in the outputs of all distribution services that go into D in fixed proportions generates a less than proportionate increase in costs due to the characteristics of this common distribution service.[8] Therefore, it is a source of increasing returns to scale.

The same example is convenient to illustrate the other two sources of returns to scale identified in the retailing literature. Let us consider first the association between store size and the average transaction basket. The quantities of items sold per store will normally increase as a result of the assortment expansion. This quantity can be viewed, by definition, as the product of the number of transactions (n) and the average basket size (q^*). Suppose the number of transactions and the average basket size increase in the same proportion as a result of assortment expansion. Sales will go up for the store with the higher level of assortment but costs will go up less than proportionately if costs increase more rapidly with the number of transactions than with the average basket size. The work of Nooteboom (1983) for Dutch supermarkets suggests that this is the case because the labor input is fixed and the increase in man-hours generated by an increase in the average basket size is less than the increase in man-hours generated by an increase in the number of transactions. Oi (1992) argues that other store inputs are related to n and q^* in a similar manner. Thurik (1981) finds evidence of a positive association between average transaction size and store size in French supermarkets. Note that this is evidence with regards to the quantity of goods sold; nonetheless, it also rests on an element of fixed costs with respect to a distribution service due to the jointness between assortment expansion and the quantities of goods sold.

Finally, the increase in assortment can also be used to illustrate the operations of scale economies as a result of demand uncertainty. The key factor in this case is the existence of idle resources as a result of the uncertainty. Suppose that cashiers and their registers are idle part of the time at the low level of assortment. When the store moves to the higher level of assortment and experiences the associated increase in the number of items sold, it becomes possible for these resources to be employed at a higher level of utilization with no or little increase in costs. Since assurance of product delivery at the desired time (through the availability of cashiers) is a common distribution service, however, it becomes possible to increase this output with minimal increases in costs when assortment and the number of items sold increase. This source of economies of scale is directly related to the quantity of goods sold but it also rests on elements of fixed costs with respect to distribution services due to the jointness between assortment expansion and assurance of product delivery at the desired time.[9]

The above discussion illustrates the difficulty of separating these different sources of scale economies in general. Nevertheless, following Bacon's dictum that truth will sooner arise from error than confusion, we shall proceed in this section by illustrating how the previous literature on economies of scale in retailing can be interpreted in terms of the special cases identified in section 4.1, that is, those captured in equations 4.5 and 4.6. In the next section, however, we present a general procedure consistent with the discussion of economies of scale above, and with equation 4.1 of the previous section. Finally in an Appendix to this chapter we present one specific functional form of a production function that captures economies of scale in the provision of assortment in a simple yet rigorous manner.

Our starting point is Ofer's (1973) careful analysis of economies of scale in the Israeli retail trade when using value added as the measure of the store's service output, D. Ofer writes the production function as follows:

$$D = AL^{\alpha}K^{\beta}e^{\gamma X}e^{u} \qquad (4.7)$$

where D is the output of distribution services, measured by value added; L is a weighted average of labor services, which we will treat here as homogeneous; and K is a two-element vector of capital services, the first one (K_1) representing fixed capital, measured by store space in square feet, and the second one representing working capital (K_2), measured as the value of inventories at the end of the year. X is a vector of dummy variables: one set capturing differences in the three cities in the sample and the other capturing differences in the sub-branches of retailing included in the sample. Finally, A is a constant and u is an error term with the usual properties of normality and identical distributions across the stores in the sample.

Estimation of production functions, including the Cobb–Douglas functional form in (4.7), with cross-section data is subject to some well-known difficulties (for example, Varian, 1984, Chapter 4), and Ofer discusses them in detail. An important one is that if any input or its quality is left out of the analysis, the assumption that the error term is uncorrelated with the explanatory variables will not hold and these will usually lead to inconsistent estimates. Ofer makes the point, however, that the city and industry dummies will capture some of the missing variables and that the remaining biases due to measurement error in within-group store variations will lead to downward biases in the estimates of returns to scale.

Equation (4.7) can be estimated with linear methods, after taking the logarithm of both sides of (4.7), and returns to scale will be properly measured[10] as

$$\text{RTS} = \alpha + \beta_1 + \beta_2. \qquad (4.8)$$

If the estimated sum of the parameters is greater than unity, we have evidence of increasing returns to scale in the provision of distribution services.

Ofer estimates equation (4.7) and its parameters for a cross-section of stores in each of three Israeli retail sectors (food, clothing and furniture).[11] The first column in Table 4.1 presents the estimates of returns to scale for the whole sample in each sector and the second one presents the t-ratio using unity as the null hypothesis. In each of the retail sectors the hypothesis of constant returns to scale is rejected against the alternative of increasing returns to scale (RTS > 1) at the 1 per cent level of significance.

The next four columns contain the results of splitting the sample for each sector into small stores (SS) and large stores (LS). A store was classified as small if it did not hire any workers so all its labor came from self employment or unpaid family members. The estimates of RTS for the sub-samples, although usually smaller, remain above unity in every case. For the stores that hire workers (LS) the results are very similar to the ones for the whole sample, especially for food and furniture. Since the range of variation for the independent variables is much smaller for the stores that hire no workers (SS), the statistical significance of the estimated coefficients is much lower in every sector than obtained for the whole sample. In sum, Ofer's study suggests considerable economies of scale in retailing with respect to the provision of distribution services.

We now turn to a study similar in methodology except that it uses a different measure of output, namely sales per establishment. We will assume, following the author, that three of the four assumptions necessary for sales to be a perfect proxy for the quantities of commodities sold apply. By the nature of the data used by Ingene (1984b) in his study of 12 retail sectors in the US, some of these assumptions are likely to apply. He uses average SMSA data on each of the 12 sectors as the basic unit of observation. Since each sector is estimated separately, there will be no gross violations of the assumptions that the prices of goods purchased from suppliers and the amount of service provided are constant across SMSAs. Similarly, one can argue that stores in an SMSA are in long-run zero profit perfectly competitive or monopolistically competitive equilibrium. In practice there will be violations of these assumptions, of

Table 4.1   Economies of scale in Israeli retailing

	RTS	t-ratio	RTS (SS)	t-ratio	RTS (LS)	t-ratio
Food	1.31	4.40	1.28	1.68	1.20	2.90
Clothing	1.26	4.73	1.26	1.43	1.10	1.41
Furniture	1.29	2.90	1.02	0.72	1.09	5.45

course, but they are not as severe as if one were combining several of these sectors, for example. Since the assumption of linear homogeneity is not imposed on the data, although it is required for sales to be a perfect proxy for Q, the results can be used as a test of the model as well.

Equation (4.7) now becomes

$$Q = AL^{\alpha}K^{\beta}e^{u}, \tag{4.9}$$

where Q stands for the quantities of goods sold, measured by sales per establishment for the particular retail branch in the SMSA; L stands for labor services, measured by employees per establishment for the retail branch in the SMSA; K stands for capital services, measured by square feet per establishment for the retail branch in the SMSA; A and u have the same interpretation as before. Returns to scale are now measured as

$$RTS = \alpha + \beta. \tag{4.10}$$

Ingene estimates (4.9) separately for 12 retail sectors using the averages per SMSA from the 1977 Census of Retail Trade as the basic unit of observation in each of the 12 regressions.

Table 4.2 presents Ingene's estimates of (4.10) for selected sectors.[12] The first three sectors are the same as in Ofer's study, ignoring variations in classification between the Israeli and the US Census. The first two columns show that the null hypothesis of constant returns to scale can not be rejected against the alternative of increasing returns to scale in any of the three sectors when using the whole sample. The next two categories were included because they were the only two retail sectors where some evidence of increasing returns was found. In the case of drugs this evidence was found for the whole sample. In the case of variety stores, there is no evidence of increasing returns for the whole sample.

Ingene also splits the sample into large stores and small stores.

Table 4.2 Economies of scale in the US retail trade

	RTS	t-ratio	RTS (SS)	t-ratio	RTS (LS)	t-ratio
Food	1.04	1.41	0.98	−0.25	1.02	0.24
Apparel	0.89	−2.72	0.86	−1.48	0.73	−9.80
Furniture	0.99	−0.21	0.98	−0.23	1.05	0.40
Drug	1.13	3.09	0.92	−1.04	1.15	1.47
Variety	0.98	−0.76	0.94	−1.05	1.20	1.70

Nevertheless the criterion is a different one. The 'representative' store for the SMSA was classified as small (SS) if it fell below the average of the representative stores for all SMSAs in terms of square feet per store. Otherwise it was classified as large (LS). There is no evidence of increasing returns for the small stores in any of the 12 sectors, including the five above. There is slight evidence of increasing returns for the large stores. Nonetheless, this evidence turns to no evidence if one uses a 1 per cent level of significance to test the null hypothesis of constant returns to scale against the alternative of increasing returns to scale. Interpreted under the assumptions that make these two studies most compelling, the results show that economies of scale in retailing arise as a result of elements of fixed costs in the provision of distribution services.[13] Of course, one can argue that this nice and neat separation is artificial because in practice the provision of distribution services and commodities to be sold is a joint activity. That is, value added (or the retail gross margin) depends on Q and sales per establishment depends on D. We shall revisit this argument but first we need to consider an alternative approach to the measurement of economies of scale.

4.3 COST FUNCTIONS

The dual approach to the analysis of production is by now well established in economics (for example, Varian, 1984). One of the reasons for its early popularity was that assuming input prices to be independent of the error terms is more persuasive than assuming input quantities, for example those in (4.7) or (4.9), to be independent of the error term. Furthermore in industries such as electricity generation, for which one could argue that the level of output was determined exogenously, the cost function approach is ideally suited for empirical work (for example Christensen and Greene, 1976).[14] In our present context, however, there is an additional reason that makes this approach attractive. In dealing with multiple outputs, it is often more convenient empirically to specify cost functions and their functional forms than the corresponding transformation functions.[15]

A multi-output cost function embodies all the relevant economic information from the transformation function in a convenient form. The best way to see this is to conceive of the cost function as generated in the following manner. The economic agent minimizes the costs of producing its given level of outputs subject to a transformation function. Hence, we can write the optimization problem, for example, as Min $p_K K + p_L L$ subject to $H(D, Q, K, L) = 0$.

The cost function can be generated by substituting the optimal choices of inputs, K and L in this case, into the objective function being minimized, which then yields

$$C = C(p_K, p_L, D, Q).$$ (4.11)

The left-hand side are the costs of retailing, which can be measured as sales minus the costs of goods sold if one assumes zero economic profits. These costs would equal the value added by the retail sector under perfect competition in retail markets, if one ignores intermediate inputs such as electricity, or gross output measured by the retail gross margin, if one does not ignore intermediate inputs. The right-hand side is the cost function, which by virtue of its construction will be non-decreasing, linear homogeneous and concave in prices of the inputs as well as increasing in the outputs (for example Fuss and McFadden, 1978).

It is useful to illustrate this process with the special transformation function in (4.6); recall that in (4.6) D was treated as a constant, assuming that F has the Cobb–Douglas form as in (4.9). The cost minimization problem subject to this particular specification of H leads to the following functional form for the cost function,

$$C = C^*(p_K, p_L)[Qg(D)]^{1/(\alpha+\beta)}.$$ (4.12)

C^* is the unit cost function, which will have the Cobb–Douglas form as well but it is not explicitly shown to keep the notation simple. We can see from (4.12) that, unless there are constant returns to scale ($\alpha + \beta = 1$), the average or unit cost function will depend on Q as argued in section 4.1.

Returns to scale on the cost side can be defined as the proportionate increase in costs as a result of an equiproportionate increase in outputs. Under this definition, we have from (4.11),

$$RTS = d\ C/C/dY/Y = C_Q\ (Q/C) + C_D\ (D/C) = S_Q + S_D$$ (4.13)

where dY/Y defines the proportionate increase in all outputs. Since we are looking at the cost side, values of RTS less than unity are now indicative of economies of scale. This definition corresponds to the one introduced by Laitinen and Theil (1978) and it is consistent with the one put forward by Baumol, Panzar and Willig (1982). There are other considerations important in the general multi-output case that we will not explore here.[16] The last reference provides an exhaustive treatment of the subject and its implications for the analysis of market structure. Sharkey (1982) provides a briefer and more accessible treatment with emphasis on the implications for natural monopoly.

To sharpen our discussion it is useful to provide an example of a specific functional form of a multiproduct cost function and show how it captures economies of scale in practice. The particular one used here is a generalization of the quadratic attributed to Braunstein by Baumol, Panzar and Willig (1982), and slightly modified for our own purposes, that is,

$$C = C^*(v, X)[\alpha_Q Q + \alpha_{QQ} Q^\beta + \alpha_{QD} QD + \alpha_D D + \alpha_{DD} D^\gamma]. \quad (4.14)$$

C^* is a unit cost function which depends on input prices (v) and other variables (X) which may shift costs, for example store formats or the presence of scanners. We will restrict all the parameters associated with D and Q to be positive for simplicity.[17] This form is useful for analyses where the interest centers on economies of scale and one is not particularly concerned about interrelations of the variations in input prices with output levels.

Application of the definition of economies of scale to (4.14) yields, after some manipulation,

$$RTS^{18} = 1 + [(\beta - 1)\alpha_{QQ} Q^\beta + (\gamma - 1)\alpha_{DD} D^\gamma + \alpha_{QD} QD]C^*/C. \quad (4.15)$$

The main implication of (4.15) is that, if the interaction term is zero or negative, declining marginal costs with respect to each dimension of output is a sufficient condition for economies of scale to exist. Declining marginal costs are ensured by the expressions in parentheses being negative. Declining marginal costs in at least one dimension of output is a necessary condition for economies of scale to exist.

To illustrate, we present the results from estimating these cost function parameters for US supermarkets.[19] β ranges from 0.9577 to 0.9834, γ ranges from 0.4567 to 0.5819 and α_{QD} ranges from 0.0684 to 0.0692 over three different surveys of one of the endogenous variables (average store price). These estimates show that there are declining marginal costs with respect to distribution services. The null hypothesis that γ is unity is rejected at the 1 per cent level of significance against the alternative that there are declining marginal costs ($\gamma < 1$) in all three cases. Similarly, they show that marginal costs with respect to the quantity of goods are either constant or declining. The point estimates imply slightly declining marginal costs but the null hypothesis that β is unity can not be rejected at the 1 per cent level of significance against the alternative that there are declining marginal costs ($\beta < 1$) in all three cases. Finally, the null hypothesis of cost complementarities ($\alpha_{QD} \leq 0$) is rejected at the 1 per cent level of significance in all three cases.

Together these results imply that there are multiproduct returns to scale for these supermarkets and that declining marginal costs with respect to distribution services are the main source of these economies of scale. For instance, an evaluation of (4.15) using the parameter estimates reported above and the mean values of the variables reported by Betancourt and Malanoski (1999, Table 1) generates estimates of RTS ranging from 0.9130 to 0.9504 over the three price surveys.

With respect to economies of scale the evidence from the early studies and the evidence from a recent one lead to the same conclusion: the provision of distribution services rather than the quantity of goods sold is the main source of economies of scale in retailing. Moreover these recent results also cast doubt on the interpretation that the difference with respect to economies of scale between Ofer's results and Ingene's results is due to the use of store data by the former and SMSA data by the latter, since these recent results are based on establishment data.

Many other aspects of the transformation process can be captured through the use of cost functions. Here, we have concentrated on economies of scale since this is a subject that has attracted considerable attention in the retailing literature. Modifications of the form in (4.14) and alternative specifications of functional forms are available in Baumol, Panzar and Willig (1982, Chapter 15). At this point, however, we turn our attention to consider another supply issue that has attracted a great deal of attention in the retail literature.

4.4   THE ROLE OF THE CONSUMER IN RETAIL SUPPLY

Oi (1992) argues that in the production of retail services the consumer supplies an essential input that has to appear as an argument in the production function alongside labor and capital. Ofer (1973) argues that sales is not an appropriate measure of output in retailing because it is the consumer rather than the store owner who determines the ratio between the goods purchased and the services provided by the store. Shaw, Nisbet and Dawson (1989) speculate that demand or marketing forces are more likely to be significant determinants of the increase in store size which has taken place than economies of scale. Finally, Berne, Mugica and Yague (1999, p.2) put forward as one of two views on retail output 'the output of the retail activity is the outcome of the encounter of the retailer with their customers'.

By specifying distribution services as an output of the retail enterprise as well as a fixed input into the household production functions of consumers it becomes possible to capture the role of the consumer in retail supply using standard tools of analysis. That is, this can be done relying on standard conceptualizations of production, such as the ones discussed in section 4.1, which do not include the consumer as an argument in the transformation function. It can also be done using sales to obtain measures of the quantity of goods sold. By identifying exactly how demand or marketing forces affect store size, we will show that the encounter aspect of retail output reduces to the endogeneity of the quantity of goods sold and the level of distribution services in an econometric framework.

We proceed by discussing one particular study which illustrates how to

capture the role of the consumer in retail supply, and we will subsequently
generalize the discussion. Betancourt and Malanoski (1999) rely on a unique
data set constructed by USDA to analyse the interactions of prices, distribution services and some aspects of competition among US supermarkets. The
data set constructed by USDA is based on three independent surveys of prices
in supermarkets across the US to construct an index of price relatives reflecting the average store price in each supermarket, p, for each of the three
surveys. Since data on sales of each supermarket is also available, this index
can be used to obtain an index of the quantity of goods sold by each supermarket, Q.

A separate store survey identifies costs and characteristics of each supermarket in the price surveys. Among these characteristics are the services
offered by each supermarket. This is done through a series of questions on
whether or not a particular service is available at the supermarket. This permits
identification of 20 components of distribution services that can be aggregated
into four of the five categories stressed here. The only distribution service not
included is accessibility of location, which is for all practical purposes fixed
when the supermarket is the unit of analysis. Based on these characteristics an
aggregate index of the distribution services offered by the store is constructed,
D.[20]

These basic variables and additional ones capturing other dimensions of
costs can be the basis for the estimation of a multiproduct cost function, for
example (4.14) in section 4.3. It is at this point of estimation, however, that the
role of the consumer in retail supply becomes important. Q is both an index of
the output of goods supplied by the store and of the consumer's demand for
these goods. Moreover, as we saw in the previous chapter, this demand function is going to depend on the price charged by the store, p, as well as on the
distribution services provided by the store, D. Both of these variables are decision variables of the store. Therefore, the essential role of the consumer in
retail supply reduces to the role of two endogenous explanatory variables in
the cost function, that is, Q and D.

Betancourt and Malanoski use the first-order conditions from their model
to generate a price and a distribution services equation and they add a demand
equation to capture the dependence of Q on the behavior of the consumer. This
yields the following equations for estimation

$$[p - w - C_Q](\partial q/\partial p)N - qN(\mu - 1) = \in_1 \qquad (4.16)$$

$$[p - w - C_Q](\partial q/\partial D)N - C_D + \mu rN = \in_2 \qquad (4.17)$$

$$Q = g\ (p, D, Y)N\in_3, \qquad (4.18)$$

where the LHS of (4.16) and (4.17) are rewrites of (2.10) and (2.11) in Chapter 2 that also incorporate the number of transactions, N, into the analysis explicitly.[21] Y is the representative consumer's income. Notice that at least the first two of these error terms ($\in_i$) would be expected to be correlated, since these two equations are the outcome of the same optimization process.[22]

The first point to be made here is that endogenous variables appear at many places in these equations. p is endogenous and it appears explicitly in all three equations. Q is also endogenous and it appears explicitly in (4.18) and in (4.16) but it also affects (4.16) and (4.17) indirectly, because it appears in marginal costs and in the slopes of the demand function. Finally, D is also endogenous and it appears explicitly in (4.18) and implicitly in (4.16) and (4.17) in the same manner as Q. Hence, estimation requires simultaneous methods. The second point to be made is that the functions in (4.16) to (4.18) are non-linear. For instance, the marginal cost functions were specified to be the ones generated by the cost function in the previous section (4.14) and the demand function was specified directly in exponential form. Therefore, estimation requires non-linear simultaneous equation methods. While the estimation problem is not trivial, these methods are in wide use now and the authors estimate equations (4.16) and (4.17) via non-linear three-stage least squares and (4.18) via non-linear two-stage least squares. The estimates for the parameters of the marginal costs functions reported in the previous section were obtained in this manner.

With respect to the role of the consumer in retail supply this study illustrates that it can be accommodated by employing estimation procedures that are currently in use in the economics literature. Moreover, these authors are not the only ones to estimate a model of retail supply that incorporates the role of the consumer without introducing the consumer into the production or transformation function. For instance, Divakar and Ratchford (1995) apply the full price model of services to estimate a derived demand for advertising and for labor to be used for in-store promotion by an establishment. In order to do so they impose the restriction on the demand side implied by the full price model, which in this case implies that the distribution service is constant (so that the time saved by the consumer in acquiring information is the same regardless of the combination of advertising and in-store promotion used by the store). The empirical analysis relies on estimation by non-linear two-stage least squares of the demand for labor by the store and the demand for quantity of goods sold by the consumer. The parameters of the derived demand for advertising are obtained from the estimates of these two equations. Thus the role of the consumer in retail supply is captured by accounting for the quantity of goods sold being an endogenous variable in the demand for labor by the store. This is accomplished through the use of a standard practice in econometrics and a bit of ingenuity by these researchers.

Both of the studies reported above require an indirect way of obtaining cost parameters because of data and other limitations in these studies. Hence, we conclude this discussion by presenting a general framework for the direct estimation of cost functions in retailing. The cost function will be given in general by

$$C = C(v, Q, D), \tag{4.19}$$

where v are the input prices of all the input costs that are included in C. Just as before, Q represents the quantity of goods sold and D is an aggregate or a vector of distribution services, depending on data availability.

One aspect of the role of the consumer in retail supply arises in the same manner as in any other setting: namely, Q is determined, at least partially, by the consumer's demand and the latter is affected by the retail price, p, selected by the retailer. A second aspect of the role of the consumer in retail supply is novel: namely, the level of distribution services, D, is also selected by the retailer and it affects the cost function directly as well as through its effect on retail demand. Hence, estimation of the cost function requires accounting for the fact that these three variables (Q, p, D) are usually endogenous. In general this can be done by specifying equations for each of them and estimating the resulting four-equation system simultaneously.[23] Alternatively, if the only purpose is estimation of the cost function, one can try to find instruments for Q and D and use instrumental variable estimation.

4.5   IMPLICATIONS FOR PRODUCTIVITY ANALYSIS

By the way of a conclusion we draw the main implications of our previous discussion for the analysis of productivity in retailing. This topic can be approached in terms of labor productivity or total factor productivity.[24] The latter approach is normally preferred at the conceptual level because it tries to capture the ability to use all resources more productively rather than just labor. The former approach is less demanding empirically and it underlies the productivity measures generated for the retail sector by BLS (for example Dean and Kunze, 1992). In both cases, however, output can be defined empirically in terms of value added, the retail gross margin or sales. Hence, our discussion in section 4.1 of the assumptions that are necessary for value added or the retail gross margin to be solely a function of distribution services and for sales to be solely a function of the quantities of goods sold is equally applicable to both approaches. That is, value added, the retail gross margin or sales are in general going to be functions of both the quantities of goods sold and the level of distribution services provided.

In the total factor productivity approach one can adopt a growth accounting framework or an econometric approach.[25] In the former case one assumes constant returns to scale and estimates productivity as a residual. The discussion in sections 4.2 and 4.3 suggests that this procedure would falsely attribute to productivity increases the consequences of larger store sizes and higher levels of distribution services. This bias would be particularly large when using value added or the retail margin as a measure of output. Incidentally, the same problem would arise in the econometric approach if one were to impose the assumption of constant returns to scale. Nevertheless, the econometric approach does not require this assumption, whereas the growth accounting framework does.[26]

One of the points emphasized in this chapter as well as throughout the book is that the output of retailing must be conceived of in at least two dimensions: the quantity of goods sold and the level of distribution services provided. Hence, the implication of this emphasis for productivity measurement is that the starting point of the econometric approach is either a transformation function, for example equation 4.1, or a multiproduct cost function, for example equation 4.11. In this sense retailing is no different from many other service industries and it can benefit from the experience of these industries. For instance, the measurement of productivity in the banking industry starts by asking the question: what is the output of banks?[27] Similarly, productivity measurement in retailing needs to start by asking the question – what are the outputs of retailing that will be considered for the retail sector or enterprise in question.

Interestingly, the staff of statistical agencies has started to recognize this issue. For instance, the staff of the Australian Productivity Commission has made this distinction between two types of outputs in a recent report on the productivity of Australia's wholesale and retail trade (Johnson et al., 2000, Appendix B). Similarly a recent study in the marketing literature, Ratchford (2003), focuses on this issue in analysing the productivity of retail food stores. In terms of the standard labor productivity measure calculated by BLS, productivity in retail food stores between 1959 and 1995 peaks in 1971 and shows a steady decline since then despite the spread of technological innovations such as scanners. Nonetheless Ratchford shows that if one estimates a multiproduct cost function, where the service dimension in terms of assortment is captured and treated as an output and the number of scanners is allowed to affect productivity, productivity in food retailing has increased over this period. Of course in this case productivity is measured in terms of decreases in a variable aggregate cost function, which is estimated using a translog functional form that satisfies the restrictions necessary for a proper cost function.

Applications of the econometric approach to productivity measurement in retailing can be undertaken using either (4.1) or (4.11) as the point of departure.

In either case, the issue of whether the analysis tries to differentiate between observations on the transformation or cost frontier and those inside the frontier arises at the time of estimation. One estimation technique, relying on (4.1) as the point of departure implicitly or explicitly, which accomplishes this differentiation is data envelopment analysis. An alternative that accomplishes the same purpose, using (4.11) as the point of departure, is the estimation of stochastic frontier cost functions. Interestingly Gong and Sickles (1992) have shown, using Monte Carlo studies, that neither technique uniformly dominates the other in the example they study.

In the specific case of retailing, data envelopment analysis is becoming popular as an estimation technique for productivity measurement (Parsons, 1994), although it has its critics (Thurik, 1994). The main implications of our analysis for this controversy are that, regardless of the estimation technique, the outputs of retailing for the purpose at hand must be carefully defined, one must allow for economies of scale, especially with respect to distribution services, and, as we saw in Section 4.4, the outputs of the retail activity should be treated as endogenous variables in the estimation if possible.

Just as in any industry where economies of scale matter, productivity measurement in retailing would benefit greatly from the availability of panel data in some form. This type of data allows the contribution of economies of scale to be separated from technical change (which can be controlled, for example, through a variety of time trends) and from efficiency differences across firms or establishments due to superior management (which can be controlled, for example, through fixed effects estimation). Some attempts at developing longitudinal data sets in the retail trade exist through the efforts of the Center for Economic Studies at the US Bureau of the Census, but their analyses of economic issues are at an early stage.

For instance, two recent studies relying on longitudinal data are Foster, Haltiwanger and Krizan (2002) and Jarmin, Klimek and Miranda (2002). The former links retail trade establishment data over three Census of Retail Trade years (1987, 1992 and 1997) and focuses on the link between establishment and industry productivity. The latter study in principle links retail trade establishments data annually from 1977–97 and focuses on entry and exit rates of firms. Not surprisingly, given that these are the first attempts at using this type of data in retailing, both studies use the data to ask the same questions that were asked of comparable data for manufacturing. The answers are similar in the second study and different in the first one. A particularly interesting result in the first one, that is, Foster, Haltiwanger and Krazin, is that most of the reallocation of output and employment in the retail trade due to the entry and exit of establishments takes place within four-digit retail sub-sectors rather than between sub-sectors. Substantively, this is perhaps the most important contrast the authors find with manufacturing.

Undoubtedly the data underlying these studies will prove quite useful in the analysis of productivity issues, but this will require the adaptation of the analysis to incorporate essential features of retailing that differ from manufacturing. One such feature is the existence of two different dimensions of output stressed here.

By way of a conclusion we present an illustration of this issue. Recall that one of the services retailers provide to consumers is accessibility of location, for example making goods and services available closer to consumers through the provision of additional establishments. Suppose between two years the number of establishments entering is twice the number of establishments exiting, there are no continuing establishments, and output and employment per establishment is the same for all entering and exiting establishments. In this setting, the productivity measure used by Foster, Haltiwanger and Krizan, that is, deflated sales per worker, will remain the same for every establishment. Thus, average productivity of establishments for the industry has not changed. Yet, if the entering establishments are half way in distance to the exiting ones, the retail sector is providing consumers with twice the accessibility of location in the end year than in the base year. This represents a significant increase in the output of one of the distributions services of the retail sector (and in consumer welfare) which is ignored because the productivity measure is not sensitive to this dimension of output.[28]

APPENDIX: A PRODUCTION FUNCTION FOR ASSORTMENT

It has become standard in the increasing returns and specialization literature, for example Ray (1998, Chapter 4), to use a specific functional form to capture the role of increasing returns in the production of suppliers services. This functional form is well suited to capture economies of scale in the production of assortment. To wit,

$$D = [(X_1)^\alpha + \ldots + (X_n)^\alpha]^{1/\alpha}, \tag{4.A1}$$

where $0 < \alpha < 1$. α is a direct measure of substitutability between the types of items, i. X_i indicates the quantities or output of type i used in the production of level of assortment D.

Output of type i is produced with labor (L_i) and another input (K), which will be assumed fixed, according to $X_i = KBL_i$. We will let $K = 1$ for simplicity. B indicates the number of items of any type that can be produced by a unit of labor. Output of type i is produced subject to diminishing returns since $\alpha < 1$. (4.A1) can then be rewritten as

$$D = [(BL_1)^\alpha + \ldots + (BL_n)^\alpha]^{1/\alpha}. \tag{4.A2}$$

The production of assortment D, given a fixed amount of labor allocated to this task $L(D)$, will be maximized by allocating labor equally among the items, so that $L(D) = nk$. n is the number of different types of items (stock keeping units, SKU, for example) and k is the number of labor units allocated to producing each type of item, i. Substituting in (4.A2) yields the following (reduced form) production function for assortment.

$$D = [n(Bk)^\alpha]^{1/\alpha} = n^{1/\alpha}\, Bk = n^\theta\, BL(D). \tag{4.A3}$$

While the production function in (4.A3) exhibits constant returns to scale with respect to increases in labor productivity (B) or the quantity of labor (either per type of item (k) or devoted to the production of assortment, $L(D)$), it exhibits increasing returns to scale with respect to increases in the number of types of items, n. That is, from the second equality in (4.A3) we have, $(\partial D/\partial n)n/D = 1/\alpha > 1$. Note that here we are keeping the amount of labor per item (k) the same among all the items, which implies an increase in the total amount of labor available to produce assortment, $L(D)$. Alternatively if we keep the total amount of labor allocated to the production of assortment, $L(D)$, the same, (4.A3) exhibits increasing returns to scale if $\alpha < 1/2$. That is, from the third equality in (4.A3) we have $(\partial D/\partial n)(n/D) = \theta$ and $\theta = (1 - \alpha)/\alpha > 1$ if $\alpha < 1/2$.[29]

Just as indicated earlier, α measures the degree of substitutability between the type of items. One would expect that the broader the assortment, for example adding categories rather than SKU within a category, the lower the degree of substitutability in production, and the lower we would expect the value of α to be. Hence, (4.A3) implies that we would expect to see stronger increasing returns for expansions of breadth than for expansions of depth. Since elements of fixed cost are likely to be a more important presence when adding breadth, this form also captures the essence of our argument in section 4.2. Incidentally, this functional form and the increasing returns it generates has also been used together with a simple economy-wide model to show how an inverted-U pattern for the share of the distribution sector arises during the course of economic development (Anderson and Betancourt, 2002).

NOTES

1. In the national accounts produced by the Bureau of Economic Analysis the retail gross margin, that is, sales minus the cost of goods sold, is used as the measure of gross output in the retail trade. On the other hand, the productivity office at BLS takes sales as its output measure. I thank Jack Triplett for this observation.

2. Incidentally, a similar argument applies to the retail gross margin. It is fine as a measure of the gross output of the distribution activity, but it will be a one-to-one measure of distribution services only under the very restrictive assumptions identified here. The main difference with respect to value added would be in the inputs that one includes in the vector X_2. In the case of value added one should only allow factor inputs such as capital and labor, whereas in the case of the gross margin one would include as well intermediate inputs such as electricity and materials.

3. This is one set of assumptions on the technology sufficient to go from (4.1) to a production function for Q, but it is not the only set of assumptions that one can use to obtain this result.

4. In section 4.3 we show how the cost function is obtained for this specific case under the assumption that F has the Cobb–Douglas form to be presented in section 4.2.

5. Sales is a measure of the gross output of the distribution activity and the production activity.

6. Similar arguments can be made about jointness or common inputs if we disaggregate distribution services into its components. Hence, the use of the general form of the transformation function is also appropriate for analyses that disaggregate distribution services into its components.

7. These authors also provide a review of the empirical evidence.

8. In simple numerical terms if the costs of assortment double when one doubles the area of a store and the volume of output in terms of items and specific distribution services associated with these items more than doubles, we have increasing returns to scale.

9. An alternative way of tying these three sources of economies of scale is by noting that there are common inputs that go into the production of distribution services and the quantities of goods sold. Insofar as expansion of the common inputs does not increase the joint outputs in the same proportion, it generates increasing returns to scale for any output that expands proportionately more than the common inputs.

10. The definition of returns to scale in this context is the proportionate increase in output (D) as a result of an equiproportionate increase in all inputs (L, K_1, K_2).

11. The results in Table 4.1 are taken from Table 3 in Ofer (1973). There are other issues treated by him which are tangential to the thrust of our discussion and will, therefore, be ignored here.

12. These results are taken from Tables 5, 6 and 7 in Ingene (1984b). Just as in the previous case we ignore issues tangential to the thrust of our discussion.

13. Ofer's study is based on individual stores whereas Ingene's study is based on aggregates for an SMSA. One can argue that the latter data are more representative of a long-run equilibrium where the process of exit and entry leads to operation under constant returns to scale.

14. For the single output case with a Cobb–Douglas technology, Mundlak (1996) shows how instrumental variable estimation of the primal problem may be preferable to the dual approach.

15. Furthermore, in terms of communicating ideas across academic disciplines or to non-academicians, it is far easier to discuss the impact of an action on costs than to discuss the impact of an action on joint outputs and its subsequent effect on costs.

16. Many of these considerations focus on the analysis of situations where one of the outputs is zero. Since our main point is that in the case of retailing neither one of these two outputs is zero, these considerations are tangential to the emphasis in this chapter although they can be relevant for the analysis of some special circumstances in retailing.

17. The main economic consequence of this restriction is that it eliminates the possibility of cost complementarity, namely a negative interaction coefficient (α_{QD}). The restriction was not imposed on the estimation discussed below and this coefficient turned out to be positive anyway.

18. Incidentally, this formula corrects a mistake in the corresponding one, equation (12), presented by Betancourt and Malanoski (1999).

19. These estimates are taken from Table 3 in Betancourt and Malanoski (1999). The essential characteristics of the data and the estimation will be presented in the next section.

20. Two alternative versions of the index using different weighting schemes were tried but they gave the same results.

21. Note that $Q = qN$, and the model of Chapter 2 is obtained when $N = 1$. Thus, aggregate demand (Q) equals the demand of the representative consumer (q) when $N = 1$.
22. Recall from Chapter 2 that r is the shadow price of distribution services and μ is the proportion of sales to the representative consumer that are lost by not meeting the competitive constraint.
23. The discussion assumes a single distribution service. In general an additional equation would be needed for every additional distribution service identified in the data.
24. Total factor productivity can be thought of as an output index deflated by an index of all inputs used in production. Labor productivity can be thought of as an output index deflated by an index of the labor input.
25. The growth accounting framework relies exclusively on price and quantity indexes of outputs and inputs. The econometric approach requires estimation of transformation or cost functions. On these issues see, for example, Caves, Christensen and Diewert (1982).
26. A related issue is the distinction between quality and output in the measurement of distribution services. This distinction is relevant for productivity measurement as well as for modeling of retail activities. One usually thinks of quality as embedded in each unit of a particular item sold. While it may be useful in some settings to view specific distribution services as simply a manifestation of quality in this sense, the same approach toward common distribution services is misleading. Treating common distribution services as a manifestation of quality that is embedded in each item eliminates their role as a source of economies of scale because it implies a fixed proportions technology in the production of distribution services and the quantities of goods sold.
27. A very comprehensive and thorough discussion of this point and other issues related to productivity measurement in banking is available in two papers and three comments in a volume edited by Griliches (1992, pp.219–300).
28. In manufacturing this does not matter because one can think of the transportation sector doing the same amount of work in the end year as in the base year. For instance, trucks travel more to the entering plants but this is canceled by their traveling less to wholesaler and retailers. In the retail trade, however, the increased travel of the transportation sector is not canceled because the consumers are the ones traveling less.
29. We are treating n as a continuous variable when in fact it is a discrete one. Nonetheless, the increasing returns argument holds in the discrete case as well. That is, keeping k $[L(D)]$ constant, D will be convex in n as long as $\alpha < 1$ $[\alpha < 1/2]$.

PART II

Interactions between retailers and consumers

5.   Multiproduct retailing

Earlier in the book, Chapter 3 to be precise, we explored several aspects of the multiproduct nature of retail demand. In this chapter we take results developed there together with features of retail supply developed in Chapter 4 and use them to heighten our understanding of several features of multiproduct retailing. Section 5.1 asks, should we focus on the prices of individual items or on the prices of items at individual stores or, more generally, at points of purchase or sale? This question becomes important precisely because retailing is normally a multiproduct activity. This feature has a variety of important and wide-ranging implications. For instance, in a somewhat lengthy Appendix I examine the interaction between the multiproduct feature of retailing, which requires the construction of price and cost of living indexes, and reliance on scanner-based data. While the underlying theory of cost of living indexes has been developed in terms of consumption, scanner data are based on purchases. The Appendix relies on recent literature to illustrate how to reconcile the difference.

Remaining sections of the chapter consider different aspects of the multiproduct nature of retailing in relation to the pricing policies followed by retailers. Section 5.2 focuses on the pricing policy of a retailer with constant distribution services, revisits some elementary results and ties the analysis to concepts introduced in Chapters 3 and 4. Section 5.3 illustrates aspects of the pricing policies of a multiproduct retailer with examples that rely on the two studies from the marketing literature discussed in Chapter 3, section 3. Section 5.4 considers the pricing policies of a multiproduct retailer with variable distribution services. While most of the argument is developed in the context of a monopolist, extensions to monopolistic competition and to strategic interactions in a duopoly are explicitly considered. Section 5.5 draws two basic implications of the previous results as well as those relevant for Internet retailing. A discussion of recent empirical studies on the Internet and an explicit comparison between conventional retailers and Internet retailers from the perspective of this book frame the argument. Finally, section 5.6 concludes with a discussion of one unique aspect of multiproduct pricing in retailing: the use of 'loss leaders'. The prior analysis in this chapter is related to two versions of this concept and to recent theoretical and empirical studies on the topic.

5.1   ITEM PRICES OR ITEM PRICES AT POINTS OF PURCHASE?

When one ignores the role of the distribution or retail sector in economic activity, or if every store were a single-product store, the answer to the question is straightforward. One should focus on item prices. This has been a typical approach in the economics literature. Nevertheless, this attitude is in the process of reconsideration in a wide variety of settings and for different reasons. Furthermore, the punchline in these settings is that item prices at individual stores matter and should be the focus of attention or at least explicitly accounted for in the analysis. We will consider several such settings in this section.[1]

One of the first settings in which this issue arises explicitly is in the attempt to do studies of the effect of concentration on price in food retailing. Some writers, for example Geithman and Marion (1993), argue that the appropriate price index for this purpose is one that measures the average price level of the same basket of market goods for all stores, firms or SMSAs. Other writers, for example Kaufman and Handy (1993), argue that the appropriate price index should measure the average price level at a store, firm or SMSA. If you have only one item, there is no 'basket of market goods' and the price of the item measures both the average price at the store, firm or SMSA and the average price of the 'basket of market goods'. If one introduces multiple items, however, any two indices constructed by this different criterion will diverge in what they measure unless all stores, for example, offer the same basket of market goods.

If manufacturers or wholesalers were the real decision makers with retailers acting as passive participants in retail markets, merely covering their costs and unable to exercise market power, measuring the average price level of the same basket of market goods across stores, firms and SMSAs would be a desirable goal. One could be interested, for instance, in the effect of market power of manufacturers on the average price of a basket of market goods purchased by consumers. If retailers are the real decision makers with manufacturers playing a passive role, however, the average price level at a store or retail firm becomes the desirable goal instead. One could be interested, for example, in ascertaining the effect of market power of retailers on the average price charged at their stores. In general one can be interested in either individual item prices or in these prices at different points of purchase or in both, depending on the purpose of the analysis and on one's view of the real decision makers at various nodes in the economic system.

For instance, one could be interested in the anticompetitive effects of a merger among two retail firms. In this case one wants to focus on what happens to the average price level at the stores of each of these firms when the other one is not around rather than on the average price level of a fixed basket of market goods that may vary across stores and firms. Such a focus is clearly illustrated by the discussion of the role of econometrics in a recent retail merger case, namely FTC versus Staples/Office Depot (Gleason and Hosken, 1998). Each side had well-known econometricians (Ashenfelter and Hausman, respectively) who disagreed on many things but they both sought to explain the same average store price index. The latter, which was proposed by Hausman, is given by

$$\log (p_{it}) = \Sigma_k \omega_k \log (p_{itk}), \tag{5.1}$$

where the index i indicates the store, t indicates time and k the category. p represents a price index and ω the share of total revenues generated by a category. Thus, the average store price at time t is a geometric mean of the price indices for the k categories.

In this particular case there were four categories in which to place the more than 7000 distinct stock keeping units (SKU) for consumable office supplies carried by a typical Staples store. The price index for each of the four categories was calculated as the following weighted average

$$p_{itk} = \Sigma_{j \in k} w_j p_{itj} \; k = 1, \ldots 4, \tag{5.2}$$

where w_j represents the share of item j in category k's unit sales. The categories were price-sensitive items, leadership items, price-insensitive items and invisible items. For most practical purposes selection of an item for these categories corresponded to the frequency with which Staples checked the price of the item.

Similarly if one is interested in economic characteristics of the distribution sector such as the existence of economies of scale in organizations operating in this sector, one wants to collapse the prices of the multitude of products at any modern store into a single or a few indicators. For instance in a recent analysis of Finnish grocery stores, Aalto-Setälä (1999) constructs a CES price index from 345 items for each of 158 grocery stores included in a cross-section. This index is given by

$$\text{CES Price Index} = \{\Sigma w_i \, [(p_i)^1 \, /(p_i)^0] \; {}^{1-\sigma}\}^{1/(1-\sigma)}, \tag{5.3}$$

where w_i are the value shares of item i in period 0, $(p_i)^1$ is the price of item i in period 1 and $(p_i)^0$ is, of course, the price of item i in period 0. These two sets of prices were gathered in 1995 and 1994, respectively. If the elasticity of substitution, σ, is zero the index collapses to a Laspeyres index, which is a widely used price index that is well known to ignore substitution possibilities.

The results of this study were not sensitive to the value of σ used and the author chose a value of 0.5 for this parameter to construct the price index used in his analysis of economies of scale.[2]

In the above study the weights were derived from a survey of consumer expenditures and one aim of the analysis was to measure the cost of living of a consumer that patronizes a particular store. Life becomes more complicated when the goal is to measure a cost of living index for society as a whole. In their discussion of the consumer price index constructed by BLS, which is a fixed basket of market goods index, the report of the Boskin commission (1996) details the shortcomings of this index as a cost of living index. Moreover, it singles out outlet bias as one of the sources of bias in the consumer price index. Namely, by drawing samples of prices from the same stores the index ignores the fact that consumers will engage in substitution against the products of the higher priced outlets, by switching to lower priced outlets, unless the additional distribution services provided by the higher priced outlets compensate them for the higher prices of these products. In a rather unique study made possible by the rotation of outlets as part of BLS procedures, Reinsdorf (1992) provides evidence that there is substitution toward lower priced outlets and that a lowering of distribution services is unlikely to explain this phenomenon.

In the previous cases the nature of the problem leads us to take into account the multiproduct nature of organizations in the retail sector through some form of aggregation. Equations (5.1) to (5.3) illustrate alternative price indexes that can be used in this aggregation process. To conclude this section, I discuss one situation where the existence of multiple products does not lead to issues of aggregation over the prices of these multiple products; instead, it raises issues of aggregation over the time at which these multiple products are priced.

Lach and Tsiddon (1996) sought to explain why in a highly inflationary situation price changes were staggered. Once the multiproduct nature of retailing is acknowledged, two alternative explanations for the staggering that is empirically observed must be distinguished. The staggering may occur because different stores change their prices at different times (across-stores staggering) or because the same stores change a proportion of the prices of their products at different times (across-products staggering), or both. In their analysis of Israeli data Lach and Tsiddon (1996) found evidence of within-store price synchronization and across-stores price staggering. Their interpretation of these results is that they provide support for menu costs explanations of sticky prices in the macro literature.

5.2 THE PRICING POLICY OF A MULTIPRODUCT RETAILER WITH CONSTANT DISTRIBUTION SERVICES

We begin with the simplest model incorporating demand and costs into the analysis. Namely, a monopolistic retailer chooses prices to maximize profits which are given by

$$\pi = pQ - C(v,Q, D) - wQ, \tag{5.4}$$

where p is the single item (Q) retail price, w is the wholesale price and C is the retailer's cost function. The latter is familiar from Chapter 4, except here all distribution services (D) and input prices (v) are assumed to be constant. The first-order condition merely implies that marginal revenues equal marginal costs, that is,

$$\partial\pi/\partial p \Rightarrow p[1 + (1/\in)] = C_Q + w, \tag{5.5}$$

where $\in$ is the own-price elasticity of demand for any one item as defined in Chapter 3.

If the price elasticity of demand and marginal costs are constant, one can solve (5.5) for the optimal price (5.6) or for the optimal mark-up (5.7).

$$p = [C_Q + w] [\in/(\in + 1)], \text{ and} \tag{5.6}$$

$$M = (p - C_Q - w)/p = -1/\in. \tag{5.7}$$

In this case (5.7) implies that the optimal mark-up should vary inversely with the absolute value of the own-price elasticity of demand as well as with marginal costs, and (5.6) implies that the optimal price varies inversely with the elasticity and positively with marginal costs. Equation (5.6) is known as the Amoroso–Robinson relation in the marketing literature (for example Simon, 1989). A similar relation is the basis for the standard analysis of price discrimination by a monopolist in the economics literature (for example Henderson and Quandt, 1980). The basic implication is the same – price is lower where demand is more elastic, that is, where the absolute value of the own-price elasticity of demand is larger.

Neither the elasticity of demand nor marginal costs are constant in general. Nonetheless, if they are approximately so, one would expect to find on average that high mark-ups are associated with low own-price elasticities and low marginal costs, and high prices with high marginal costs and low own-price elasticities. If the absolute value of the own-price elasticity of demand increases with price, the association between high prices and mark-ups and low own-price elasticities will be weaker than if it decreases with price. Similarly, if marginal costs are increasing with price, which implies decreasing marginal cost curves with respect to output, the association between high marginal costs and low mark-ups is attenuated while the association between high marginal costs and high prices is accentuated.

To capture the multiproduct nature of retailing emphasized here, let us have the retailer choose the prices of all items to maximize profits. Thus, (5.4) remains the same but p, w and Q can now be interpreted as vectors instead of scalars. If for simplicity we suppose there are only two items or elements in these vectors,[3] the first-order condition for item 1 now implies

$$\partial \pi / \partial p_1 \Rightarrow p_1 (1 + \in_{11}) = (C_1 + w_1)\in_{11} - (p_2 - C_2 - w_2)(Q_2 / Q_1) (\in_{21}),$$
$$(5.8)$$

where C_i represents the marginal cost of retailing good i, p_i and w_i represent the retail and wholesale price of good i, respectively, and the price elasticities of demand ($\in_{ij}$) are defined as in Chapter 3.

By manipulating (5.8) we obtain

$$p_1 = (C_1 + w_1)(\in_{11} / (\in_{11} + 1)) - (p_2 - C_2 - w_2)(Q_2/Q_1) (\in_{21})/(\in_{11} + 1).$$
$$(5.9)$$

Hence, the first term in (5.9) shows that the same relation between price and the own-price elasticity of demand and marginal cost that existed before, equation (5.6), continues to operate in the multiproduct case. Essential features of what is new in the multiproduct case can be seen from the second term in (5.9). The latter implies that if two items are gross substitutes ($\in_{21} > 0$), the price of item 1 will be higher in the multiproduct setting than it would have been in the single product one associated with (5.6). On the other hand, if they are gross complements ($\in_{21} < 0$), the price of item 1 in the multiproduct setting will be lower than it would have been in the single product one associated with (5.6).[4] If they are gross independents ($\in_{21} = 0$) and marginal costs are also independent, the choice of price for item 1 will not be affected by the choice of price for item 2 and (5.9) collapses to (5.6).[5]

A similar expression to (5.9) holds for item 2 but note that one of the insights of Chapter 3 is that the cross-price elasticities are not symmetric, $\in_{21}$ is not equal to $\in_{12}$. Since the consumption effects depend on the use of the item as an input in the household production function of commodities, their magnitudes can be quite different. A related insight from Chapter 3 is that most items will tend to be gross complements: that is, $\in_{ij} < 0$. Thus, the average store price in a multiproduct store will tend to be lower than the price in a single-product store. More generally, given the same number of products, the average store price of stores that provide breadth of assortment, by stocking products that are net independents, will tend to be lower than the average store price of establishments that provide depth of assortment, by stocking products that are net substitutes.

5.3   ILLUSTRATIONS

Mulhern and Leone (1991) define the following pricing strategy as implicit price bundling, 'the price of a product is based on the multitude of price effects that are present across products without providing consumers with an explicit joint price.' One way of illustrating this strategy is to use the results of their study, presented in Table 3.1, in the following conceptual experiment. Consider the effect on profitability of changing a regular price of cake mix. If we assume an initial equilibrium in which all prices are $1, then a 1 per cent decrease in the price of Duncan Hines cake mix generates a 1.62 per cent increase in quantities of DH cake mix purchased as well as a 3.07 per cent increase in the quantities of frostings from Betty Crocker, Duncan Hines and Pillsbury for a net increase in revenues of 1.85 per cent for the retailer, assuming for illustrative purposes that cake mix and frosting contribute in equal proportion (0.5) to revenues. If marginal costs are constant, this represents the increase in profits. A similar experiment can be conducted for other brands.

This illustration is somewhat artificial but it serves to illustrate three important points. First, the gross complementarity across the two categories in this study means that part of the benefits to retailers of lower regular prices on Duncan Hines cake mix come from the increased consumption of Betty Crocker, Duncan Hines and Pillsbury frosting by their customers. Under our assumptions and the results in Table 3.1, this is the price change that increases the profits of the retailer the most. Second, this also illustrates the conflict between the interests of the manufacturers and the interests of the retailers. Under the same circumstances and assuming also constant marginal costs for the manufacturers, the profits of the manufacturer (DH) will be increased more by a decrease in the price of their frosting than in the price of their cake mix.

A third important point that can be illustrated with this example is a limitation of the approach. Namely, in general, profit maximization is attained by choosing all the prices simultaneously, not by performing the individual price experiment described above. I address the general case in section 5.4. Here, the discussion continues by focusing on the implications of this analysis for special deals or price promotions when this limitation does not arise. One can think of the limitation not arising for deals for two different reasons: one is that the manufacturer may choose the week its brand is on special offer; the other is that, while the retailer does the choosing, the use of features and displays is difficult to do for more than one brand. In any event in the data used by Mulhern and Leone (1991), there were substantial differences in the number of weeks that the different brands were on offer. For instance, the store brand frosting was never on offer and the store brand cake mix was on offer 1 per cent of the weeks for the store shown in Table 3.1. Yet, the BC brands of cake mix and frosting were on offer 35 per cent and 36.2 per cent of the weeks covered by the study. Finally, DH and P cake mix, for example, were on offer 12.6 per cent and 17.5 per cent of the weeks, respectively.

Mulhern and Leone evaluate the effect of special deals or promotions on profits in terms of experiments designed to capture the implicit price bundling strategy. For instance, they evaluate the impact of a Pillsbury cake mix price promotion on retail profits by comparing profits during a special deal week with baseline profits during regular price weeks under different scenarios. These scenarios incorporate the relevant effects from other brands, cross-category effects, marginal costs changes due to promotional allowances and display or feature effects in the estimates of profitability. An interesting result of their analysis is that the display or feature effect of special deals, which they interpret as a signaling device, is what generates the greatest contribution to store profitability under the assumption of constant marginal costs for the retailer.

Blattberg, Briesch and Fox (1995), in their discussion of how promotions work, emphasize several results as empirical generalizations consistent with a number of studies. By the way of a conclusion to our first illustration, it is useful to identify explicitly four results of Mulhern and Leone that fall in their category of empirical generalizations. Promotions have sizable own-price effects. Like regular prices, promotions affect complementary categories and the cross-promotional effects of brands are asymmetric. These two effects stem from the multiproduct nature of retail demand and provide the basis for the pricing strategy that Mulhern and Leone (1991) call implicit price bundling. Finally in-store displays and feature advertising have strong effects on item sales. Both of these activities can be viewed as the provision of specific distribution services about particular items in the form of information.

One of the features that follows from the multiproduct nature of retailing is that the basket of market goods offered by different stores may be different, or that the prices charged by different stores for the same basket of market goods may be different. According to HKMR (1995), 'Micromarketing seeks to customize retailing policies to exploit differences across stores in consumer characteristics and the competitive environment'. One such policy is a pricing strategy that maximizes profits by charging different prices at different stores in response to different characteristics of consumers that affect their demand elasticities.

The study by these authors discussed in Chapter 3 estimates a category price elasticity that differs across stores for each of 18 categories.[6] They also used characteristics of consumers in the market area of each of the 83 stores to explain variations in these category price elasticities. It turns out that consumer characteristics are more powerful in explaining these variations than characteristics of the competitive environment facing each store in all 18 categories. Since all the stores belong to the same chain, HKMR compare the implications of adopting a pricing strategy consistent with micromarketing with the current pricing policy of the chain.

Everyday pricing policies had been chosen by assigning stores to three pricing zones on the basis of competitive considerations. There was no relation between the zones to which the stores were assigned and the price sensitivity indicated by the category elasticities. Our discussion of (5.6) and (5.9) shows that with a micromarketing pricing policy lower price zones should have been associated with category price elasticities with high absolute values or price-sensitive categories. Similarly, a uniform, chain-wide strategy was the pricing policy for promotions. Once again the results of the previous section suggest that a simple micromarketing policy would be to have smaller cuts in stores that are price sensitive. Of course, as HKMR point out, the costs of accumulating, updating and processing the necessary information for a micromarketing pricing strategy to be implemented need to be included before concluding that the earlier policies were suboptimal.

5.4   THE PRICING POLICIES OF A MULTIPRODUCT RETAILER WITH VARIABLE DISTRIBUTION SERVICES[7]

One can think of the analysis in this section as simply an extension of the analysis in section 5.2. Indeed, the starting point is the same, equation (5.4) defining profits, but with two qualifications. All the variables on the right-hand side of (5.4) are here defined as vectors, and distribution services (the vector D) are no longer assumed constant. The simultaneous choice of prices and distribution services leads to the following first-order conditions after manipulation.

$$\alpha_i = \Sigma_k \, \alpha_k \, [(p_k - C_k - w_k)/p_k] \, (-\in_{ik}) \, k, \, i = 1, \ldots, N \qquad (5.10)$$

$$\eta_i = \alpha_i \, {}^*M_i \in_{is} \quad i = 1, \ldots N, \, s = 1, \ldots, N \qquad (5.11)$$

$$\eta_j = \Sigma_i \, \alpha_i \, {}^*M_i \in_{ij} \quad j = 1, \ldots, J \qquad (5.12)$$

where k, i index items or products, s indexes specific distribution services, and j indexes common distribution services.[8] M is shorthand for the mark-up as expressed in the term within square brackets in (5.10). $\eta_i = C_i (D_i/C)[\eta_j = C_j (D_j/C)]$ is the elasticity of costs with respect to the ith specific [jth common] distribution service. α_i is the share of the ith item in total revenues ($p_i q_i/\sum_j p_i q_i$) and α_i^* is the share of the ith item in the total costs of retailing ($p_i q_i/C$).

Equation (5.10) is a generalization to N products or items of (5.6) or (5.9). Its economic implications are similar to those found in section 5.2 and it captures the basic insight from the earlier literature on market basket pricing (for example Preston, 1962), which we will express as

> *Proposition 5.1*: High values of the own- and cross-price elasticities of demand ($-\in_{ik}$) lead to low prices and mark-ups, due to the profitability of charging a higher price when items are inelastic or gross substitutes.

The main difference in our setting, however, is that distribution services could affect the outcome since they would enter the analysis if the marginal cost of the item (C_k) depended on the level of the distribution service or if the price elasticities of demand depended on the level of the distribution service. In general this will be the case, but it will not change the prior conclusion.[9] If we assume that η_i (η_j) increases with distribution services (D) and with the quantities of items (Q) and that $\in_{is}$ ($\in_{ij}$) decreases with distribution services, we can add to the previous proposition based on (5.10) that the low prices or mark-ups generated by the high price elasticities in (5.10) also lead to lower levels of distribution services, which can be seen from (5.11) and (5.12).

Distribution services also generate the following

> *Proposition 5.2*: High distribution services elasticities of demand ($\in_{is}$, $\in_{ij}$) imply the choice of high prices and high levels of distribution services by retailers.

This is easiest to see from (5.11) where, under the same assumptions about the elasticities as in the previous paragraph, one can perform the conceptual experiment of considering two situations such that in A, the distribution services demand elasticity is high relative to the situation in B. Starting from an initial position of equilibrium in B with a given mark-up, a move to A can be accomplished by increasing D, which will lead to a reduction in the value of the distribution services elasticity and an increase in the cost elasticity on the left-hand side. Increases in the levels of D increase the quantities of the items demanded (Q), and this increases marginal costs, which reduces mark-ups. Hence, it leads to an increase in prices in A which serves to restore the mark-up levels. A similar analysis can be made of exogenous changes in the marginal cost elasticity of distribution services and it leads to the following

Proposition 5.3: Low elasticities of marginal costs with respect to distribution services (η_i, η_j) imply the choice of high prices and high levels of distribution services by retailers.[10]

While the above arguments were made in terms of specific distribution services, the same arguments hold for any one common distribution service as given by (5.12). The main difference is that the increase in distribution services and prices to restore equilibrium in response to these exogenous changes would be spread out over all the items in the assortment rather than concentrated on a single item. Notwithstanding, there is a noteworthy situation where specific and common distribution services respond differently to an exogenous change: namely, an expansion in the assortment. It is useful to summarize the difference in the following way.

Proposition 5.4: Retailers who provide common distribution services and find it profitable to expand their assortments are likely to increase the levels of these common distribution services and lower their prices; retailers who provide specific distribution services and find it profitable to expand their assortments are likely to lower the levels of these specific distribution services and raise their prices.

To establish this proposition, let us consider first a firm that provides only specific distribution services. The expansion of assortment modifies (5.11) as follows

$$\eta_i = \alpha_i * M_i \in_{is} \qquad i = 1, \ldots N + 1, s = 1, \ldots, N + 1. \qquad (5.11)'$$

With prices and marginal costs (C_i) given, at the old level of distribution services (5.11)$'$ can not be an equilibrium because $\alpha_i *$ in (5.11)$'$ decreases as a result of the increase in total costs due to the new item in the assortment and the specific distribution service associated with it. Hence, under the assumptions made above about the demand elasticities for distribution services and the cost elasticities for distribution services, specific distribution services in the N previously existing items must decrease in order to restore equilibrium after the new item in the assortment is introduced. Incidentally, this holds, no matter how profitable the new $(N + 1)$ item is in the assortment. Alternatively, given the old level of specific distribution services, at the old prices (5.11)$'$ can not be an equilibrium and for the same reason as before. In order to restore equilibrium for the N previously existing items in (5.11)$'$ mark-ups and thus prices must increase. In general, adjustment to the assortment expansion will rely on both instruments: prices and distribution services.[11]

Consider now a second type of firm that provides only common distribution services. As a result of expanding the assortment, the first-order condition (5.12) becomes

$$\eta_j = \Sigma_i \, \alpha_i \, {}^*M_i \in_{ij} + \alpha_{N+1} \, {}^*M_{N+1} \in_{(N+1)j} \qquad j = 1, \ldots, J. \qquad (5.12)'$$

If prices are given and the marginal cost of providing the ith item is not affected by the change in assortment, the first term in (5.12)′ relative to (5.12) will be smaller and for the same reason as before. The second term in (5.12)′, however is positive and if the expansion of assortment is sufficiently profitable it will dominate the decrease in the first term. Hence, the RHS of (5.12)′ will be larger than the RHS of (5.12). This will then require an increase in the common distribution service to bring the two sides into equilibrium. If distribution services are given, on the other hand, a lowering of prices will be required to bring the RHS of (5.12)′ into equilibrium with the LHS. In practice both instruments will be used, but the pattern of association remains the same as long as the proviso indicated in note 11 is also met in this case.

While the above argument has been developed in terms of the retailer as a monopolist, it is easy to extend it to a monopolistically competitive setting by introducing a competitive constraint just as we did in Chapter 2, section 5. It yields the following modifications of the first-order conditions.

$$\alpha_i = \Sigma_k \, \alpha_k \, [(p_k - C_k - w_k)/p_k] \, [(-\in_{ik})/(1 - \mu)] \, k, \, i = 1, \ldots, N \quad (5.10)''$$

$$\eta_i = \mu(r_i \, D_i/C) + \alpha_i \, {}^*M_i \in_{is} \qquad i = 1, \ldots N, \, s = 1, \ldots, N \qquad (5.11)''$$

$$\eta_j = \mu(r_j \, D_j/C) + \Sigma_i \, \alpha_i \, {}^*M_i \in_{ij} \qquad j = 1, \ldots, J \qquad (5.12)''$$

These three equations can be viewed as the generalization of the model in Chapter 2, section 5 to n items and specific as well as common distribution services, or as the generalization of the model in this section to allow for competition among retailers.

From (5.10)″ we see that the main effect of competition on this equation is to increase the value of the price elasticities of demand, since μ is less than unity, and if there is a given level of distribution services this will lower prices. From (5.11)″ and (5.12)″ we see that competition introduces a positive term on the RHS of each of these first-order conditions, because the shadow price of distribution services (r) is always positive. In view of the arguments underlying Proposition (5.4) with respect to common distribution services, if prices are given, adding a positive term through the introduction of competition is likely to generate higher levels of distribution services. If prices are not given, however, the result on distribution services is ambiguous, because a lowering of prices can lower the mark-ups on the RHS of (5.11)″ and (5.12)″ sufficiently to counteract the effect of the positive term introduced by competition. This is simply a generalization of the case analysed in Proposition 2.5 of Chapter 2.

Extensions of this analysis to incorporate strategic interactions requires a change in modeling approach. Nonetheless, it has already been undertaken in the literature. In a clever paper Lal and Rao (1997) use a standard game theoretic approach to explain the coexistence in equilibrium of two firms, each offering two products, where one adopts an everyday low pricing (EDLP) strategy whereas the other one engages in promotional pricing (PROMO). The most important implication of their analysis for our purposes is (p.60) 'we show that EDLP and PROMO strategies are positioning strategies, rather than merely pricing strategies, with different elements: price/promotions, service and communications.' Thus, in their multiproduct setting the two firms choose prices and two distributions services (in-store service, which is a dimension of assurance of product delivery, and public communication of their strategy with respect to prices and service, which is a dimension of information) taking into account the position of their rival on these dimensions.

Their model specification postulates two types of consumers: those with a high opportunity cost of time (time constrained) and those with a low opportunity cost of time (cherry pickers). Since there are only two stores assumed to be located at the opposite ends of a line, while both types of consumers are uniformly distributed along this line, accessibility of location or convenience will differ for consumers according to their store choice and all consumers will make some trade-off between price and convenience in the form of accessibility of location. It is also assumed in their model that the time constrained consumers have a higher willingness to pay (or demand) for the in-store service, which is costly to produce. Not surprisingly in the equilibrium where one store adopts the EDLP strategy and the other adopts the PROMO strategy, the EDLP store offers lower prices (on average) and lower services than the PROMO store. Their model also implies that the PROMO store offers higher services in order to attract more of the time constrained consumers. Some empirical evidence in favor of these last two results is presented in their paper.

5.5   IMPLICATIONS: THE INTERNET

An important implication of the analysis of the previous section is that it provides the basis for understanding a couple of stylized facts of modern retailing. First, there seems to be a trend toward retail formats with broader and deeper assortments. While assortment expansion is normally viewed as one of the factors in the rise of the conventional supermarket and the demise of the corner grocery store,[12] for example, it takes on the role of main factor in the continuation of this process that we observe in recent decades with the replacement of conventional supermarkets by other formats. For instance, sales of conventional supermarkets[13] in the US decreased from 73.1 per cent of supermarket sales in 1980 to 42.6 per cent in 1989 and to 19.3 per cent in 1997, while at the same time sales of superstores[14] increased from 17.7 per cent in 1980 to 30.6 per cent in 1989 and to 43.2 per cent in 1997. The main difference between these two formats is the deeper and broader assortments of the superstores relative to the conventional supermarkets. Incidentally, the number of establishments in each category moved in the opposite direction.[15] Thus, the first half of Proposition 5.4 allows us to understand how the broader and deeper assortments of superstores allow them to provide greater accessibility of location (a common distribution service) and prices low enough to take market share steadily away from conventional supermarkets during the last two decades.

Similarly, it is well known that department stores have higher 'retail gross margins' than grocery stores in general and supermarkets in particular. One explanation for this difference is that department stores provide more services. Our analysis suggests that it is not more services in general, but more specific distribution services in particular. Since both department stores and supermarkets have broad assortments, one intuitive explanation for the difference in margins suggested by Proposition (5.4) is that the higher retail margins of the department stores are generated by their need to charge higher prices in order to cover the higher levels of specific distribution services provided, for example, through their sales personnel. Incidentally, grocery stores provide more of at least one service than department stores, namely accessibility of location, but it is a common distribution service. This explanation is also supported by two robust empirical results reported in Chapter 2, section 7: that is, retail organizations or sectors that provide high levels of output and high levels of accessibility of location tend to have low 'retail gross margins', and retail organizations that provide high levels of specific distribution services (and, thus, have high payrolls) tend to have high 'retail gross margins'.

Perhaps most importantly, the results of the previous section have substantial implications for the analysis of Internet retailing. To draw these implications out it is useful to ask, what are the main differences between Internet retailing and conventional retailing in terms of the approach in this book? First the Internet lowers the costs to the retailer of providing broader and deeper assortments, since it eliminates all storage costs at the point of sale. One would expect this feature alone to result in a substantial assortment expansion by Internet retailers relative to conventional ones, which is what is observed.[16]

Second, this assortment expansion is combined with the provision of greater accessibility of location for acquiring possession of the item than at the store, through the direct shipping of the item to the customer's home. Third, this level of accessibility of location provided is now explicitly priced rather than bundled with the price of the item. It is useful to pause at this point in the comparison to note the main implication of the previous characteristics. They imply that Proposition 5.4 applies to Internet retailing. That is, a cost reduction in the provision of assortment leads to an expansion in the provision of assortment and of another common distribution service (accessibility of location) by the Internet retailer, and presumably to a lowering of prices.

In one of the most careful comparisons of prices offered by Internet retailers and conventional retailers carried out to date, Brynjolfsson and Smith (2000) find that Internet retailers charge lower prices than conventional retailers for the same homogeneous product. In a comparison of prices between eight conventional retailers and eight Internet retailers offering 20 compact disks, and a similar comparison for 20 books, over the February 1998–May 1999 period, they show that Internet retailers charge lower average prices of $2.16 per book and $2.58 per CD than conventional retailers. This lower average prices result is robust to corrections for taxes, shipping and handling and travel time. With respect to other issues, they find: 1) Internet retailers tend to have lower minimum prices and more frequent price changes than conventional retailers; and 2) there is a substantial amount of price dispersion in both distribution channels; indeed dispersion can be greater for the Internet channel with some measures, for example, the standard deviation. The last result is viewed by the authors as inconsistent with search cost theory and they suggest that the explanation may lie in other services, including those provided by trust and brand.[17] They offer as evidence the following fact: Internet retailers that also have conventional outlets charge a price premium for books (CDs) of 8.7 per cent (8.6 per cent) compared to those that operate exclusively on the Internet.

Subsequent research by Smith and Brynjolfsson (2001) relies on choices in an Internet 'shopbot' (EvenBetter) to explain price dispersion in the Internet book market. A shopbot is an Internet service that provides product and price information from numerous competing retailers. In this particular case, in addition to the price information on the book wanted by the customer the shopbot returned information provided by retailers on acquisition time, delivery time, shipping costs and taxes, among other things. Choices made through their last click by consumers visiting this site between August and November of 1999 provide the basic data for their analysis.

One of their main findings is that store brand has a substantial impact on choice even after price, shipping costs and delivery time are included. They interpret this as the result of reducing uncertainty on the actual delivery time, which is a non-contractible service.[18] It is also consistent with our analysis in terms of the need for the retailer to provide assurance of product delivery to the customer. Indeed, the intangible nature of Internet transactions (for example you can not inspect the item directly) requires the Internet retailer to provide a higher level of this distribution service than a conventional retailer (where you can, for example, touch the item). Finally, they also find that the impact of shipping costs on choice is much greater than the impact of item price. While they find this result difficult to understand, it is easily explained in our framework. The unbundling of the price charged for this distribution service from that of the item to be acquired allows the consumer to substitute for the service while still acquiring the good by going to the conventional store. Demand is more sensitive when there are more substitutes.

Returning to the comparison between the Internet and conventional retailers from the perspective in this book, there are some additional differences worth mentioning. First, the Internet eliminates or substantially lowers the costs to the retailer of providing the common distribution service ambiance at the point of sale. Second, it increases the costs to the retailer of providing a given level of assurance of product delivery at the desired time or in the desired form for each item, due to the inability of the consumer to acquire the product at the time and place of purchase. This is consistent with the existence of a price premium for hybrid retailers and it also provides a rationale for price dispersion in the Internet as we just saw in the analysis of the shopbot. Third, the Internet lowers the costs of providing some types of information specific to the items, for example, prices and some physical characteristics, while increasing the costs of providing other types of information, for example browsing through the book or listening to the CD. Moreover, the relative size of these costs is very sensitive to the state of technology available to the consumer and the retailer.[19]

5.6 'LOSS LEADERS'

No topic is more appropriate to conclude our discussion of multiproduct retailing than 'loss leaders'. First, in its strictest interpretation of pricing below marginal cost, loss leading is an intrinsically multiproduct subject. For, a single product firm that prices below marginal cost ceases to exist! Second, in its broader interpretation of taking into account gross complementarities in setting prices, loss leading leads to a brief extension of topics addressed earlier in this chapter. Finally, it has become an important topic in terms of recent literature that stresses the multiproduct nature of retailing. Indeed, an important empirical contribution to this literature argues that a 'loss leader' model is the only one (of four considered) consistent with scanner data on peak demand for a particular supermarket chain (Chevalier, Kashyap and Rossi, 2003) (hereafter CKR).

Perhaps the easiest place to begin is by revisiting the discussion associated with the pricing policy of a simple two-item retailer as captured in equation (5.9) of section 5.2. It is clear from this equation that loss leading in the sense of pricing below marginal costs makes no sense in the case of gross substitutes or gross independent items, because it would lead to a lower or the same price for the profitable product and a greater or the same quantity purchased of the one offered at a loss. That is, a necessary condition for loss leading, in the sense of pricing below marginal cost, is the existence of gross complementarities that increase the price of the profitable product and lower the quantities purchased of the one sold at a loss when the price of the profitable one rises.

Summing up, the strict version of loss leading in this simple setting is merely a special or extreme form of a more general phenomenon. Namely, in a multiproduct setting gross complementarities lead to a lower average store price. In the strict version of loss leading this average store price includes at least one price below marginal cost. In the broader version of loss leading this lower average store price need not include any price below marginal cost. While loss leading in the strict sense of pricing below marginal cost may or may not be a rare phenomenon, loss leading in this broader sense is definitely a widespread phenomenon and it is in this broader sense that the term is used in recent empirical literature (thus, our use of the quotation marks).

In section 5.4 the results of section 5.2 are extended to allow for more than two items explicitly and for the choice of distribution services. This extension is captured in equations (5.10), (5.11) and (5.12). By itself the extension to more than two products brings no new insights to this issue, but allowing for distribution services provides two new insights. First, the provision of a specific distribution service with an item is inconsistent with the use of that item as a loss leader in the strict interpretation of this term. Under the strict interpretation of loss leading, equation (5.11) implies the impossibility of a negative mark-up times a positive number equated to a cost elasticity that must be positive. Second, common distribution services are consistent with the existence of loss leading in its strict form since a negative mark-up plays a similar role in equations (5.10) and (5.12). More generally, the endogenous choice of distribution services, especially common distribution services, does not diminish the extent of loss leading in its broader sense of generating a lower average store price due to the prevalence of gross complementarities. On the contrary, it enhances the ability of a firm to absorb the loss leader by manipulating another dimension of the environment.

Nowhere is this potential role of distribution services clearer than in an important paper on loss leading by Lal and Matutes (1994). The authors develop a duopoly model where consumers are uniformly distributed along a line of unit length and face at each end of the line a firm that competes for their patronage by selling two goods. These goods are assumed independent in consumption. Since it is costly to travel to the store, however, there are gross complementarities in the purchasing behavior of consumers in our terminology. These two firms can advertise prices at a fixed cost per good and the advertisements reach all consumers. The authors characterize their model in terms of a game with stages where the players resolve their uncertainties at different stages. Both consumers and firms have rational expectations.

Advertising in their model acts as a commitment device whereby informing consumers of prices on one good limits how much surplus a firm can extract from the consumer at the store on the other good, even if reservation prices are charged on the unadvertised product. The authors show that a unique equilibrium where all consumers buy both goods at either one of the two stores and both firms advertise the same good at a price at or below marginal cost is likely to arise when the reservation price on the unadvertised good and the fixed cost of advertising are high relative to the opportunity cost of shopping. While advertising acts as a commitment device in their model, it can also be viewed in terms of our discussion as an indicator of information as a common distribution service. This distribution service provides consumers with information that assures acquisition of both goods at a 'low' average store price given the gross complementarities introduced by shopping costs in the form of transport costs.

A recent paper by Hosken, Matsa and Reiffen (2001) uses BLS data on over 350 000 items that generate over 16 000 price series which can be grouped into 20 categories of goods to obtain three main conclusions. First, stores seem to have a regular price and most deviations from that price are downward; for example in 18 out of 20 categories[20] the percentage of products at the modal price is greater than 50 per cent (Table 5) and in all 20 categories the number of products below the modal price is significantly higher than the number of products above the modal price (Table 6). Second, within a category the same items are regularly put on sale; for example, the percentage of price series experiencing a sale of 15 per cent or more in the second year given that a similar sale took place the first year is significantly higher than the percentage of price series experiencing a sale the second year given no sales in the first year for all 20 categories (Table 9). And third, the probability of a sale seems to be highest when demand for that item is highest; for example in five categories identified as having seasonal demands[21] the probability of a sale is higher in the high demand period than in the low demand period (Table 10). Thus, 'loss leading' in the broad sense of having a lower average store price seems to occur often, tends to rely on the same items within a category to generate store traffic, and happens most frequently at times of peak demand.

Another recent empirical study, mentioned earlier (CKR), uses scanner data to test the implications of four different models of pricing behavior at times of peak demand.[22] The neoclassical perfect competition model under diminishing returns implies that prices should increase at times of peak aggregate demand or peak idiosyncratic demand. Hence it is inconsistent with the evidence in Hosken, Matsa and Reiffen (2001) discussed above, as well as with similar evidence presented by CKR for items identified as experiencing seasonal or peak demands (Table 6).[23]

Warner and Barsky (1995) develop a model that generates cyclical demand elasticities due to economies of scale in search. With a fixed cost of search it is optimal to search more during high purchasing periods, and consumers are more price-sensitive when overall demand is high. CKR test this implication by estimating a demand model that allows the price elasticities to vary at peak demand periods. Their results are inconsistent with this implication of the Warner and Barsky model. They find (Table 6) that only in 4 out of 11 categories[24] are there statistically significant increases (at the 1 per cent level) in price sensitivity as a result of the Christmas high demand period. For 3 categories there is no statistically significant increase (at the 1 per cent level) in price sensitivity due to Christmas high demand period. Furthermore, in 3 categories there is actually a statistically significant decrease (at the 1 per cent level) in price sensitivity due to the Christmas high demand period! CKR find similarly mixed results for the Thanksgiving high demand period.

Rotemberg and Saloner (1986) develop a model in which prices should be lower in periods of peak aggregate demand, because the gains from defecting out of tacit collusion agreements are highest during these periods and thus these agreements should be harder to sustain at these times. While this model (and the same is true of Warner and Barsky) gives no prediction as to which prices or margins should be lowest during the peak aggregate demand period, CKR point out that both models are inconsistent with price declines that don't apply to all items at peak periods. Yet for 6 of the 7 categories[25] where they identify Christmas as an aggregate demand peak but not as an idiosyncratic demand peak, prices in the category increase at Christmas time (Table 3). Moreover, 4 of the 6 increases are statistically significant at the 1 per cent level. Finally, they also run a regression with an overall or aggregate price index based on 29 categories for which they could get data, and they find that overall prices are slightly higher at Christmas.

According to CKR, 'loss leader' models such as that of Lal and Matutes are the ones most consistent with their evidence because they provide a rationale for why retailers accept lower prices or margins[26] on goods experiencing a surge in demand, whether or not that demand surge corresponds to an aggregate demand peak. For instance, one of their most statistically robust and economically powerful results is a lower price for tuna during Lent which is an idiosyncratic peak. More importantly, these models have no difficulty with the finding that prices or margins are slightly higher at Christmas for non-holiday season items. Finally, they also find some direct evidence in favor of these models in the sense that the same variables that identify periods of peak demand also play an important role in explaining the percentage of category sales accounted for by advertised deals (Table 7). All of these results, however, support the broad version of 'loss leaders' models. The latter do not require price to be below marginal cost, are based on the gross complementarities emphasized throughout the chapter and on the important role of distribution services stressed in the book.[27]

APPENDIX: THE NATURE OF RETAIL DATA AND THE CONSTRUCTION OF PRICE INDEXES

Recently economists have become interested in the use of scanner data to construct price indexes. According to Feenstra and Shapiro (2003) (hereafter FS) they have three potential advantages over survey sampling: they include the universe of products sold (instead of just a sample of products); they are available at very high frequencies (on a weekly basis rather than on a monthly basis for example); and they provide simultaneous measurement on prices and quantities (instead of just measurement on prices). Realizing these potential advantages, however, raises other issues.

For instance, one issue they address is that the standard cost of living concept is based on the measurement of consumption, but scanner data measures purchases. Thus, FS adapt the model of Chapter 3 to develop an expression for the cost of living related to purchases. That is, purchases (q) are treated as inputs or retail items and they are chosen in the first stage subject to a quasi-convex functional relationship between consumption (x) and purchases, that is, $f(q,x) \leq 0$.

In the second stage utility is maximized by choosing consumption (x), given a vector of consumption of all other goods (z) and a budget constraint that uses the cost function generated in the first stage ($C(p, x) \leq I$, where I is income). This yields optimal purchases as $q = C_p [p, g(p, z, I)]$. FS show that an equivalent result can be obtained in the following single stage problem: Choose q and x to minimize expenditures through purchases while satisfying the quasi-convex relation between consumption and purchases and given that utility is above or equal to an exogenously given level (U^*). In this alternative, but equivalent, formulation optimal purchases are given as $q = E_p (p, z, U^*)$. Since purchases in this formulation relate directly to an expenditure function with utility explicitly included, it can be used to construct a cost of living index.

The distinction between purchases and consumption generates potential problems for the construction of cost of living indexes. More specifically when the data on purchases are available at high frequencies, which is the case with scanner data, they require accounting for the possibility of inventory behavior by consumers, that is, buying for storage during sales and not buying at normal or everyday prices after sales. FS address this issue by differentiating between the planning horizon, which they assume to be a 'year' (either 1 or 0), and the purchase intervals which consist of 'weeks' [$t = 1, \ldots, T$] within the year for any one year. They assume a translog expenditure function over any one year, which is given by

$$\ln E = \alpha_0 + \sum \alpha_t \ln p_t + \sum_s \sum_t \gamma_{st} \ln p_s \ln p_t \qquad s, t = 1, \ldots, T. \qquad (5.A1)$$

The authors restrict the parameters to impose symmetry and linear homogeneity in prices but allow the first-order parameters to depend on z and U. That is,

$$\alpha_t = h_t (z, U), \text{ where } t = 0, \ldots, T. \qquad (5.A2)$$

Hence the share of weekly expenditures on the category of interest for any one week over the year (s_t), for example the authors used tuna in their analysis, depends on annual utility and on the exogenous variables, that is,

$$s_t = \alpha_t + \sum_s \gamma_{st} \ln p_s \qquad t = 1, \ldots, T. \qquad (5.A3)$$

Thus, exogenous changes in annual utility or the consumption of goods other than tuna can affect the expenditure function and the share of annual expenditures spent on tuna each week in a non-neutral way, since the only restriction on (5.A2) is that $\sum_t \alpha_t = 1$ (for $t = 1, \ldots, T$). Nonetheless it is still possible to construct an annual cost of living index based on data on purchases and prices.

A cost of living index is the ratio of expenditures needed to obtain a given level of utility at two different sets of prices, for example using period 1 as a reference we have

$$[COL]^1 = E(p^1, z^1, U^1)/E(p^0, z^1, U^1). \qquad (5.A4)$$

A 'true' cost of living index can be constructed as the geometric mean of period 0 and period 1,

$$COL = \{[COL]^1\}^{1/2} \{[COL]^0\}^{1/2}. \qquad (5.A5)$$

FS prove that if annual expenditures take the translog form with the restrictions indicated above, then the annual cost of living index in (5.A5) can be computed as the following Tornqvist index.

$$\text{COL} = \exp\left\{\sum_t 1/2[s_t^0 + s_t^1]\ln(p_t^1/p_t^0)\right\}. \tag{5.A6}$$

Extending the analysis to allow for different varieties (i) within the tuna category and using period 0 modal prices (these are the non-sale prices) as the base, we have

$$\text{COL} = \exp\left\{\sum_t \sum_i 1/2[s_i^0 + s_{ti}^1]\ln(p_{ti}^1/p_i^0)\right\}, \tag{5.A7}$$

where $s_{ti}^1 = p_{ti}^1 q_{ti}^1 / \sum_t \sum_i p_{ti}^1 q_{ti}^1$. The expenditure share in the base period is constructed using the average quantity at the modal price. Thus, p_i^0 and s_i^0 do not differ over the weeks.

The authors obtained weekly scanner data on the value of sales and quantity sold, among other things, from AC Nielsen's academic data base on 316 varieties of canned tuna over a period of two years (1993 and 1994) for 690 stores covering ten different regions of the US. This allowed them to calculate the 'true' cost of living index in (5.A7) for each store and average it over all the stores in a region. The index shows the improvements in the cost of living due to the existence of sales. This index is compared with a fixed base Laspeyres, a chained Laspeyres, a fixed base geometric, a fixed base Tornqvist and a chained Tornqvist.[28] We present the fixed base Tornqvist index, COL$'_t$, for illustrative purposes

$$\text{COL}'_t = \exp\left\{\sum_i 1/2[s_i^0 + s_{ti}^1]\ln(p_{ti}^1/p_i^0)\right\}, \tag{5.A8}$$

where $s_{ti}^1 = p_{ti}^1 q_{ti}^1 / \sum_i p_{ti}^1 q_{ti}^1$. That is, this index was computed over varieties of tuna for each store, each week. Subsequently, it was averaged over the weeks for each store and over the stores in a region to compare with the true cost of living index. It was the index giving the closest results to the true index in (5.A7).[29]

If one wants maximum accuracy, then (5.A7) should be used to calculate the cost of living. Nonetheless, this index is making annual comparisons. Sometimes one may want to report price indexes at higher frequencies. Indeed, BLS provides many of its series on the basis of monthly intervals. Since the fixed base Tornqvist is quite close to the 'true' one and it is constructed with data available at weekly intervals, it can be used to create a monthly price index without much loss of accuracy. By contrast the other indexes can lead to large inaccuracies, especially the chained ones.[30] Furthermore, the authors go on to show that an important reason for the inaccuracy of the chain indexes is inventory behavior by consumers.

NOTES

1. Incidentally, these comments are easily expanded to include Internet retailing or to cover mail order retailing. Indeed, section 5.5 addresses the issue of item prices at the Internet explicitly. Here we emphasize the generality of our points by referring to item prices at individual points of purchase rather than just to item prices at individual stores in the section heading.

2. The author found economies of scale with respect to turnover in his analysis, but he also assumed distribution services were constant across the stores.

3. We will discuss the generalization to k items explicitly in section 5.4.

4. Unless we allow for pricing below marginal cost. For clarity of exposition we will assume no 'loss leaders' in this strict sense in this section and the following ones. This topic is taken up explicitly in section 5.6.

5. While the direction of the price adjustment relative to the simple assortment is entirely determined by the sign of the cross-price elasticity, the magnitude of the adjustment depends on the magnitude of the cross-price elasticity, the magnitude of the profit margin and the relative importance of item 2 to item 1 in the assortment.

6. The average over the stores of the category price elasticity for any category can be obtained by adding the numbers in the last two columns of Table 3.2 that correspond to the category.

7. The bulk of this section draws heavily from Betancourt and Gautschi (1993a).

8. For notational simplicity we assume that each specific distribution service is associated with one and only one item and that each common distribution service is associated with all the items. The analysis is easily extended to incorporate other alternatives but the notation is cumbersome. Incidentally, it is possible that no specific distribution service is provided for an item.

9. Betancourt and Gautschi (1993a) provide a comparative statics analysis in the appendix to that paper where the conditions for Proposition 5.1 (as well as 5.2 and 5.3 below) to hold exactly are identified.

10. This proposition may appear surprising at first sight, since in the quality literature the higher costs of producing higher quality are associated with higher prices (for example Moorthy, 1988). Our result arises because higher costs in our model can arise due to a steeper marginal cost function for items or for distribution services. If we assume that the source of the higher costs is the marginal cost function for items, instead of the one for distribution services, we get the same result as in the quality literature.

11. Of course we are assuming that the changes in prices and/or distribution services also equilibrate the extension of (5.10) to this case, namely

$$\alpha_i = \Sigma_k \, \alpha_k \, [M_k] \, (-\in_{ik}) + \alpha_{N+1} \, [M_{N+1}] \, (-\in_{i(N+1)}) \, k, \, i = 1, \ldots, N+1. \qquad (5.10)'$$

12. See the discussion in Chapter 7.

13. Defined as a grocery store, primarily self-service in operation, providing a full range of departments and having at least $2.5 million in annual sales in 1985 dollars.

14. Superstores contain greater variety of products than conventional supermarkets, including specialty and service departments, and considerable non-food (general merchandise) products.

15. All figures were taken from either Table 1364 in the 1991 US Statistical Abstract or Table 1284 in the 1999 US Statistical Abstract.

16. For instance, Brynjolfsson and Smith (2000) report that barnesandnoble.com carry an assortment of about 3 million titles while a Barnes & Noble superstore carries an assortment of about 175 000 titles. Brynjolfsson, Smith and Hu (2003) estimate the value to consumers of the increased variety, or depth of assortment for books provided by the Internet channel at approximately 1 billion dollars in 2000.

17. More recently Pan, Ratchford and Shankar (2002) find that the heterogeneity in observable distribution services they could measure explained from 5 per cent to 43 per cent of the variation in prices in a hedonic regression for each of eight categories of products, including

books and CDs. Their data sources were price quotes and service evaluations from BizRate for November 2000. Measures of trust and brand don't explain much in their analysis.

18. Waldfogel and Chen (2003) find that the use of an information intermediary that provides evidence on reliability (in addition to price) lowers Amazon shopping by 25 per cent. The use of an information intermediary that provides only price information lowers Amazon shopping by only 10 per cent.

19. For instance, using the same eight categories as in the study cited in note 17, Ratchford, Pan and Shankar (2003) results (Table 8) show that price dispersion decreased substantially between November 2000 and November 2001.

20. The two exceptions are eggs and bananas.

21. These categories are ground beef and hot dogs (peak demand during summer barbeque season), canned soup (peak demand during fall and winter), eggs (peak demand around Easter), and peanut butter (peak demand during back-to-school planning).

22. In contrast to the BLS data, scanner data permits the identification of brands and stores and is available at higher than monthly frequencies.

23. These authors identify periods of peak demand for beer, oatmeal, tuna, snack crackers, cheese, canned soup and 'eating soup'. For specific brands and forms within each of these categories they use regressions to estimate the impact of various peak periods (for example cold weather, Christmas, Labor Day) on prices. The average of these regression coefficients over the different brand and forms within a category is negative for 13 of the 14 peak periods experienced by these seven categories (Table 4).

24. The categories are the same seven cited in the previous note plus analgesics, cookies, dish detergent and regular crackers.

25. These categories were identified by CKR as analgesics, dish detergent, cookies, crackers, tuna, oatmeal and 'eating soup'.

26. These authors try to control for movements in marginal cost by looking primarily at wholesale prices, w in our notation, and make a convincing argument that their findings for retail prices apply to retail margins. Note, however, that the latter are defined as $(p - w)$ or what we have called earlier the retail gross margin. The marginal cost of retailing is very difficult to measure but I think their arguments would go through even if the right concept were used, namely $(p - C_Q - w)$.

27. Mention should also be made of a forthcoming paper by Hosken and Reiffen (2004) using the BLS data on prices. They find their results to be inconsistent with inter-temporal models of price discrimination (for example Pesendorfer, 2002), and with Varian's model of sales.

28. All the comparisons are available in Table 4 of Feenstra and Shapiro (2003).

29. The smallest difference between these two indexes over the ten regions using 1992 as the base year is 0.001. That is, in the West-Northwest region the value of the cost of living index was 0.977 according to (5.A7) and 0.978 according to (5.A8) averaged over weeks and stores. Similarly, the largest difference between these two indexes using 1992 as the base year is 0.019, and it obtains for two of the ten regions.

30. The largest difference for any one region between the 'true' cost of living and the fixed base Laspeyres, which is the equivalent of (5.3) with σ set to zero and averaged over weeks and stores, is 0.074. That is about four times larger than for the fixed base Tornqvist. On the other hand, the largest difference between the 'true' cost of living index and the chained Laspeyres is 0.267. That is about 14 times larger than for the fixed base Tornqvist.

6. Is packaging service provision or price discrimination?

In this chapter I analyse a retail business practice that has as an important feature, perhaps as its most important one, the shifting of distribution costs across market boundaries: namely, packaging. This feature of packaging is usually absent from the modern literature on the topic. This literature focuses on the price discrimination aspects of packaging. I will use this introduction to embed the topic of packaging in the broader price discrimination setting to which it belongs, but I will devote most of the rest of the chapter to bring out the consequences of its being a mechanism for providing different levels of distribution services through the shifting of distribution costs across market boundaries.

Whenever one observes more than one package of the same item available, one enters the world of commodity bundling. It is, thus, useful to start by relating this type of bundling to the bundling discussed in Chapter 2. There we identified two types of bundling as fundamental characteristics of retail markets: the bundling of distribution services with the items or services explicitly sold at retail, and the bundling of distribution services among themselves. Packaging of items explicitly sold at retail into a small and a large package, for example, can be viewed as a third type of bundling, which the literature refers to as commodity bundling, or it can be viewed in terms of one of the two types of bundling described as fundamental characteristics of retail markets in earlier chapters. That is, the small package provides a high level of the distribution service assurance of product delivery in the desired form bundled with the items explicitly sold that are contained in the small package.

There is a substantial literature on commodity bundling. A seminal point of departure for the modern literature is the work of Adams and Yellen (1976).[1] It eliminates what one may consider two fundamental explanations for bundling: preferences (complementarity of demand) and technology (economies of scope). Instead, it focuses on commodity bundling as a mechanism for price discrimination between heterogeneous consumers. It defines three possible strategies for a monopolist selling two package sizes of the same items. Offering just the large size, which is called pure commodity bundling; offering both sizes with the large one priced at a discount, which is called mixed commodity bundling; and, implicitly, offering the small size which would be simple monopoly pricing or the pure components strategy in their terminology.

Subsequent work proceeds by relaxing the assumptions made by Adams and Yellen (1976) but, by and large, preserves the emphasis on commodity bundling as a form of price discrimination. Lewbel (1985), for example, extends their results by showing that there can be a profit incentive to bundle in the presence of substitutes and a profit incentive not to bundle in the presence of complements. McAffee, McMillan and Whinston (1989) characterize mixed commodity bundling as an optimal strategy in very general terms, by deriving the results in terms of joint probability distributions for the reservation values of consumers rather than in terms of discrete consumers, and by allowing for premiums as well as discounts, and they extend the result to a duopoly. More recently, the literature stressing the price discrimination aspect of commodity bundling has moved to the incorporation of strategic interaction features, for example Carbajo, de Meza and Seidman (1990) and Matutes and Regibeau (1992). Finally, commodity bundling as a price discrimination device is the sole view presented in discussions of this topic even in the best modern textbooks on industrial organization (for example Pepall, Richards and Norman, 1999).

Of special relevance to our present purposes are three other contributions. Two of them stress the so-called fundamental reasons for commodity bundling. Chae (1992) assumes an extreme form of economies of scope in the distribution technology and demonstrates that pure commodity bundling can increase profits and consumer surplus relative to a pure components strategy. This analysis and its application to the subscription television market is described by the author as a case of natural bundling. Salinger (1995) shows that when pure commodity bundling lowers costs (economies of scope), it tends to be more profitable when demands are positively correlated (goods are complements) and stand-alone production is expensive. Finally, Gerstner and Hess (1987) analyse mixed commodity bundling in a setting where consumer heterogeneity in storage and transaction costs is used to explain discounts, premiums and package sizes in terms of price discrimination.

To conclude this brief review, mention should be made of a recent article in marketing that aims at synthesizing the literature on bundling, Stremersch and Tellis (2002). If we follow their terminology, packaging can be classified both as a form of product bundling and as a form of price bundling. They define product bundling 'as the integration and sale of two or more separate products or services at any price. This integration provides at least some consumers with added value'. If we view a package as a combination or bundle of the items explicitly sold with the distribution service assurance of product delivery in the desired form, then packaging is a form of product bundling. Price bundling is defined as 'the sale of two or more separate products in a package at a discount, without any integration of the products.' If we view packaging as merely bringing together different numbers of the items explicitly sold, we can view it as price bundling unless there is uniform pricing of each item across packages. The latter is rarely observed.[2]

Why is the interpretation relevant? In these authors' own words, price bundling 'may be optimal because it is a form of price discrimination between different consumer groups'. With respect to product bundling, however, they assert that it 'may be optimal because it creates added value for consumers, saves costs, and creates differentiation in highly competitive markets.' Therefore, the welfare implications of the two interpretations are dramatically different.

In section 6.1 I show how the natural bundling of a distribution service, assurance of product delivery in the desired form, with the items sold at retail, which is a fundamental characteristic of the technology of retail markets, leads to a pure commodity bundling equilibrium in retail markets when all consumers are identical. Section 6.2 proceeds to demonstrate that the existence of an additional distribution service, assortment, and its natural bundling with the previous one leads to mixed commodity bundling equilibria in retail markets when all consumers are identical. Section 6.3 draws the implications of the previous results for the explanation of discounts, premia and package sizes.

The first three sections stress the shifting of distribution costs across the market boundary between consumers and retailers as fundamental determinants of the commodity bundling associated with packaging and the role of intertype competition in determining the main stylized facts of commodity bundling. Since all consumers are identical, price discrimination across consumers is impossible. In section 6.4, we introduce consumer heterogeneity into the analysis and show how these considerations continue to prevail. Consumer heterogeneity simply increases the variety of package sizes available in equilibrium. An illustration using the packaging of potato chips is provided in section 6.5. A brief conclusion brings out the welfare implications of our results.

6.1   PURE COMMODITY BUNDLING EQUILIBRIA (PCBE): STORAGE COSTS

In order to relate our analysis to the existing literature while highlighting the fundamental characteristics of retail markets identified here, we follow the assumptions and definitions in Adams and Yellen (1976) as much as possible. In particular, throughout this chapter, the definitions of the strategies available to the decision makers are logical extensions to our case of these authors' definitions. That is, we identify an equilibrium as a pure components equilibrium if there exists one type of firm selling small packages in equilibrium. An equilibrium is a pure commodity bundling equilibrium if there are two specialist types of firms: one offering a small package and one offering a large package. Finally, we identify an equilibrium as a mixed commodity bundling equilibrium if there are at least two types of firms: a generalist offering a small and a large package and either one or both of two specialists, a firm offering a small package and/or one offering a large package.

In contrast to Adams and Yellen, and all of the references cited in the introduction, we will assume homogeneous consumers through the device of a single representative consumer. This is not because we believe all consumers to be the same, but because it provides a mechanism that brings out as sharply as possible the importance of cost shifting in the packaging decision at the retail level. From this perspective, packaging can be viewed in many instances as an instrument for offering consumers higher levels of assurance of product delivery in the desired form (small packages), which reduces consumers' storage costs, at the expense of the retailer incurring a higher level of storage costs due to the provision of a higher level of this output. This will be the view adopted in this section. It also allows us to relate the analysis immediately to the model of competition in Chapters 2 (section 5) and 4 (section 4).

If we assume one distribution service to be variable, assurance of product delivery in the desired form, and all others to be constant at the same level for every firm, it immediately follows from this model that:

Proposition 6.1: Imperfect competition is a necessary condition for a pure commodity bundling equilibrium to exist.

With perfectly competitive behavior, profit maximization by the retailer implies $p = C_Q + w$ and $r = C_D/N$.[3] Hence, the retail price equals the marginal costs of retailing plus the price per item paid to suppliers[4] and the consumer's shadow price for the distribution service equals the marginal cost per transaction of producing this level by the retailer. Given an increasing marginal cost function for distribution services,[5] a firm providing small packages will provide a higher level of distribution services at any given p than one providing large packages, since the main determinant of costs of providing this distribution service is the number of packages. That is, with the same total number of items it takes more space, materials and labor to provide small packages than large packages.

Perfect competition leads to a pure components equilibrium in retail markets. The firm providing the higher level of distribution services will lead the consumer to experience a lower shadow price of the distribution services[6] and, thus, a lower level of expenditures in attaining the same level of utility.

Hence, with homogeneous consumers, only the firm that provides the highest level of distribution services will survive in the market and a PCBE is not feasible. Another way of interpreting this result is that, as we saw in section 2.6, perfect competition eliminates the natural bundling that exists between distribution services and the items explicitly sold at retail. Thus, it eliminates a fundamental reason for commodity bundling.

By definition a pure commodity bundling equilibrium implies the existence of intertype competition: that is, a small package firm coexisting with a large package firm in the same market. Under what conditions can this happen? The next proposition summarizes our main result.

Proposition 6.2: Given imperfect competition,[7] quantity discounts are necessary for a pure commodity bundling equilibrium to exist with homogeneous consumers.

For this equilibrium to exist the representative consumer must be indifferent between the two types of firms. This implies that the expenditures of the consumer at each type of firm must be the same, other things being equal. That is,

$$E[p(A), D(A), D_-, p', Z] = E[p(B), D(B), D_-, p', Z], \qquad (6.1)$$

where A identifies the small package retailer and B the large package retailer. Thus, $p(A)$ [$p(B)$] is the price per item of the small [large] package retailer and $D(A)$ [$D(B)$] is the level of assurance of product delivery in the desired form for the small [large] package retailer. D_- is the level of other distribution services offered by both retailers, p' are the prices of other items purchased by the consumer outside this market and Z are the levels of the consumption activities; all three will be assumed constant at the same level while patronizing both types of firms. By definition $D(A) > D(B)$, which implies that the left-hand side of (6.1) is less than the right-hand side if $p(A) \leq p(B)$. This follows from the fact that the expenditure function must be decreasing in D and increasing in p. Hence, quantity discounts, that is, $p(A) > p(B)$, are necessary for this equilibrium to be possible. Otherwise, the consumer could not be indifferent between these two types of firms.

Are quantity discounts sufficient for a PCBE to exist? The answer is yes. With identical costs conditions *ex ante*, we can rewrite the first-order conditions in Chapter 4, section 4, as follows:

$$[p - C_Q - w] - (p/\in)(1 - \mu) = 0; \qquad (6.2)$$

$$(p/\in)(1 - \mu)(\partial q/\partial D) + [\mu r - C_D /N] = 0. \qquad (6.3)$$

If the level of imperfect competition is the same for both types of firms, in the sense that μ is the same for both, and since N can be normalized at unity, the existence of quantity discounts implies restrictions on (6.2) and (6.3), that is, $dp/dD > 0$. Starting from a pure components equilibrium where the second-order conditions are satisfied for the small package firm, we can show that these restrictions merely assure that the second-order conditions will also be satisfied for the large package firm. Since the argument is intricate, we present it in an Appendix.

The differential shifting of storage costs across market boundaries associated with intertype competition in a pure commodity bundling equilibrium requires quantity discounts. This result provides insight into a very commonplace observation with respect to one particular form of intertype competition in retail markets: namely, the offerings of items in large packages by warehouse stores are accompanied by substantial quantity discounts relative to the offerings of the same items in smaller packages by supermarkets, convenience stores or vending machines.

6.2   MIXED COMMODITY BUNDLING EQUILIBRIA (MCBE): STORAGE COSTS AND SHOPPING COSTS

In this section we have the objective of demonstrating that the natural bundling that occurs among distribution services, in particular between assurance of product delivery in the desired form (which determines the storage costs associated with package size) and assortment (which determines the shopping costs associated with travel, time and adjustment efforts of multiple trips), can lead to mixed bundling equilibria in retail markets where a generalist can coexist with a specialist.

Our main result can be stated in terms of the following proposition.

Proposition 6.3: Given imperfect competition,[8] the existence of more than one distribution service, each of which is valued by the consumer, is a necessary condition for mixed commodity bundling equilibria to exist in a retail market with homogeneous consumers.

For the equilibrium to exist, the consumer must be indifferent between patronizing a specialist (A) selling small packages and a generalist (C) selling a mixed bundle of small and large packages. This requires

$$E\,[p(C), D(C), D\_(C), p', Z] = E\,[p(A), D(A), D\_(A), p', Z], \qquad (6.4)$$

$D(A) > D(C)$, because the small package retailer provides a higher level of assurance of product delivery in the desired form; and $D\_(A) < D\_(C)$, because the small package retailer provides a lower level of assortment. $p(A)$ is the (average) price per item of the small package retailer and $p(C)$ is the (average) price per item of the mixed bundle retailer.

If we assume that the (average) price per item offered by both retailers is the same, $p(A) = p(C)$, and that the number of items desired by the consumer is the same, then equilibrium requires that the lowering of consumer expenditures from the higher level of assurance of product delivery at the specialist, compensate the higher expenditures due to the lower level of assortment and vice versa for the generalist or mixed bundle retailer. These trade-offs are consistent with the properties of the expenditure function, in which each distribution service operates as a fixed input, as long as the consumer has a positive valuation for each of the distribution services. If the consumer does not value storage costs (D) or shopping costs $(D\_)$, these trade-offs become impossible and mixed bundling equilibria can not exist.

Sufficient conditions require additional assumptions. We illustrate why, with one special case that is of particular interest in the context of retailing. In detailed analyses of features of retail markets one often finds the following linear characterization of the consumer's transaction costs technology, which is derived from the classical inventory model (for example Whitin, 1952 and Oi, 1992).

$$TC = s(Q/P) + h(P/2), \tag{6.5}$$

where s is the shopping cost per trip and h is the storage cost for the average number of items held per period, and P is the number of items in a package. As P increases, shopping costs go down and storage costs go up. With only one consumer, and given s, h and Q, there is only one optimal package size trading off shopping and storage costs, and mixed commodity bundling equilibria are not feasible.

A sufficient condition for the mixed bundle equilibria to exist in the homogeneous consumer setting with this linear in prices (s, h) transactions technology is to introduce a carrying constraint on the consumer while patronizing the small package specialist.[9] More generally, note the following relation for the price per item at the two types of retailers

$$p(C) = (P/Q)p(S) + [(Q - P)/Q] \, p(L) = \alpha p(S) + (1 - \alpha)p(L) = p(A). \tag{6.6}$$

Since P and Q can be assumed constant, a sufficient but not necessary way of satisfying this equation is uniform pricing by the mixed bundle retailer, that is, $p(S) = p(L)$, or the price per item of the small and large package are the same. Since Q is arbitrary, the optimal size of the large package $(Q - P)$, and consequently the proportion of items in the large package (1– α), increases with Q in this type of equilibrium.

Summing up, the bundling of these two distribution services, each of which is valued by the consumer, is a natural source of commodity bundling in retail markets. The particular type of mixed commodity bundling equilibrium analysed here is selected to stress this point by keeping the price per item at both types of retailers constant and at the same level. In section 6.1, however, we chose to keep the level of all distribution services but one constant and at the same level for both types and looked at the trade-off between prices and the other distribution service. Hence we will conclude this section by analysing a similar case where the level of assortment is assumed fixed at both types of stores but at a different level for each type.

More specifically, the level of assortment at the specialist $D\_(A)$ will be fixed at a value (one package size) lower than the level of assortment at the generalist $D\_(C)$ (two package sizes). In this setting, the imposition of a carrying constraint on the consumer, who therefore must make more trips at the specialist than at the generalist, allows for different trade-offs between the two distribution services at the specialist and at the generalist. With homogeneous consumers this assumption suffices to generate a mixed commodity bundling equilibrium with a specialist providing items in small packages and a generalist providing them in small and large packages.

In equilibrium, the expenditure function of the consumer at the two types of retailers is given by (6.4) again. The differences from the earlier case are that no constraint is placed on the relation between $p(A)$ and $p(C)$ and that while $D\_(A) < D\_(C)$, each of them is assumed constant. The constancy of assortment for each type of firm allows us to rely on equations (6.2) and (6.3) of section 1 in this chapter for the analysis of each type of firm. For (6.4) to be satisfied in this case, the consumer's trade-off between price and assurance of product delivery in the desired form at the specialist must be such that it also compensates for the lower level of assortment at this type of retailer relative to the generalist.

In order to bring this out we will assume that the price per item of the small package is the same at both types of retailers, that is, $p(A) = p(S)$. In this setting a premium implies $p(L) > p(A)$ and a discount implies $p(L) < p(A)$. Thus, the price per item at the generalist is given by

$$p(C) = \alpha p(A) + (1-\alpha)p(L). \tag{6.7}$$

For any value of α, $0 < \alpha < 1$, it follows from (6.7) that a premium for the large package implies $p(C) > p(A)$ and a discount implies $p(C) < p(A)$. Can the consumer be indifferent between both retailers in both of these settings? The answer is yes.

If there is a discount, the higher price per unit of the small package retailer (which increases the expenditure function, E) is compensated by a higher level of assurance of product delivery in the desired form (which decreases E) and this must be valued highly enough by the consumer (the difference must be negative) to compensate also for the higher level of shopping costs. If there is a premium, the lower price of the small package retailer plus the higher level of assurance of product delivery in the desired form (both of which decrease E) must be sufficient to compensate for the higher level of shopping costs. Hence, premiums, discounts and, as we saw earlier, uniform prices are all feasible in MCBE, because of the natural bundling among distribution services as well as between distribution services and the items sold at retail.

If cost conditions are identical *ex ante* for both types of firms, equilibrium in this case requires that $C [Q, D(A), D\_(A)] > C [Q, D(C), D\_(C)]$ if a discount prevails, so that revenues for the small package retailer can exceed costs by the same amount as the smaller revenues for the mixed bundle retailer (with the lower price per item) exceed costs. Similarly, $C [Q, D(A), D\_(A)] < C [Q, D(C), D\_(C)]$ must hold for a premium to prevail in equilibrium. Both conditions are feasible, since they depend on the relative contributions to costs of providing a given combination of a level of assortment (through the availability of a different number of packages at each retailer on any one trip) and a level of assurance of product delivery in the desired form (through the total number of small packages). This discussion generates an empirical implication.[10]

Proposition 6.4: Premiums should be associated with high costs for the mixed bundle retailer and discounts should be associated with low costs for the mixed bundle retailer.

Interestingly, Agrawal, Grimm and Srinivasan (1993) present evidence that provides partial support for this hypothesis. For a sample of 16 supermarkets, 600 brands and 62 products, they calculate the number of packages in a brand offered at a premium relative to the total number of packages and average this magnitude over all brands and stores for each product in their sample. This generates a dependent variable, Y, that measures the relative frequency of a premium in a product. In a logit regression on $Y/(1 - Y)$ of a dummy variable that takes the value of 1 if the product must be refrigerated at the store and a value of zero otherwise, they obtain a positive coefficient which is statistically significant at the 10 per cent level while controlling for other variables.[11] The costs of providing any combination of assurance and assortment are higher in the refrigerated environment.

Similarly, Walden (1988) finds a positive and statistically significant coefficient (at the 5 per cent level) for a dummy variable indicating whether or not a product requires refrigeration in an OLS regression with the following dependent variable: the percentage difference in price per unit or item in a package between large package sizes and the smallest package size. A dummy variable indicating whether or not the product needed to be frozen was also positive and statistically significant (at the 1 per cent level) in this regression. The reference category for both of these dummy variables was that the product only required shelf space. This analysis was based on 875 comparisons over 55 products taken from the consumer product list of a major southeastern supermarket chain and it includes other characteristics of the products as control variables.

6.3   DISCOUNTS, PREMIUMS AND PACKAGE SIZES: STYLIZED FACTS

Given the empirical evidence just cited in support of Proposition 6.4, we can view the association between premiums and high costs for a mixed bundle retailer as a first 'stylized fact' of packaging. This raises two questions: are there any other 'stylized facts' of packaging? And, can these other 'stylized facts' be explained by the models presented here?

Perhaps the most robust finding or 'stylized fact' established by the empirical literature on packaging is that a large proportion of products sold in large size packages are sold at a discount. For instance, Gerstner and Hess (1987) found for a North Carolina supermarket that of 472 brands sold in two package sizes, 91.5 per cent of the large packages were sold at a discount with 7.2 per cent sold at a premium and 1.3 per cent sold under uniform pricing. Agrawal, Grimm and Srinivasan (1993) summarize other supermarket studies and present some evidence of their own. The latter shows that 80 per cent of all packages were discounted while 18 per cent sold at a premium and 2 per cent sold under uniform pricing. The other studies generate similar results.[12] This is what one would expect in light of Proposition 6.2. Nonetheless this empirical evidence comes from supermarkets, which are an example of a mixed bundle retailer. Thus it would be more convincing to explain this second 'stylized fact' in terms of the model in section 6.2, which will be accomplished after explaining the next 'stylized fact'.

A third, less noticeable 'stylized fact' of packaging is that products sold at a discount are usually sold in larger sizes than products sold at a premium. For instance, Gerstner and Hess (1987, Table 1) show that for the 91.5 per cent of the brands which were offered at discounts, the average size ratio was above two (2.26), that is, $(1 - \alpha)/\alpha = (Q - P)/P > 2$. On the other hand, for the 7.2 per cent of brands offering premiums, the average size ratio was below two (1.78), that is, $(1 - \alpha)/\alpha = (Q - P)/P < 2$.

Can the model of the previous section shed any light on this more subtle finding? The answer is yes. Intertype competition leads to (6.4) holding. The mixed bundle retailer has to choose a price, $p(C)$, and a level of assurance of product delivery, $D(C)$, given his level of assortment $D_{-}(C)$. If in addition Q $(= K_1)$ is the same for both types of retailers, then with only two package sizes and P fixed at the specialist's level, the large package size $(Q - P)$ is fixed, so that the level of assurance of product delivery of the mixed bundle retailer is also fixed. Hence, the only variable under the control of the mixed bundle retailer to select $p(C)$ in (6.2) is the price of the large package, $p(L)$, as can be seen from (6.7).

What happens if Q increases to a new level, K_2? Given P (the package size of the specialist), $p(A)$ goes down which decreases $p(C)$ in (6.7), and $(Q - P)$ goes up, thereby increasing $(1-\alpha)$ in (6.7), which lowers the level of assurance of product delivery in the desired form provided by the mixed bundle retailer. Finally, the mixed bundle retailer chooses $p(L)$ so that the new $p(C)$ allows (6.4) to hold at the higher level of Q. Since assurance of product delivery in the desired form is now lower, however, this requires a lower $p(C)$ (thus a lower $p(L)$) than in the absence of a change in the large package size in order to get the consumer to purchase the new level of Q. So, the larger is Q, the lower are $p(A)$, $p(L)$, and $p(C)$, and the higher is $(Q - P)$ and, thus, the size ratio as well as vice versa.

Therefore, we have

Proposition 6.5: Given intertype competition, the small package size of the specialist and the same level of output of items for both types, the higher is this level of output the more likely are discounts to arise and this will be associated with high size ratios; the lower the level of output the more likely are premiums to arise, and this will be associated with low size ratios.

Proposition 6.5 fully explains this more subtle 'stylized fact' of packaging identified by Gerstner and Hess (1987). Furthermore, it provides insight into the explanation of the more robust finding in terms of a mixed commodity bundling equilibrium. If products sold at a discount are the ones with a high level of demand, Proposition 6.5 explains the association between discounts and large package sizes that we frequently observe in mixed bundle retailers such as supermarkets. Support for this view is provided by the empirical evidence in Agrawal, Grimm and Srinivasan (1993). They find that a high propensity to buy a product in large sizes, measured on a scale of 0 for 'don't buy' to 5 for 'I usually buy the product in the largest size', is explained mainly by a high level of demand, measured as the mean response of the answers to the questions of 'my household uses a lot of this product' and 'my household can not do without this product' with the answers given on a five-point scale from 'strongly disagree' to 'strongly agree'.

Fourth is another less than obvious 'stylized fact' identified by Gerstner and Hess (1987, Table 6). They show that the size of the discount is positively correlated with the size ratio, and the size of the premium is also positively correlated with the size ratio. To explain this stylized fact with the model of the previous section, note that our earlier analysis forced the mixed bundle retailer to produce the same level of output as the specialist, which in turn fixed the large package size for any given Q. Hence, the mixed bundle retailer could only control $p(L)$. Suppose instead that $Q(A)$ can differ from $Q(C)$. Equilibrium on the consumer side is affected as follows: the right-hand side of (6.4) does not change as long as P is given, but the left-hand side is different in that the mixed bundle retailer now controls two variables, $p(L)$ and the size of the large package $[Q(C) - P]$, that influence $p(C)$, and one ($Q(C)$) that influences $D(C)$ directly.

Consider first a situation in which a discount prevails, that is, $p(L) < p(A)$ and thus $p(C) < p(A)$ for any α in (6.7) and (6.4) holds. Suppose we increase the size of the discount relative to the previous one so that in the new equilibrium the distance between $p(A)$ and $p(C)$ in (6.7) is longer than when $Q(A) = Q(C)$. In contrast to the earlier situation, however, the mixed bundle retailer can reach this new lower price per item equilibrium by lowering $p(L)$, which increases the size of the observed discount, or by increasing the size ratio at the original $p(L)$, which increases the intertype discount. In practice one would expect to observe both instruments used and thus the positive correlation.[13] Suppose instead that a premium prevails, that is, $p(L) > p(A)$ and thus $p(C) > p(A)$ for any α in (6.7). If we increase the size of the intertype premium in this setting so that the distance between $p(C)$ and $p(A)$ is longer, the mixed bundle retailer can attain this intertype premium by increasing the observed premium $[p(L)]$ or by increasing the size of the large package or any combination of both.[14]

More generally, we have

Proposition 6.6: When the mixed bundle retailer is not constrained to offer the same number of items as the specialist, the size ratio $((Q - P)/P)$ and the price per item of the large size package $(p(L))$ act as complements in arriving at a given price per item of the bundle offered to the consumer $(p(C))$.

6.4   CONSUMER HETEROGENEITY AND THE NUMBER OF PACKAGE SIZES

One of our aims in the previous discussion was to explain as many aspects of the commodity bundling associated with packaging as possible without appealing to consumer heterogeneity. In this section we consider additional insights offered by introducing consumer heterogeneity into our approach. We consider first the pure commodity bundling equilibria.

Assume that consumer (1) values storage more than the other one (2). Following the argument in section 6.1, it is feasible that equation (6.1) holds for each consumer separately. Thus, we have

$$E^1 [p(A1), D(A1), D_-, p', Z] = E^1 [p(B1), D(B1), D_-, p', Z] \text{ and} \quad (6.8)$$
$$E^2 [p(A2), D(A2), D_-, p', Z] = E^2 [p(B2), D(B2), D_-, p', Z].$$

This implies that we have two pure commodity bundling equilibria with four types of specialist retailers ($A1$, $B1$, $A2$, $B2$). The first question that arises is, can the two consumers be indifferent between the small package specialists, $E^1(A1) = E^2(A2)$?

The high storage cost consumer (1) demands smaller packages. In terms of the model of section (6.1), this follows from equation (6.3). The shadow price of the distribution service, r^1, is higher for consumer 1, at any level of D. That is, given D, the value of an additional unit of the distribution service must be higher for the high storage cost consumer. So if (6.3) holds for consumer 2 at a given value of D, it will be positive at that value of D for consumer 1. Therefore, equilibrium for 1 will require a higher value of D, because the shadow price is decreasing in the distribution service. This higher level of the distribution service will require a higher price per item of the commodity. Thus, we have $p(A1) > p(A2)$ and $D(A1) > D(A2)$ in (6.8), if $E^1 = E^2$.

Therefore, we have

Proposition 6.7: The introduction of consumer heterogeneity in storage costs generates pure commodity bundling equilibria with greater heterogeneity in package sizes.

One way of proceeding would be to generate similar results for the mixed commodity bundling equilibria analysed in section 6.2. The same logic would lead us to obtain the same results for each type of consumer so we would have two MCBE in which the results of sections 6.2 and 6.3 would apply for each equilibrium and in which introducing consumer heterogeneity would increase the number of package sizes. This case, however, is not as interesting analytically or empirically as the following alternative: is consumer heterogeneity sufficient to generate a mixed commodity bundling equilibrium in which the mixed bundle retailer offers more than two package sizes?

In order to analyse this case we start with the small package specialist, who will cater to the consumer with high storage costs by providing the smallest size package this consumer is willing to pay for. If we assume that the package size of the specialist must be offered to the patrons of the mixed bundle retailer, then a mixed commodity bundling equilibrium with three packages requires on the consumer side that,

$$E^1 [p(A), D(A), D\_(A), p', Z] = E^1 [p(C^1), D(C^1), D\_(C^1), p', Z] = $$
$$E^2 [p(C^2), D(C^2), D\_(C^2), p', Z]. \qquad (6.9)$$

Both consumers use the small package specialist as the reference point for the mixed bundle retailer. The one with high storage costs (1) can be in equilibrium (the first equality in (6.9)) by the same arguments as in section 6.2, and behaves with respect to discounts, packages and premiums as in section 6.3. This implies, of course, that $D\_(C^1) > D\_(A)$ and $D(C^1) < D(A)$. Premiums or discounts prevail according to whether $Q(C^1) = Q(A)$ is low or high enough. If high, a bigger large package size is chosen and if low, a smaller sized large package is chosen. In order to make a comparison with consumer 2, however, it is necessary to consider the optimization problem of the mixed bundle retailer offering the three package alternatives.

Profits to be maximized are defined as $[p(C^1) - w] Q(C^1) + [p(C^2) - w]$ $Q(C^2) - C [Q(C^1) + Q(C^2), D(C^1), D(C^2), D\_(C^1), D\_(C^2)]$. This maximization now requires keeping both types of consumers at the store, so it is subject to one constraint for each type of consumer market. Namely, both equalities in (6.9) must hold simultaneously. The level of assortment in each market is given and at the same value for the mixed bundle retailer, that is, $D\_(C^1) = D\_(C^2)$. So the retailer will design one combination of small package and large package for each consumer market by choosing $D(C^1)$ and $D(C^2)$, or the levels of assurance of product delivery in the desired form. In addition, the retailer will choose an effective price per item, $p(C^1)$ and $p(C^2)$, for each consumer market.

Just as we did earlier we will assume the size of the small package P and the price per item of this size package to be given at the value of the small package retailer, that is, $p(S) = p(A)$. Thus, the choices of an effective price per item for each bundle and a level of assurance for each type of customer imply a choice of the price per package of the large package for each customer, $p(L^i)$, which can be seen from (6.7), and a level of $Q(i)$, since P is given. Below we present the first-order conditions for profit maximizing stemming from the four choice variables of the mixed bundle retailer offering three packages.

$$[p(C^i) - C_{Q(i)} - w] - [p(C^i)/\in](1 - \mu) = 0, i = 1, 2. \qquad (6.10)$$

$$[p(C^i)/\in](1 - \mu)\partial q(i)/\partial D(i) + [\mu r^i - C_{D(i)}/N] = 0, i = 1, 2. \qquad (6.11)$$

Just as before, if (6.11) is satisfied for the low cost of storage customer at a particular value of D, the high cost of storage customer can not be in equilibrium at that value of D because $r^1 > r^2$.[15] Since r is decreasing in the distribution service, the retailer will choose to offer a higher level of this service to the high cost of storage customer. This implies that $D(C^2) < D(C^1)$ in (6.9). Therefore, the only way (6.9) can hold is if $p(C^2) < p(C^1)$, which is consistent with (6.10) if, for example, the marginal costs of providing more items increases when this is done in smaller packages, that is, $C_{QD} > 0$.

Therefore, we have

Proposition 6.8: The introduction of consumer heterogeneity in storage costs generates package size variety in mixed commodity bundling equilibria, including one in which a mixed bundle retailer offers more than two package sizes.[16]

6.5   AN ILLUSTRATION

Reality is far more complex than the models of price discrimination in the commodity bundling literature cited in the introduction, or than the models of cost shifting in the natural bundling analysis of previous sections. Indeed, it includes features left out of the analysis in both cases. For instance, both approaches ignore the role of the manufacturer in selecting price per item and package sizes. Whatever the role of the manufacturer, however, retailers make choices with respect to commodity bundling by choosing the subset of packages that they stock in their stores and, thus, offer their customers. Hence, it is useful to conclude our discussion of packaging with an illustration of these choices for one particular commodity by a variety of retail establishments in the Washington metropolitan area.

We have gathered data on package sizes and prices of one brand of potato chips (Utz no preservatives) at four different types of retail establishments in the Washington area: a vending machine, a convenience store,[17] two supermarkets from the same chain[18] and a warehouse store. We present this information in Table 6.1, where we include the package price, the quantity in a package (q) and the price per item in a package, $p(C)$, experienced by a consumer when purchasing a particular package at an establishment type. The first thing that one observes is that there is variety in package sizes, which implies consumer heterogeneity in terms of our model as well as opportunities for price discrimination in terms of the commodity bundling literature.[19] This variety also implies consumer segmentation within and across retail formats.

Within the convenience store retail format, for example, the existence of four different package sizes suggests that their customers differ in at least three relevant dimensions of their demand for potato chips. These could be willingness to

Table 6.1 Typical potato chips package offerings in the Washington DC area

	Package Price ($)	$p(C)$ price per item(¢)	q Package Quantity
Small Package Specialist (Vending Machine)			
Pack 1	0.55	2.75	20[1]
Pack 2	0.75	2.14	35
Generalist 1 (Convenience Store)			
Pack 1	0.69	1.97	35
Pack 2	0.99	1.23	80
Pack 3	1.49	1.24*	120
Pack 4	1.99	1.10	180
Generalist 2 (Supermarket A, moderate income neighborhood)			
Pack 1	0.99	1.23	80
Pack 2	1.49	1.24*	120
Pack 3	1.99	1.10	180
Pack 4	3.79	0.94	400
Generalist 2 (Supermarket B, middle income neighborhood)			
Pack 1	1.49	1.24*	120
Pack 2	1.99	1.10	180
Pack 3	2.99	1.06	280[2]
Pack 4	3.79	0.94	400
Large Package Specialist (Warehouse Club)			
Pack 1	4.49	0.80	560[2]
Pack 2	5.69	0.59	960
Pack 3	8.79	0.72*	1200[1]

Notes:
*An asterisk indicates premium within or across types of stores in the following sense. Since we have ordered the packages by their sizes (number of items), the asterisk indicates that there is another package with fewer total items and the same or lower price per item.
1. The package size of the large package specialist is obtained by putting together in a box 60 packages of the smallest size available at the small package specialist.
2. The package size of the large package specialist is obtained by binding together two packages of the smaller size available at supermarket B.

store, level of quantity demanded and either willingness to make purchase trips and/or consumption activities for which the commodity is demanded.[20] Across retail formats consumer segmentation suggests two potential PCBE and two potential MCBE.

First, there is a potential PCBE between the smallest package of the vending machine (20 items) and the smallest package of the convenience store (35 items). The package at the convenience store is offered at a 0.78 cents per item discount. Note that a utility maximizing consumer is very unlikely to purchase the largest package of the vending machine (35 items) if the latter were located outside a convenience store, since the price per item is higher, while the number of items is the same. This offering seems geared to accommodate the larger demand of a segment of vending machine customers. Second, there is another potential PCBE between the largest package of the two supermarkets (400 items) and the smallest package of the warehouse club (560 items). The latter is offered at a discount of 0.14 cents per item. Note that this PCBE would have an unusual feature. Namely, since in this case the 'larger' package is made up of two smaller ones, the risk of spoilage of items that are not consumed when the package is opened is smaller for the 'larger' package.

It is also useful to discuss one PCBE that is unlikely to exist because the two retail formats target different types of consumers. For instance, a consumer of the vending machine's smallest package for 60 days pays $24.21 more than a patron of the warehouse club for the same number of items over the 60-day period in the same daily package. The latter customer often must travel a fairly long distance to the warehouse for a purchase, store these packages at home over the 60 days, and remember to carry one of them every day to the consumption location. It is safe to assume that the representative customers of these two specialists are two very different types of consumers. Hence, pure commodity bundling equilibria are unlikely to exist in this case.

With respect to mixed commodity bundling equilibria, one potential equilibrium is between a convenience store and supermarket A (moderate income neighborhood). Here the two formats compete for a segment that values small packages more than one-stop shopping in relative terms. The last three offerings of the convenience store overlap with the first three offerings of supermarket A. Similarly, another potential MCBE is between a convenience store and supermarket B (middle income neighborhood). Here the two formats compete for a segment that values one-stop shopping more than small packages in relative terms. The last two offerings of the convenience store overlap with the first two offerings of supermarket B.

Not surprisingly, in view of this heterogeneity, we find some evidence of price discrimination. In particular Table 6.1 suggests that there are three incontrovertible cases of price discrimination. Both the convenience store and supermarket A price discriminate against the consumer of the 120 items package. Only a consumer with a strong preference for larger quantities would buy this package at these two stores, since at least one smaller package size is available at a lower price per item. Supermarket B also discriminates against this consumer through the unavailability of the lower price per item alternative. Finally, the higher price per item of the largest package at the warehouse club is not necessarily evidence of price discrimination, because the packaging alternatives are very different. Pack 2 is a package that contains the chips whereas Pack 3 is a box that contains 60 small packages that contain the chips. Hence, the costs of packaging are higher for the 'larger' package.

Among the most important benefits of intertype competition in retailing is that it prevents or ameliorates both explicit price discrimination and implicit price discrimination through non-availability. Thus, a consumer who wants to avoid the premium associated with the 120 chips package at Supermarket B or the price discrimination through non-availability of the 80 and 35 chips packages can accomplish both by patronizing a nearby convenience store to acquire either the 80 or 35 chips packages. Intratype competition, on the other hand, would force this consumer to travel substantially farther to another supermarket, for example A, and there one would only have access to the 80 chips package. Consumers who value accessibility of location highly are the ones who benefit the most from the intertype competition provided by the convenience store.

Finally, the benefits of intertype competition are intimately related to the distribution services that define the types of retail establishment. That is, the result in the previous paragraph is not an accident. Consider the consumer of Pack 3 at supermarket B. It is likely that there is price discrimination against this consumer.[21] This is considerably mitigated by the existence of the large package specialist where the same package can be obtained at 0.26 cents less per item provided the consumer is willing to purchase, and thus store, two packages at a time. Since these warehouse clubs are less conveniently located than most supermarkets, consumers with low storage costs who can shop less frequently, and as a result value accessibility of location less, are the ones who benefit the most from intertype competition in this case.

6.6   CONCLUDING REMARKS

Our analysis brings out two important aspects of retail systems for the understanding of packaging. First, the natural bundling that exists among distribution services and between these services and the items sold at retail provides a fundamental rationale for the commodity bundling associated with packaging in retailing. Second, intertype competition in retailing is exceedingly powerful and important from the point of view of welfare in the analysis of packaging. For it ameliorates, and in some cases it may eliminate the consequences of the use of commodity bundling through packaging as a form of price discrimination. This has been ignored in the prior literature, stressing the price discrimination aspects of packaging.

From this perspective, our discussion of packaging brings out important policy issues in retailing. Consider the frequent restrictions on retail space and retail hours that are imposed on retail systems through legislation all over the world, going back at least to the Middle Ages. These restrictions have the unfortunate consequence of preventing or eliminating intertype competition. Space restrictions limit or eliminate warehouse and other large stores from certain areas; restrictions on hours eliminate or limit convenience stores. By preventing these types of retail forms from existing or limiting their viability, these restrictions accentuate the negative welfare consequences of any price discrimination through packaging that may exist in a market.

More generally, similar welfare issues arise with respect to other dimensions of distribution services. For instance, assurance of product delivery at the desired time in the form of extended hours can lead to the welfare-enhancing charging of different prices when it is more costly to provide extended hours. Of course, it can also lead to price discrimination of consumers by charging different prices to consumers with different preferences for the timing of their shopping. In principle both interpretations are equally valid from an economic point of view.

APPENDIX: QUANTITY DISCOUNTS ARE SUFFICIENT FOR A PCBE TO EXIST

The second-order condition at the pure components equilibrium is simply the condition for a constrained maximum in the two-variable case. The latter can be stated in terms of the second derivatives (F_{ij}) of the objective function, where F is the objective function presented in Chapter 2, section 5, and the derivatives of the constraint in that objective function $(-q, -r)$. Namely,

$$(G + H)qr - r^2 X - q^2 Y > 0, \text{ where } G = F_{12}, H = F_{21}, X = F_{11}, \text{ and }$$
$$Y = F_{22}. \tag{6.A1}$$

Taking the total differential of the first-order conditions with respect to the endogenous variables we find

$$Xdp + G \, dD = 0 \tag{6.A2}$$

$$Hdp + YdD = 0. \tag{6.A3}$$

Quantity discounts imply $dp/dD = - G/X = -Y/H > 0$. Hence if Y and X are less than zero, quantity discounts imply G and H are greater than zero, which in turn implies the second-order condition (6.A1) is satisfied. Therefore, when the second-order condition is satisfied at the pure components equilibrium for the small package firm, quantity discounts are sufficient to ensure that they will be satisfied at the pure components equilibrium for the large package firm. Thus, they are sufficient for a pure commodity bundling equilibrium to exist.

All we need to prove now is that X and Y, which are given below, are negative.

$$X = [1 - C_{QQ}(\partial q/\partial p)N](\partial q/\partial p)N + (p - C_Q - w)(\partial^2 q/\partial p^2)N$$
$$+ (1 - \mu)N(\partial q/\partial p), \text{ and}$$
$$Y = -C_{QD}(\partial q/\partial D)N + (p - C_Q - w)(\partial^2 q/\partial D^2)N - C_{DD} - \mu N E_{DD}.$$

If we have a monopoly situation $\mu = 0$ and the last term on the right-hand side of Y vanishes, but the sum of the other three terms must be negative because they are just one of the second-order conditions for the two variable profit maximization case. The last term on the right-hand side of Y must be negative because the expenditure function is convex in D, that is, $E_{DD} > 0$. Hence, we have established that $Y < 0$ under monopoly and is very likely to be negative under imperfect competition. Furthermore, quantity discounts then imply that $H > 0$. Since $H = G$, by the continuity of the objective function, then $G > 0$. But, quantity discounts then imply $X < 0$.

NOTES

1.   This work also provides references to the earlier literature.
2.   To prevent confusion note that there are three types of bundling I have identified in the book. For instance, the bundling of distribution services by themselves described in Chapter 2, which these authors ignore. The bundling of distribution services with the goods or services explicitly priced, also described in chapter 2. These authors call it product bundling and it was labelled simply as bundling in the introduction, Chapter 1. Finally, there is the bundling of the explicit goods or services in different packages, that is, what we have called commodity bundling and what these authors refer to as price bundling if there is a discount.
3.   This follows, for example, from setting the disturbance terms on the right-hand sides of (4.16) and (4.17) to zero and μ to unity.
4.   Following the literature cited in the introduction, we are assuming that the retailer gets the items from suppliers at the same price per item regardless of the packaging.
5.   As we saw in Chapter 2, section 6, perfect competition is inconsistent with a decreasing marginal cost function for distribution services.
6.   We saw in Chapter 3 that the shadow price of distribution services is decreasing in distribution services.
7.   Imperfect competition in this model can be justified in terms of an exogenously given distribution service, for example location. Firms can vary in the distance at which they are located from a mass of consumers concentrated at a point. This suffices to generate the possibility that a firm with an inferior offering in terms of price or the variable distribution service survives in equilibrium. This is true for both types of firms, which can be assumed to be located at the same point or distance from the mass of consumers.
8.   The same motivation for imperfect competition as in the previous note applies here.
9.   Incidentally, Gerstner and Hess (1987) introduce a similar constraint in their analysis.
10. If cost conditions *ex ante* differ between the two types of firms, these cost inequalities will not hold exactly. Nonetheless, one would expect the empirical implication to continue to hold as a general tendency rather than as an exact result.

11. This study will be discussed further in the next section.
12. These other studies as well as Agrawal, Grimm and Srinivasan were not as meticulous as Gerstner and Hess in limiting their comparisons to brands offering just two package sizes.
13. This implies a larger $Q(C)$ and a lower $D(C)$ for the representative consumer on the left-hand side of (6.4), which is feasible.
14. This implies a smaller $Q(C)$ and a higher $D(C)$ in (6.4), which is feasible.
15. We are assuming, of course, the same number of customers in both markets.
16. Incidentally, in the three-package case, the medium size package is sold at a premium relative to the large package and it can be sold either at a premium or at a discount relative to the small package.
17. A quick check of three other convenience stores belonging to the same chain in the area showed the same four package size and price offerings.
18. On the other hand, a quick check of supermarkets from the same chain in the area revealed different offerings. The supermarket chosen in a higher income area offers larger package sizes than the one chosen in a lower income area.
19. While this heterogeneity is necessary for second and third degree price discrimination to exist, for example Carroll and Coates (1999), it is not sufficient to conclude that there is price discrimination. Furthermore, one wants to exclude all other possible sources of differential costs explanations for price differences.
20. Interestingly, the prediction for the mixed bundle retailer that the next to largest package is sold at a premium relative to the largest package is confirmed for the three generalists in Table 6.1.
21. An increase of 60 chips in going from Pack 1 to Pack 2 leads to a drop in price per item of 0.14 cents. Hence, one would expect a similar or greater drop in price per item in going from Pack 2 to Pack 3, since the increase in the number of chips is 100 and the type of plastic bag use in the packaging is the same. Instead, we observe a drop in price per item of only 0.04 cents.

7. Retail forms and the provision of distribution services

In this chapter we focus on retail forms and the distribution services that characterize them. In section 7.1 we present the main trends identified in the literature for food stores and interpret them in terms of the distinctions relevant to understand retail output developed in Chapter 4. This interpretation leads us to concentrate on the level of assortment as one of the main, if not the main, defining characteristic of modern supermarkets. Section 7.2 develops a model of assortment, inspired by the work of Messinger and Narasimhan (1997), to analyse intertype competition. This model also provides an alternative way of capturing this type of competition to the one used in the model of the previous chapter. Section 7.3 shows how this model indeed collapses to the one actually estimated by Messinger and Narasimhan and discusses the econometric evidence provided by these authors on the choice of assortment by supermarkets.

Section 7.4 develops a model along the lines of those considered in Chapter 6 to analyse the choice of assortment by retailers in a setting of spatial competition. This model was inspired by the work of Bhatnagar and Ratchford (2000). It generalizes the model of section 7.2, by allowing location to vary in equilibrium, and it generalizes Bhatnagar and Ratchford (2000), by allowing for imperfect competition, general functional forms and varying levels of market demand. Generality is bought at the price of lack of differentiation between depth and breadth of assortment. This difference and its implications for the classification of retail forms become the subject of section 7.5, which is explicitly related to the work of Bhatnagar and Ratchford (2000) in terms of assumptions and empirical results.

Section 7.6 considers non-store retailers. The main sub-category in this group is in a process of transition, characterized by its change of name from the old Standard Industrial Classification (SIC), catalogue and mail order houses, to the new North American Industrial Classification (NAICS), electronic shopping and mail order houses. In both cases the retail form provides high levels of assortment, certain types of information, and maximum accessibility of location in exchange for providing limited assurance of product delivery at the desired time and no information associated with direct experiencing of the item. We conclude in section 7.7 with a discussion of shopping centers and shopping malls. These retail agglomerations provide high levels of assortment breadth and depth. In addition, malls often provide considerable entertainment services. Yet, they offer limited accessibility of location to many of their customers.

7.1   FOOD STORE TRENDS AND THEIR INTERPRETATION

One feature of food stores worth stressing is that their total output, measured by sales in constant dollars, has been increasing. For instance, BLS data reported by Oi (1992, Table 4.3) shows a steady increase between 1959 and 1987.[1] The increase in constant dollar sales reflects a food sector that is producing more distribution services and turning over a greater quantity of goods. Nonetheless, the same source shows that sales in constant dollars per hour increased until 1979 and decreased between 1979 and 1987. What is the meaning of this last trend? The recent decrease in constant dollar sales per hour is explained by a rapid increase in extended hours, especially those offered by supermarkets. For instance, by 1988 over 50 per cent of the large supermarkets (more than 35 000 square feet of selling area) were open 24 hours, seven days a week, Oi (1992, Table 4.5). This process was facilitated by the elimination of the so-called blue laws in most of the states of the US (or the delegation of their enforcement to the counties). Extended hours is a mechanism for providing the distribution service assurance of product delivery at the desired time. Thus what the data show is that one of the outputs of distribution services, assurance of product delivery at the desired time, has been increasing faster than the other components of total output between 1979 and 1987. This trend says nothing about productivity.[2]

A second characteristic of food stores worth stressing is that not all of the components of total output have been increasing. From 1940 to 1980, sales in constant (1967) dollars went from 25.6 million to 86.7 million (Oi, 1992, Table 4.4). The same source, however, shows that sales per store, also in constant (1967) dollars, went from 57 000 to 519 000 over the same period. This much more rapid rate of growth was accompanied by an absolute decrease in the number of stores, which went from about 447 000 to 167 000. Thus, the output of food stores went up in terms of the quantities of goods turned over and some distribution services, but it went down in terms of at least one distribution service: namely, accessibility of location. US consumers had to travel farther to their food stores in 1980 than they did in 1940.

Food stores are divided by the US Bureau of the Census into grocery stores and specialized food stores (meat, fish and retail bakeries). Nonetheless, grocery stores take the lion's share of sales by food stores, for example 94.5

per cent in 1990 and 93.6 per cent in 1998. Grocery stores are further subdivided into convenience stores, supermarkets and superettes. The latter are basically small supermarkets, having annual sales of less than 2.5 million in 1985 dollars. Supermarkets are the dominant sub-category with 70.6 per cent of sales by food stores in 1990 and 70.4 per cent in 1998.[3] Consequently, the rest of the discussion in this section concentrates on this sub-category.

The supermarket as an institution made its appearance early in the 20th century, according to Oi (1992). Among its main characteristics in the early phases were the elimination of free delivery and credit. Thus, cash and carry, self-service and low prices made possible by locating in lower rent suburban areas defined its early existence. In more recent years some of these features have changed, for example credit extension. Notwithstanding, the most salient feature of this institution in the last two decades of the 20th century is an evolution toward the provision of increasingly broad assortments to its customers.

Direct information over time on this distribution service is difficult to obtain, but the indirect evidence is more than sufficient to establish our point. The supermarket category consists of six sub-categories: conventional supermarkets, warehouses, superstores, combination food and drug, superwarehouses and hypermarkets.[4] The last four categories provide broader assortments than both conventional supermarkets and warehouses and they may provide deeper assortments as well.[5] Relying on data for the supermarket category from the US Statistical Abstracts (1991, Table 1364; 2000, Table 1280), one must conclude that there has been a substantial shift toward the provision of broader assortments to food store customers over the last two decades. Table 7.1 summarizes the information. The four categories with broader assortments have experienced substantial and steady increases in their share of sales and in their share of the number of stores.

In evaluating this information one should note that the total number of food stores decreased between 1980 and 1998 (from 253 400 to 244 300) while total sales of food stores increased (from 220.2 billions in current dollars to 443.0 billions in current dollars). This represents a continuation of the trend for food stores between 1940 and 1980 identified in our earlier discussion.[6]

Table 7.1   The evolution of supermarket assortments: 1980, 1990, 1998

	Share of number of food stores			Share of food stores sales		
Conventional	8.3	13.7	10.4	52.1	24.6	13.4
Warehouses	0.6	3.4	2.2	3.0	9.0	4.4
Other supermarkets	1.4	7.8	11.3	16.2	37.0	52.7

7.2   ASSORTMENT CHOICE AND INTERTYPE COMPETITION

In this section we adapt the model of Chapter 2 to analyse the assortment problem and to illustrate an alternative way of capturing intertype competition to the one employed in Chapter 6. The retailer wants to maximize profits while keeping the representative consumer at the store just as in Chapter 2. The main difference with both Chapter 2 and Chapter 6 is in the specification of intertype competition through the expenditure function of the representative consumer. The latter will be given by

$$E(p^S, D^S, D\_^S, p^{NS}, D^{NS}, D\_^{NS}, p', Z). \tag{7.1}$$

p^S is the average price charged by the supermarket for its assortment and D^S is the level of assortment provided by the supermarket. Both of them are choice variables for the supermarket, just as in previous cases. $D\_^S$ is the level of another distribution service, or a set of them, which will be assumed constant at a given level. p^{NS} is the average price charged by the intertype or non-supermarket competitors which will be taken as given. D^{NS} is the level of assortment of the intertype competitors, which will be inversely related to the level of assortment of the supermarket and will be discussed further below. $D\_^{NS}$ is the level of another distribution service, or a set of them, for the intertype competitors, which will be assumed constant but at a different level than that of the supermarket. This will make it possible for the consumer to be willing to patronize both competitors.

It is helpful to indicate the economic setting underlying this specification. Suppose the intertype competitor is a convenience store. $D\_^S$ and $D\_^{NS}$ would represent in this case accessibility of location, for example, which is a distribution service that the convenience store provides at a higher level than the supermarket, that is, $D\_^S < D\_^{NS}$. This relation will be taken as given at these different levels for both types of stores. The consumer patronizes both of them but at different times, of course. Alternatively, the intertype competition could be a specialist such as a liquor store. In this case the distribution service, $D\_^S$ and $D\_^{NS}$, would make most sense interpreted as depth of assortment, which the specialist again provides at a higher level than the supermarket. This provides the basis for the supermarket competing with the other type of store without necessarily driving the other type of store out of the market or vice versa, since the supermarket provides a higher level of breadth of assortment with respect to the specialist and of both breadth and depth with respect to the convenience store.[7]

Another new feature of the specification is the relationship of the assortments in the two types of store. Since assortment is a decision variable for the supermarket, the latter will incorporate in its decision making when it increases assortment that this will have an impact on the level of assortment provided by the intertype competitor at the given retail price of the intertype competitor. In reality the intertype competitor is likely to respond, but not necessarily through the level of assortment because the supermarket is likely to have an advantage in providing this dimension of output. Since we are focusing here on the supermarket, we will ignore the possible response of the intertype competitor through the change in other distribution services. This is less limiting than it seems, since we are also assuming that these changes will not drive the intertype competitor out of the market.

The retailer's problem is to maximize profits by choosing p^S and D^S subject to (7.1) being less than what the consumer would spend at an alternative supermarket, E',

$$\text{Max } L = p^S Q - C(v, Q, D^S, D\_{}^{NS}) - wQ + \mu N \, [E' - E(.)], \text{ where} \quad (7.2)$$

$E(.)$ is the function in (7.1).[8] The first-order conditions are given by

$$[p^S - C_Q - w] - [p^S/\in] \, (1-\mu) = 0. \quad (7.3)$$

$$[p^S - C_Q - w] \, \partial q/\partial D^S + \mu[r^S - r^{NS}] - C_D/N = 0. \quad (7.4)$$

And, of course, the constraint in (7.2) must be binding or

$$E' - E(p^S, D^S, D\_{}^S, p^{NS}, D^{NS}, D\_{}^{NS}, p', Z) = 0.$$

Thus, the main difference with the model in Chapter 6 is that the retailer will set the level of the distribution service, assortment, taking into account the marginal contribution to profits that he or she obtains by switching a unit of assortment from the intertype competitor, instead of using the full contribution of a unit of assortment to lowering the expenditures of the consumer. This can be seen by comparing (7.3) and (7.4) with (6.2) and (6.3).

What is the essence of assortment from the point of view of the consumer? The value of a higher level of assortment is in the provision of one-stop shopping. Its marginal valuation for the consumer is given by the difference in the two shadow prices. It could be affected by all of the variables in the expenditure function of the consumer in principle. The consumer marginal valuation of one-stop shopping will be greater, the greater the difference between the shadow prices of assortment for the two intertype competitors.

A couple of special cases will be useful in highlighting the main implications of the model. Suppose there is perfect competition, that is, $\mu = 1$. (7.3) and (7.4) will collapse to:

$$p^S - C_Q - w = 0, \text{ and} \tag{7.5}$$

$$[r^S - r^{NS}] - C_D/N = 0. \tag{7.6}$$

Thus, the average retail price will equal the marginal cost of selling an additional item. Furthermore, the marginal value of one-stop shopping to the consumer will equal the supermarket's marginal cost per customer of providing an additional unit of assortment.

Suppose that there is an exogenous change in the consumer's valuation of one-stop shopping, so that the first term in (7.6) increases; equilibrium can be restored by increasing the level of assortment, if the marginal costs of assortment are increasing in assortment. Presumably the higher level of assortment at supermarkets decreases the valuation of assortment there by the consumer, and the lower level at the intertype competitor increases the valuation of assortment there. In the price equation the higher level of assortment will lead to a higher marginal cost of providing the average item, assuming the usual situation where $C_{QD} > 0$. Thus, it leads to an increase in price.

What happens if the marginal costs of assortment are declining with respect to assortment? First, equilibrium is no longer assured; in general, it will require the marginal valuation of one-stop shopping to decrease more rapidly than the marginal costs of assortment per transaction. In this latter case, the argument with respect to the price equation remains as before so we would expect to observe a higher price associated with the higher level of assortment.

One possible exogenous factor to the retailer that may increase the value of one-stop shopping to the consumer is, of course, the consumer's wage rate. But there are other factors, for example the availability of refrigeration or of automobile transportation. Both of these factors lower the costs of increasing the size of the transaction for the consumer. Their effect would be similar to the one just analysed. Similarly, if the intertype competitor increases price, this allows the supermarket to respond by increasing prices and distribution services in the settings just described.

Suppose instead that the supermarket operates as a monopolist, hence $\mu = 0$. In this setting there is no intertype competition, since the latter occurs through the consumer's expenditure function which plays no role in the monopoly setting. Equations (7.3) and (7.4) become

$$[p^S - C_Q - w] - p^S/\mathcal{E} = 0, \text{ and} \tag{7.7}$$

$$[p^S - C_Q - w]\partial q/\partial D^S - C_D/N = 0. \tag{7.8}$$

Nevertheless, if the marginal costs with respect to assortment are increasing, the analysis goes through in the same fashion as before, in the sense that exogenous changes that disturb the equilibrium condition in (7.8) will lead to adjustments where price and distribution services move in the same direction. If the marginal costs with respect to distribution services are decreasing in assortment, however, restoring equilibrium in (7.8) can require the average retail price and distribution services to move in opposite directions.[9]

An important economic implication of these results is

Proposition 7.1: For a lower retail price to be associated with a higher level of assortment in this model two conditions are necessary: declining marginal costs with respect to distribution services and some form of imperfect competition.

7.3 ECONOMETRIC EVIDENCE ON SUPERMARKETS

The simple model presented in the previous section can be used to generate the one developed by Messinger and Narasimhan (1997) to analyse the choice of assortment and average price by supermarkets. Their model is the special case of (7.5) and (7.6), the perfect competition case, that results from making the following two assumptions: constant returns to scale with respect to turnover or the quantity of output of goods sold; the representative consumer's utility is constant at its maximum level when patronizing the supermarket and the other store.

Constant returns to scale allows (7.5) to be rewritten as

$$p^S - w = C_Q(v, D^S, Q) = C^*(v, D^S) = \alpha + \beta \ln D^S + \gamma z + u_1 \qquad (7.9)$$

From the assumption of constant returns to scale, we have that average cost must equal marginal cost and, thus, the second equality in (7.9), where C^* is the unit cost function. The third equality in (7.9) simply reveals the main functional form adopted by these authors for their unit cost function in the empirical setting (equation (9) in their paper), where z is a vector of variables that can shift the cost function[10] and u_1 is a disturbance term.

The second assumption allows (7.6) to be rewritten as

$$q(dp^S/d\,D^S) = [r^S - r^{NS}] = C_D/N = p'\,(h - t) + u_2 \qquad (7.10)$$

The first equality in (7.10) relates our formulation to their assumption of constant utility. If the latter is constant in the expenditure function, the total differential of the expenditure function allowing the supermarket retail price and assortment in both stores to change implies that the first equality must hold. The second equality simply restates (7.6), just as the first equality in

(7.9) restates (7.5). Finally, the third equality in (7.10) follows from an assumption made by Messinger and Narasimhan. It shows the functional form adopted by the authors to capture the consumer's shopping cost differential[11] in their equation for the average price at the supermarket, that is, equation (10) in their paper.

In our notation this equation is given by: $(10)'\ p^S = p^{NS} + p'(h - t) - g(Z)/D^S + u_2$, where u_2 is a disturbance term and $g(Z)$ is the utility value in monetary units of one-stop shopping. $(10)'$ implies that $p'(h - t) + u_2 = p^S - p^{NS} + g(Z)/D^S$. The authors also assumed that the consumer purchases only one unit from any category. In this case, $q = 1$ in (7.10), and we can write $d\,p^S/d\,D^S = p^S - p^{NS} + g(Z)/D^S$. That is, the change in average price at the supermarket as a result of a unit change in assortment will equal the difference in the average price between the supermarket and the non-supermarket plus the utility value in monetary units of one-stop shopping, $g(Z)$, per unit of assortment, D^S. By (7.10) this must equal the implicit shopping cost differential of the representative consumer, $[r^S - r^{NS}]$. Finally, we can write $(10)'$ as (7.11) in terms of our notation, that is,

$$[p^S - w] = [p^{NS} - w] + p'(h - t) - g(Z)/D^S + u_2. \tag{7.11}$$

Differentiating (7.9) and (7.11) with respect to assortment shows that $\partial[p^S - w]/\partial D^S = \beta/D^S$ from (7.9) and $\partial[p^S - w]/\partial D^S = g(Z)/[D^S]^2$ from (7.11). Hence, we can rewrite (7.11) as

$$[p^S - w] = [p^{NS} - w - \beta] + p'(h - t) + u_2. \tag{7.12}$$

For empirical purposes it is also useful to express (7.9) in reduced form by using (7.11) to eliminate $[p^S - w]$ from (7.9), which yields

$$\ln D^S = [(p^{NS} - w - \alpha - \beta)/\beta] + [(h - t)/\beta]p' - [\gamma/\beta]z + [u_2 - u_1]/\beta. \tag{7.13}$$

(7.12) and (7.13) were the two reduced forms estimated by the authors. They used as the dependent variable in (7.12) the average gross retail margin as a percentage of sales for a sample of US supermarkets chains surveyed annually by Cornell University. And, as the dependent variable in (7.13) they used the average number of different items per supermarket store in the US. As their measure of the consumer's wage rate, the authors used real disposable income. The results were obtained for an aggregate time series of observations between 1961 and 1986 using feasible generalized least squares to correct for first-order serial correlation.

Two results are especially interesting in our context. First, the reduced form estimates for the assortment equation show a strong and robust positive relationship between the equilibrium level of assortment and their proxy for the consumer's wage rate, real disposable income. The t-ratio for the coefficient is positive and greater than five (Messinger and Narasimhan, 1997, Table 5). This result also holds for a similar analysis using cross-section data across the 48 contiguous states of the US for 1991 (Messinger and Narasimhan, 1997, Table 11). In this variant, assortment is defined in terms of average square feet per store. The result also holds while adding other variables to the relationship in the time series regression (not reported in the published version), for example road mileage and the adoption of refrigerators.

Second, the authors' specification allows them to obtain an estimate of the average value of one-stop shopping for the consumer. $(p^S - w)/p^S$ and p' can be evaluated at their mean values. The estimation generates estimated coefficients for $(h - t)$ and $[p^{NS} - w]$ expressed as a percentage of sales. Hence, (7.12) and (7.13) can be used to obtain an estimate of $g(Z)$ [$= \beta D^S$] expressed as a percentage of sales. This estimate of the value of one-stop shopping is 2.37 per cent with the method described here. The average supermarket gross margin, $p^S - w$, is slightly higher than the estimated margin at other stores, $p^{NS} - w$. The premium for shopping at the supermarket relative to the intertype competitor is 0.96 per cent as a percentage of sales with the method described here.[12]

Taking these results at face value implies that customers of supermarkets pay more on average to these retailers for providing broader and/or deeper assortments but the utility value to these customers of these assortments is on average more than what they pay to retailers. While the authors discuss a number of other issues, and we will return to one of them later (namely the extension of their analysis to shopping centers), the discussion in this section captures the essential aspect of their contribution. A simple equilibrium model of assortment choice by supermarkets reveals two things upon empirical implementation. Increases in the consumer's opportunity cost of time are a driving force toward increasing assortment by supermarkets and the resulting outcomes benefit consumers.

While the previous model is especially attractive, because of its unique focus on assortment, it is not the only econometric study on supermarkets that stresses distribution services, including assortment. Betancourt and Malanoski (1999) have implemented empirically a model of supermarket behavior in which they assume imperfect competition and no explicit intertype competition. The main features of this model were described in Chapter 4, section 4, including their reliance on data for individual supermarkets. Here we merely report two of their empirical results that are particularly relevant in the present context.

First, these authors found that an index of distribution services[13] had a positive and statistically robust impact on the demand for supermarket products.

More generally, a 1 per cent increase in distribution services generates increases ranging from 0.38 per cent to 0.42 per cent in the quantity demanded of supermarket products for the average supermarket in their sample (Table 2). Second, they obtained estimates of the shadow price of this index of distribution services, r in equation (4.17), or the monetary value of the change in utility as a result of adding a unit of these distribution services. These estimates can be viewed as the annual value to supermarket patrons of increasing assortment by, for example, adding an area for a delicatessen with employee assistance. They ranged from 2.88 per cent to 2.97 per cent of the value of average supermarket sales in the sample, which is similar to the gain from one-stop shopping estimated by Messinger and Narasimhan.

7.4   EXTENSIONS: ASSORTMENT AND SPATIAL COMPETITION

In this section we extend the previous analysis in the spirit of Bhatnagar and Ratchford (2000) by allowing for spatial competition. We begin by extending the model of Chapter 2 to a situation where the retailer chooses prices and a distribution service, which will be interpreted as assortment, in a setting where accessibility of location is given from the perspective of the individual supermarket but is determined by the process of entry and exit of firms.

Just as before, the retailer's problem is to maximize profits subject to the expenditure function of the representative consumer, $E(.)$, being less than what the consumer would spend at an alternative supermarket, E'. The retailer now chooses an average price, p, and a level of assortment, D_1, given another distribution service, D_2, and accessibility of location D_-. The latter is determined by the fact that stores of the same type are located along the circumference of a circle and customers are uniformly distributed with n customers per unit of distance. The marginal customer of the focal store (our representative consumer) is located at a distance of $d/2$ from the store, and adding the customers on both sides of the store generates $N = nd$. The store would like to make this distance as large as possible, but it can only affect it indirectly.

Bhatnagar and Ratchford assume perfect competition and allow the process of entry and exit of stores to determine the equilibrium level of accessibility of location in our terminology, note that $[D_- = - d.]$,[14] through the zero profit condition. I will assume imperfect competition but allow the equilibrium level of accessibility of location to be determined by the process of entry and exit through the zero profit condition. What makes imperfect competition possible is the existence of a second distribution service constant at a given level, D_2. This implies that the store need not lose all its patronage when it does not match the assortment and price offerings of the adjacent supermarket competitor, because its level of D_2 can keep the consumer patronizing the store if constant at a higher value than that of its adjacent competitor.

More precisely, we have

$$\text{Max } L = p\,Q - C(v, Q, D_1, D_2, D\_) - w\,Q + \mu N\,[E' - E(.)]. \qquad (7.14)$$

The first-order conditions are given by

$$[p - C_Q - w] - [p/\in](1 - \mu) = 0. \qquad (7.15)$$

$$[p - C_Q - w]\partial q/\partial D_1 + \mu[r_1] - C_1/N = 0. \qquad (7.16)$$

$$E' - E(p, D_1, D_2, D\_, Z) = 0. \qquad (7.17)$$

While this is sufficient for a short-run equilibrium, a long-run equilibrium with respect to location requires no incentive for entry and exit, namely

$$p\,Q - C(.) - w\,Q = 0 \Rightarrow p - w = m = C(.)/Q = C(.)/qnd. \qquad (7.18)$$

One way to make progress is to introduce special assumptions that bring out different aspects of the problem. One can first look at the implications of the choice of average price for the location equilibrium by keeping assortment constant. In this setting, the zero profit condition (7.18), the expenditure function of the consumer, (7.17), and (7.15) can be used to find the characteristics of optimal levels of accessibility of location (distance) or patronage, d or N, and average store price or margin, p or m.

From the expenditure function of the consumer, it follows that, given the level of assortment and imperfect competition, accessibility of location and price must satisfy $-E_p\,dp - E_{D\_}\,dD\_ = -q\,dp + r_{D\_}\,dD\_ = -q\,dp + r_{D\_}\,d(-d) = 0$. This implies

$$\partial d/\partial p = -q/r_{D\_} < 0. \qquad (7.19)$$

From the long-run equilibrium condition, it follows that $d = C/[p - w]qn = C/mqn$ and, thus,

$$\partial d/\partial p = -d/m - Cn\{m - C_Q\}\partial q/\partial p = -d/m - Cn\{[p/\in](1 - \mu)\}\partial q/\partial p, \qquad (7.20)$$

where the last equality follows from (7.15). (7.19) and (7.20) imply

$$q/r_{D\_} = d/m + Cn\{[p/\in](1 - \mu)\}\partial q/\partial p = d/m - Cn(1 - \mu)q. \qquad (7.21)$$

If we assume perfect competition among stores ($\mu = 1$), the second term on the right-hand side of (7.21) vanishes. Since this second term is negative whereas the other two are positive, we have our first result. Namely,

Proposition 7.2: Given the size of market demand (q) and willingness to pay for location (r_{D_-}), perfect competition among stores leads to equilibria with a higher average price and margin, p and m, but smaller distances (d) between the stores than in a setting of imperfect competition. That is, $\partial d^*/\partial \mu < 0$ and $\partial m^*/\partial \mu > 0$.

In order to facilitate the exposition, consider first the effect of market demand and willingness to pay for location in the perfectly competitive case. Exogenous increases in market demand (q) lead to equilibria in which the distance between stores is farther apart and the average price charged by stores is lower than prior to the change. Similarly, exogenous increases in the willingness to pay for location (r_{D_-}) lead to equilibria with higher average prices and smaller distances between stores. These results are similar to the ones obtained by Bhatnagar and Ratchford (2000) who find that margins decrease while patronage increases with population density, whereas margins increase while patronage decreases with consumer transport costs. In their case population density and consumer transport costs play a similar role to the one that market demand and willingness to pay for location play in our case and patronage plays a role in their case similar to distance in ours.[15] The role of margins and average price are the same in both analyses.

Under imperfect competition the same results as above hold for the effect of willingness to pay for location on distance. Similarly, the effect of willingness to pay on the average price would be a higher average price, but in this case it is attenuated by the fact that the increase in price in the second term of (7.21) also helps to restore the equilibrium. If the demand curve is linear in price, the second term in (7.21) becomes $- Cnq(1 - \mu)$. It also follows in this case that exogenous increases in market demand, q, increase distance, but by a bigger value than under perfect competition, and decrease average price, by a bigger absolute value than under perfect competition. Thus, we have

Proposition 7.3: Under both perfect and imperfect competition, exogenous increases in market demand (q) and exogenous *decreases* in willingness to pay for location (r_{D_-}) lead to equilibria with stores located farther apart and charging lower average prices. That is,

$$\partial d^*/\partial q > 0, \ \partial d^*/\partial r_{D_-} < 0, \ \partial m^*/\partial q < 0, \ \text{and} \ \partial m^*/\partial r_{D_-} > 0.$$

Imperfect competition generates additional results. That is, if we maintain the assumption of a linear demand curve, exogenous increases in the costs of retailing (C) and in population density (n) lead to equilibria with longer distances among stores and lower average prices. That is, $\partial d^*/\partial C > 0$, $\partial d^*/\partial n > 0$, $\partial m^*/\partial C < 0$, and $\partial m^*/\partial n < 0$. It also follows from (7.21) that increases in competition for the consumer's dollar $(\in)$ lead to equilibria with smaller distances among stores and higher average prices. That is, $\partial d^*/\partial \in < 0$ and $\partial m^*/\partial \in > 0$. Not surprisingly, the latter result is similar to the one on competition from other stores, that is, Proposition 7.2.

Similarly to what was done in Chapter 6, it is of interest to consider here an alternative analysis in which we allow assortment to change while keeping the average price or margin constant. This will allow us to derive the characteristics of optimal levels of accessibility of location or distance and optimal levels of assortment by using the zero profit condition (7.18) and the expenditure function of the consumer (7.17) with the first-order condition for assortment (7.16).

From the expenditure function of the consumer, it follows that, given the average price and imperfect competition, accessibility of location and assortment must satisfy $-E_{D1} dD_1 - E_{D_-} dD_- = r_1 dD_1 + r_{D_-} d(-d) = 0$. This relation implies

$$\partial d/\partial D_1 = r_1/r_{D_-} > 0. \tag{7.22}$$

From the first-order condition (7.16) and the relation $N = nd$, we have $[p - C_Q - w]\partial q/\partial D_1 + \mu r_1 = C_1/nd$, which implies $Ad = C_1/n$, and, thus

$$\partial d/\partial D_1 = \{C_{11}/n - d\,[\partial A/\partial D_1]\} \,/\, \{A + [\partial A/\partial d]\} \tag{7.23}$$

where $A = \{[p - C_Q - w]\partial q/\partial D_1 + \mu r_1\} > 0$. Note that $[\partial A/\partial D_1] < 0^{16}$ and we will assume $[\partial A/\partial d] = 0$ to simplify the exposition.[17] (7.22) and (7.23) imply

$$r_1/r_{D_-} = \{C_{11}/n - d\,[\partial A/\partial D_1]\}/A = \{C_{11}/n - (C/mqn)\,[\partial A/\partial D_1]\}/A, \tag{7.24}$$

where the second equality follows from (7.18).

Just as before exogenous increases in the willingness to pay for location (r_{D_-}) lead to equilibria where stores are closer together, since d in the first equality in (7.24) must decrease if we keep assortment constant. By (7.22) this will also imply that optimal assortments will have less breadth or depth if we adjust to this change by keeping d constant. Increases in the willingness to pay for assortment (r_1), on the other hand, lead to equilibria with stores farther apart, since d in the first equality in (7.24) must increase if we keep assortment constant. By (7.22) this will also imply that optimal assortments will have greater breadth and/or depth. The signs of these impacts will be the same under imperfect and perfect competition.[18] Thus, we have

Proposition 7.4: Under both imperfect and perfect competition, increases in the willingness to pay for location and *decreases* in the willingness to pay for assortment lead to equilibria with stores operating closer together and offering shallower and narrower assortments. That is, $\partial d^*/\partial r_1 > 0$; $\partial d^*/\partial r_{D-} < 0$; $\partial D^*/\partial r_1 > 0$; and $\partial D^*/\partial r_{D-} < 0$.

Finally, increases in population density (n) will lead to equilibria with stores farther apart ($\partial d^*/\partial n > 0$) if the marginal costs of assortment provision are increasing in assortment, or closer together ($\partial d^*/\partial n < 0$) if marginal costs are decreasing in assortment. Optimal assortments will be broader and deeper in the former case ($\partial D^*/\partial n > 0$) and narrower and shallower in the latter case ($\partial D^*/\partial n < 0$). Our analysis here has kept prices and margins constant. If we allow them to change, however, then the lowering of m^* associated with an increase in n, which was established in the analysis of the previous case when assortment was given, allows a smaller reduction in D^* when marginal costs are decreasing. This can also be characterized as an increase in the equilibrium level of assortment, D^*, relative to the setting where m^* was constant, which illustrates the main aspect of Proposition 7.1 in a different setting, namely, the critical role of decreasing marginal costs with respect to a distribution service in generating an association between lower prices and higher levels of the service.

Some perspective on the importance of this feature is provided by the work of Bagwell and Ramey (1994) on coordination economies in retail markets. These authors develop a basic model in which decreasing marginal costs with respect to the selling technology (K) (a bundle of distribution services in our terminology) and cost complementarities[19] between this technology and product variety (V) (assortment in our terminology) are essential assumptions. In this setting equilibrium outcomes for the firm have increases in assortment associated with lower prices. Thus, this basic model exhibits coordination economies, that is, lower prices and greater variety offered to consumers, and higher expected profits for retailers.

In this context the authors go on to show that retail advertising in the presence of consumer search costs can generate equilibria where firms are fewer than without the advertising, and consumers are better off in terms of the deals that they are offered with advertising than without advertising. This result is driven by the existence of coordination economies for the firms in the analysis. In turn, the existence of coordination economies requires decreasing marginal costs for distribution services together with cost complementarity between these distribution services and assortment.

7.5 DEPTH, BREADTH AND A CLASSIFICATION OF RETAIL FORMS

While our results in the previous sections by and large apply to both breadth and depth of assortment, they are especially relevant for breadth of assortment. In addition, we have assumed previously homogeneous consumers. Bhatnagar and Ratchford (2000), on the other hand, emphasize the distinction between breadth and depth, introduce consumer heterogeneity in the form of segments of consumers and rely on both to provide a classification of retail forms. In this section, each of these issues is taken up together with some basic empirical tests presented by these authors.

A well accepted distinction between depth and breadth of assortment is that depth is identified by the number of varieties within a product line or category, whereas breadth is identified by the number of product lines or categories. This is the definition adopted by Bhatnagar and Ratchford (2000) and employed here.

Somewhat related to these definitions are the demand-based definitions suggested by Betancourt and Gautschi (1990). There depth of an assortment is defined by the number of net substitutes stocked in the assortment, while breadth of an assortment is defined by the number of net independent items stocked in the assortment.[20] In comparing actual assortments, however, the demand-based definitions are limited by the difficulty of identifying net substitute and net complement items in practice. For instance, the analysis in Chapter 3 suggests that demand-based definitions of net substitutes and complements may vary with the calendar unit used for the analysis.

Another reason for the difficulty in identifying net substitute and net complement items in practice is heterogeneity among consumers or the existence of different segments, for instance depth or convenience or one-stop shopping. These segments are usually identified in terms of the determinants of their demand. Search costs within and between stores provide the most basic rationale for consumers' demanding depth, for example Moorthy, Ratchford and Talukdar (1997). In this context Bhatnagar and Ratchford (2000) stress the following features of the demand for depth: consumers' perception of heterogeneity in a category, their prior information on the items, and their perceptions of substitutability among the items. Similarly, they view one-stop shopping as the primary basis for the demand for breadth with in-store search costs as a link between depth and breadth.[21]

On the supply side these authors view depth and breadth as multiplicative dimensions of output in terms of increasing costs. Furthermore, they assume that these costs increase at an increasing rate, with marginal costs increasing faster for breadth than for depth. This last assumption is justified as follows: within a category it is assumed that only net substitutes are stocked; between categories all goods are net independents. Running out of all items in a category forces the consumer to leave the store (in their model consumers buy one item from each category of breadth) whereas running out of an item within a category merely means a consumer can substitute for another item. Hence, higher inventories in breadth than in depth are required.

Based on the depth dimension, the authors classify the following retail forms into three groups from low to high : Convenience Stores; Supermarkets, Department Stores and Superstores; Specialty Stores. Based on the breadth dimension, the authors classify these same retail forms from low to high into three groups: Convenience Stores, Specialty Stores; Supermarkets, Department Stores; Superstores. This classification provides a useful although incomplete starting point for classification of retail forms. It leaves out some retail forms, for example non-store retailers and shopping centers, and some dimensions relevant to the differentiation of retail forms, for example distance. We consider this type of issue in sections 6 and 7.

Here, we conclude by discussing three propositions on the relation between retail margins and store types that Bhatnagar and Ratchford test empirically. First, they find evidence that the retail margins of convenience stores are higher than the retail margins of supermarkets for a time series of gross margins between 1972 and 1994. While this proposition is consistent with their particular analysis, this is also what one would expect to find on the basis of Proposition 7.3 and 7.4. That is, a segment that values accessibility of location (r_D) highly, namely those who patronize a convenience store, should end up in equilibria with higher margins, closer stores and narrower and shallower assortments than those who value accessibility of location less, for example those who patronize supermarkets.

Second, they find evidence that the gross margins for specialty stores are higher than for the corresponding categories of department stores on the basis of data for 1994 from the National Retail Federation. This proposition is consistent with their particular analysis when one assumes that the market segment is smaller for the specialty stores. It also follows from the analysis in the previous section. The analysis associated with Proposition 7.3 implies that, under imperfect competition, a decrease in population density leads to equilibria with higher margins for any given depth or breadth of assortment.

Third, they find evidence that the gross margins of superstores are higher than those of conventional supermarkets based on a preliminary survey. Similar results are obtained by Leibtag (2002) based on a national sample collected by BLS to construct the producer price index for the food store category in the year 2000. Once again this proposition is consistent with their analysis and with the analysis of the previous section and for the same reason, namely assuming that the superstore market segment is smaller than the conventional supermarket segment.

While these tests are interesting and encouraging from the point of view of our approach, they are clearly limited in their scope since they don't control for many other relevant aspects of these comparisons. In designing more suitable tests, particular attention should be given to the issue of whether or not there are declining marginal costs or other features of increasing returns with respect to the provision of assortment. Bagwell and Ramey (1994) assume decreasing marginal costs in distribution services, implicitly including breadth of assortment; Bhatnagar and Ratchford assume increasing marginal costs in both depth and breadth of assortment. In section 7.4 the discussion allows for both possibilities with respect to marginal costs and it makes a difference to the final outcomes with respect to equilibrium assortment.[22]

7.6 NON-STORE RETAILERS

Some versions of non-store retailing have been around for many years.[23] Yet recent technological changes, especially the advent of the Internet, are likely to enhance the importance of some sub-categories within this category in the future. In other words one would expect this form of retailing to generate a greater proportion of retail sales in the 21st century than it did in the 20th century.[24] Table 7.2 provides information on which to base this somewhat speculative prediction. Before discussing the table, however, we need to address a prior issue.

Unfortunately technological changes have also led to the need for restructuring our industrial classification systems. These changes have been implemented by the Bureau of the Census in 1997 and they lead to a serious break in continuity for most of the time series on the retail trade due to non-comparability of coverage. Thus, Table 7.2 presents information under both the old classification of retail industries (SIC) and the new classification of retail industries (NAICS). In the old system the main three entries in this category are catalogue and mail order houses, merchandising machine operators and direct selling establishments; in the new system the first category becomes electronic shopping and mail order houses, the next two categories remain the same (at least in name since direct selling establishments are not comparable in both classifications)[25] and fuel dealers are added to the category. In both cases, however, it can be seen from Table 7.2 that the first sub-category represents the lion's share of category sales in 1999, 80 per cent under SIC and 67 per cent under NAICS.

With the SIC classification one sees that the proportion of retail sales by non-store retailers increases during the last 15 years of the 20th century from 0.02 to 0.04. Furthermore, the proportion of non-store retail sales by the category catalogue and mail order houses also increases during this period from

Table 7.2   Retail sales by non-store retailers (billions of current $)

Category	1985	1990	1995	1997	1999
1. Retail Sales (SIC)[1]	1375	1845	2359	2611	2995
2. Non-store Retailers	28	46	73	90	114
3. Catalogue & MO	16	27	51	65	90
4. (2/1) (3/2)	(0.02) (0.57)	(0.02) (0.59)	(0.03) (0.70)	(0.03) (0.72)	(0.04) (0.80)
5. R. Sales (NAICS)[2]	–	–	2259	2509	2863
6. Non-store Retailers	–	–	96	116	138
7. Elec. Sh. & MO	–	–	53	70	93
8. (6/5) (7/6)	–	–	(0.04) (0.55)	(0.05) (0.60)	(0.05) (0.67)

Notes:
1. This row of figures and the next two are based on the Standard Industrial Classification, SIC, US Statistical Abstract (2000, Table 1275) (MO stands for mail order).
2. This row of figures and the next two are based on the North American Industrial Classification System, NAICS, US Statistical Abstract (2001, Table 1020) (Elec. Sh. stands for electronic shopping).

0.57 to 0.80. Indeed sales by catalogue and mail order houses increase more rapidly than non-store retail sales (they go from 0.0114 to 0.0320 as a proportion of retail sales during this period). Using the NAICS classification one sees that from 1995 to 1999 non-store retail sales go from 0.04 to 0.05 as a proportion of retail sales; electronic shopping and mail order houses sales go from 0.55 to 0.67 as a proportion of non-store retail sales; and electronic and mail order sales go from 0.0220 to 0.0335 as a proportion of retail sales.

A need for using both classifications arises because the two classifications differ in fundamental ways. For instance, just as noted earlier, fuel dealers are included in the totals for non-store retailers under NAICS but they are not included under SIC. Similarly the category of electronic shopping and mail order houses for NAICS is not comparable to the category catalogues and mail order houses for SIC in that the sales figures under NAICS can not be estimated within 3 per cent from the SIC data. Nonetheless the general trends for non-store retailers are similar with both classifications.

Last but not least, it is useful to note that in 1999 e-commerce sales, defined as sales of goods and services over the Internet, extranet, EDI or other online system, represent 12.5 per cent of the category electronic shopping and mail order houses, 8.5 per cent of the category non-store retail sales and 0.5 per cent of the category retail sales.[26] Thus, e-commerce activities classified as electronic shopping and mail order represent 76.4 per cent of all retail sales classified as e-commerce. These data are available in US Statistical Abstract (2001, Table 1038). One would expect e-commerce in particular to grow rapidly in the 21st century, since the penetration of the market by personal computers and the concomitant Internet access is most likely to reach its peak during this period.

It is instructive to consider in detail a study that analyses competition between mail order houses and retail stores in the early part of the 20th century (Michael, 1994), for two reasons. First, the author emphasizes in his analysis the importance of several distributions services, albeit in some cases giving them different names than are used here, and second these distribution services are also relevant for analyses of competition between Internet retailing and brick and mortar retailing. In addition, existing analyses of the Internet tend to ignore the cost side while Michael's analyses emphasizes the cost side. Furthermore, since the Internet is at an incipient stage as an institution whereas mail order houses are at a very mature stage, Michael's analysis of mail order houses can highlight aspects of competition that are yet to arise in the case of Internet retailing.

In our earlier discussion of the Internet in Chapter 5 (section 5.5), we stressed that one of its features was the ability to provide much broader and deeper assortments than conventional retailers and that this led to their charging lower prices. The same phenomenon applies to the comparison between mail order houses and retail stores. The provision of extensive assortments through catalogues, while more expensive than the provision of extensive assortments through the Internet, is much cheaper than the provision of extensive assortments at the retail store and for the same reason, namely the savings on storage costs. In his comparison of mail order and retail stores, Michael implicitly assumes assortments to be the same by framing the problem in terms of a merchant considering two distribution channels for any one item. On the other hand, this assumption allows him to concentrate on the insights provided by the role in the comparison of three other distribution services.

Michael views any channel as performing two basic functions: providing transportation, or what we label accessibility of location, and breaking bulk, or what we label providing assurance of product delivery in the desired form (small packages as in Chapter 6). Merchants using the mail order channel ship directly to consumer homes while if they use the retail store channel they ship in bulk to the stores and consumers will provide the remainder of the transportation needed when they patronize the store. The mail order channel provides greater accessibility of location to consumers but incurs higher costs than the retail store. This is what one would also observe with the Internet.[27] In order to break bulk for the consumer the mail order channel does it once while the retail store has to do it at least twice (packaging for sending the items to the store and packaging for selling the items to consumers). In sum, Michael concludes that at low levels of population densities mail order will experience a cost advantage whereas at high levels the retail store has the cost advantage.[28]

The mail order channel can also be viewed as providing descriptive information through the catalogue at lower cost than the retail store, but with no possibility of inspection of the item. According to Michael this led the mail order houses to offer guarantees which raise costs, but by less than the savings from information provision through the catalogue. This information aspect is hard to separate from our earlier argument on assortment provision through the catalogue substantially lowering costs relative to the retail store channel,[29] since storage at the retail store becomes irrelevant in the case of the catalogue as well as in the case of the Internet. What is relevant in both cases but absent from Michael's discussion is that assurance of product delivery at the desired time is higher in the retail store channel for the items that are actually stocked at the store.

In any event, Michael (1994, Table 3) provides some empirical evidence for his basic argument that increases in population density diminish the cost advantage of mail order houses. Perhaps more importantly in a modern context, he notes that as the major mail order firms lost this cost advantage they changed their organizational form by expanding rapidly their opening of retail stores in the 1920s. Out of five exclusively or mainly mail order houses in the 1920s, two (Sears and Montgomery Ward) became primarily retail stores with a mail order business, another two (Chicago Mail Order and National Bella Hess) tried the same idea but failed and closed in the 1960s, and the last one (Spiegel) tried the same idea and also failed but was able to retreat to a niche as an exclusively mail order house. One suspects that a similar fate may await some of the successful Internet firms. Since we have already seen some bricks and mortar firms become Internet suppliers as well, however, it is likely that either the cost advantages associated with the Internet channel and/or the features of demand for distribution services especially met by this channel are not easily competed away by other channels or eliminated by exogenous changes in the environment.

7.7   SHOPPING CENTERS AND SHOPPING MALLS

Shopping centers and shopping malls have become ubiquitous in the United States during the second half of the twentieth century. In this time period they have also spread to other developed countries. Furthermore, the diffusion of this retail form to developing countries has already started. For instance, an important industry trade association, the International Council of Shopping Centers, has among its news releases (18 July 2002) on its website (www.icsc.org) an announcement of the first conference on shopping center development in Mexico and Central America.

Centers and malls come in various sizes and forms. According to the Shopping Center Development Handbook, McKeever and Grifffin (1977): the smallest ones are neighborhood shopping centers with less than 100 000 square feet of gross leasable area and typically they have a supermarket or drugstore as an anchor; the next smallest ones are community shopping centers with 100 000–300 000 of gross leasable area and at least one type of department store as an anchor; the next category are regional centers or malls with 300 000–750 000 square feet of gross leasable area and at least one full line department store as an anchor; finally, we have the super-regional with 750 000 to over 5 million (West Edmonton Mall) square feet of gross leasable area and at least three department stores as anchors.

All of these categories have experienced substantial growth in terms of numbers, gross leasable area and sales in recent decades. We can use data from the US Statistical Abstract to obtain an approximate idea of the characteristics of this growth process in the 1990s. Retail sales in the first three categories of Table 7.3 have grown in this decade at an annual rate of 5.1 per cent and in the last category at an annual rate of 5.2 per cent. The rate of growth of numbers and gross leasable area is also positive for all four categories. Nonetheless, it exhibits far greater variability across the four categories.[30]

Table 7.3   Shopping centers in the 1990s[1]

Type[2]	Neighborhood	Community	Regional	Super-regional
Numbers				
1990	23 231	8 756	1 102	357
2000	45 115	10 958	1 424	410
Gross Leasable Area (GLA) (million of square feet)				
1990	1 125	1 197	618	457
2000	1 383	1 514	790	526
Retail Sales (billions of current dollars)				
1990	205.1	179.5	91.7	77
2000	342.8	300.0	152.8	129.8

Notes:
1. The numbers in the table are from US Statistical Abstract (2001), Table 1045.
2. Neighborhood, are centers with less than 100 001 million square feet of GLA; 'Community' are centers with 100 001–200 000 million square feet of GLA; 'Regional' are centers with 400 001 to 800 000 million square feet; and 'Super-regional' are centers with more than a million square feet. The only category that corresponds exactly to the one used by the Handbook is the neighborhood category.

One can view the expansion of the neighborhood shopping centers as another illustration of the drive toward one-stop shopping and the expansion of assortments that has characterized the supermarket category. Indeed, Messinger and Narasimhan (1997) in the study discussed in section 7.3 use data on the average square footage of shopping centers to estimate one of the relationships suggested by their model of supermarkets, equation (7.13). They obtain a positive relationship between square footage and personal income in a cross-section regression across states of the US. Nevertheless they rightly note as a caveat that in the case of shopping centers there is no single authority controlling the setting of all prices and marketing activities of the individual stores, which is the assumption underlying their model.

What one finds in shopping centers, however, is a single authority (the developer) determining the number and type of stores that are included in the center, the rental prices that the stores are charged, and the provision of common facilities and inputs at given costs. Our discussion of demand in Chapter 3, section 5, brought out how the common distribution services of one retailer are usually gross complements with most of the items in the assortment of other retailers. This feature, which is asymmetric across different retailers, provides one basis for the formation of retail agglomerations on the demand side. In a shopping center setting this implies that a developer who incorporates these considerations in deciding how to allocate space to different tenants can generate higher profits than one who ignores these considerations.

Eppli and Shilling (1995) demonstrate this result in a simple theoretical setting where anchor tenants induce patronage for non-anchor tenants but non-anchor tenants have no effect on the patronage of the anchor tenant. For any given rental rate per square foot for these types of tenants, profit maximization by the developer allocates the quantities of retail space leased to each type by internalizing the patronage effects of the anchor tenant. Furthermore, they show that developers' profits increase with the strength of the patronage (or gross complementarity) effects. Nevertheless, there is no attempt in the literature to estimate directly the gross complementarities generated by the distribution services provided by different stores in a shopping center. There is, however, an ingenious attempt to estimate indirectly the value of the external economies generated by department stores as anchors in regional and super-regional shopping malls.

Pashigian and Gould (1998) start from the assumption that department stores generate mall traffic and, thus, create external economies by indirectly increasing sales and/or reducing promotion costs of smaller mall stores. They then set out to measure the size of these external economies by looking at the rent per square foot paid by various store types. Their data shows department stores leasing space at a median cost of $1.95 per square foot in super-regional malls and $3.00 in regional malls. By way of contrast note that the next category of stores, clothing and accessories, leases space at a median cost of $18.58 per square foot in super-regional malls and $15.42 per square foot in regional malls. A regression explaining median rent per square foot across store types in terms of median sales per square foot and a dummy for department stores leasing space in the mall yields an estimated rent subsidy for the anchors of 81 per cent. Including store size as an additional variable leads to an estimated rent subsidy for the anchor of 72 per cent. The subsidy is interpreted as the compensation paid by the developer for the external economies generated by the department stores.

One difference between super-regional malls and regional malls found by Pashigian and Gould is that the ratio of the median GLA for department stores in the two types of malls is substantially above unity (1.6) while the ratio for other types of store is at or below unity. The ratio of median sales per square foot, however, is barely above unity for department stores and substantially higher for every other type of store. Meanwhile the ratio of median rent per square foot is 0.7 for department stores and at or above unity for every other type, except recreation (0.9). They explain these differences in terms of department store anchors providing greater external economies in super-regional malls than in regional malls.

While Pashigian and Gould don't mention it, their argument implies that recreation activities in malls, especially in super-regional malls, generate external economies as well. Not surprisingly, one of the trends in super-regional malls has been the addition of recreation facilities. One very dramatic example of this trend is the largest mall in the world, West Edmonton Mall, which attained its current size in its third phase of expansion by doubling the size of the mall with the addition of primarily recreation activities.[31] In a study of consumers at three super-regional malls, Bloch, Ridgway and Dawson (1994) identified four types of patrons: the traditionalists and minimalists who go to the mall for multi-purpose or single purpose purchases, respectively, and who comprise 56 per cent of their sample; the enthusiasts who go to the mall for purchasing, usage of the mall and experiential consumption and who comprise 24 per cent of the sample; and, the grazers who go to the mall primarily for experiential consumption but, in so doing, purchase goods and services and who constituted 20 per cent of their sample. Thus, for a substantial group of consumers (44 per cent of them), visiting a super-regional mall entails engaging jointly in consumption and purchasing activities.

By way of a conclusion we consider a study that analyses similarities (and implicitly differences) within and between community centers and regional malls in Calgary and Edmonton. West (1992) argued that community centers or regional malls should be similar in several ways, reflecting that a developer's desire to maximize profits would lead to similar choices at the same level in the shopping center hierarchy. The main difference between these two shopping center categories in West's view was that malls would contain the same type of stores as community centers plus additional store types.

He defined two main store types in both mall and centers as M stores catering to multiple-purpose shoppers on a multiple purpose trip and C stores catering to comparison shoppers on a multiple purpose trip. Examples of the latter would be department stores and clothing stores of various types; examples of the former would be supermarkets and specialty food stores of various types. His main result in the present context is that there is greater similarity among store types between malls than between community centers.[32] Since malls, by definition, start with a full line department store as an anchor whereas community centers, by definition, allow for different types of department stores as anchor, this result is to be expected. The gross complementarities generated by different types of anchors are different and they should also vary in their attractiveness to different types of stores among the non-anchor stores.

NOTES

1. BLS uses a sales measure of output in constant dollars at the three-digit level.
2. This point is conceptually the same as the one made by Ratchford (2003) with respect to assortment, which is cited in our discussion of productivity in Chapter 4. In addition, one should note that Oi's work (1992, Table 4.4) also reveals that this decline in sales per hour did not take place in department stores.

3. The information presented in this paragraph comes from the US Statistical Abstract (2000), Table 1280.

4. Conventional supermarkets are primarily self-service, have a full range of departments and at least 25 million of annual sales in 1985 dollars. Warehouses provide limited product variety, fewer services and incorporate case lot stocking and shelving practices. Superstores contain greater variety of products than conventional, and considerable non-food products. A combination food and drug store contains a pharmacy, a non-prescription drug department and greater variety of health and beauty aids than conventional. A superwarehouse offers expanded product variety and often service meat, deli or seafood departments. Finally, a hypermarket is a very large store offering a greater variety of general merchandise and personal care products than other grocery stores.

5. Incomplete but reliable evidence for this assertion is provided by Leibtag (2002, Table 6). Using the sample of stores that BLS uses to construct the producer price index for food stores in 2000, he finds the following average number of stock keeping units for four of these six categories: Superstores, 63 273; Combination Food and Drug, 108 039; Conventional Supermarket, 34 946; and Warehouses, 21 141.

6. By the way, the source for the earlier figures cited was Oi's work and he took his numbers from the *Progressive Grocer*. The more recent figures cited here are from the US Statistical Abstract. The two sources obviously differ.

7. Demand conditions under which this type of situation arises are discussed in Chapter 3, section 5.

8. Recall from Chapter 2 that the constraint captures the idea of offering the consumer at least as good value as she could obtain at the next best alternative store. Also recall that $Q = Nq$ where N can be interpreted as the number of customers, q is the demand of the representative costumer, r is the shadow price of distribution services and $\in$ is the price elasticity of demand in absolute value.

9. This is consistent with (7.7). For instance, if the price elasticity of demand is constant, a necessary condition for (7.7) to be consistent with a decrease in price when distribution services increase is that there also be declining marginal costs with respect to the quantity of output, $C_{QQ} < 0$.

10. In practice the authors used proxies for input prices (v) such as hourly earnings of workers in grocery stores, real prime interest rate, and a construction price index relative to the consumer price index.

11. p' represents the consumer's wage rate and h and t are the constant marginal costs to the consumer in terms of time of shopping at the non-supermarket and at the supermarket, respectively.

12. The authors estimate an alternative to (7.12) using operating costs as a percentage of sales as the dependent variable. This yields values of 2.24 per cent for the average value of one-stop shopping and 1.56 per cent for the premium.

13. This index was composed of 20 categories and it captured dimensions of four of the five categories of distributions services stressed here, including assortment. For instance, the index gave higher values to stores having bakeries, deli, meat or fish areas with employee assistance. The only distribution service not included was accessibility of location.

14. An increase in accessibility of location from the point of view of the consumer implies a decrease in distance between stores from the point of view of the retailer.

15. Among other differences between their analysis and ours is that they use a specific functional form for the cost function and they differentiate between breadth and depth of assortment while restricting market demand (q) to unity for the products of any one department or category.

16. This follows from the properties of the demand function discussed in Chapter 2 (section 5) and Chapter 3 (section 1).

17. This expression merely affects the size of the denominator in (7.23), which must be positive.

18. The main impact of perfect competition is to make the first term in A zero and to increase the size of the second term in A. Hence, it is not clear whether or not it enlarges or reduces the impact of exogenous changes.

19. Cost complementarities require that the marginal costs of assortment be decreasing in the provision of other distribution services and vice versa.

20. See Chapter 3, section 2, for a definition and discussion of net independent and complements in this context.
21. Along the same lines, one would view accessibility of location as the primary determinant of the demand for convenience.
22. Parenthetically, Proposition 5.4 (Chapter 5, section 4) on the distinction between common and specific distribution services is insightful in this context. It suggests that expanding depth by adding an item to an assortment operates as a specific distribution service while expanding breadth by adding a whole category of items to an assortment operates as a common distribution service. The latter are more likely to exhibit decreasing marginal costs or other features that lead to increasing returns.
23. For example mail order houses were one of the business innovations of the second half of the 19th century (Chandler, 1977).
24. Palmer (1997), for example, argues that the formats represented by catalogue, cable TV and the web are projected to grow 50 times faster than the in-store format.
25. Not comparable means that NAICS sales or receipts can not be estimated within 3 per cent from SIC data.
26. On the other hand, e-commerce sales in 1999 represent 5.3 per cent of total sales by merchant wholesalers (US Statistical Abstract, 2001, Table 1039). That is, they are more than ten times larger than retail sales.
27. In the case of the Internet the merchant would most likely use Federal Express or its equivalent instead of the postal service.
28. The same would be true of the Internet and for similar reasons.
29. This illustrates the jointness of provision among distribution services. In this case between assortment and information.
30. Incidentally, total shopping center retail sales for 2000 reported in Table 1045 represented 38 per cent of total retail sales for 2000 reported elsewhere in the US Statistical Abstract.
31. A fourth phase of expansion was under active consideration in the summer of 2002.
32. This is partly due to the larger presence of multi-chain firms in malls than in community centers. For instance, he finds that the proportion of C store firms that are owned by multi--chain firms in malls is 0.555 while in community centers this proportion is 0.159. Similarly, the proportion of M stores in malls that are owned by multi-chain firms is 0.179 while in community centers it is 0.085.

PART III

Interactions between retailers and other agents

8. Channel issues

Just as indicated in the introduction to the book, in this chapter attention is focused on a subset of interactions between retailers and their suppliers or channel issues in which distribution services play or can play a particularly important role in determining the nature of these interactions. Section 8.1 discusses how the distribution of economic power in a channel can be affected by who controls the level of distribution services. Section 8.2 summarizes recent empirical evidence on the distribution of power in a channel in light of the previous discussion. Section 8.3 considers a dramatic illustration of the exercise of economic power in a channel by a retailer, namely the possible lock-out of Betamax video rentals through the choice of assortment levels by video shops.

Section 8.4 discusses the direct and indirect profit incentives retail firms have to become complex organizations through backward integration, moves into new markets, and the addition of product categories or varieties. Our discussion identifies the role of distribution services in these processes and relates these incentives to the evolution of Wal-Mart and the introduction of private labels or store brands. Finally, section 8.5 indicates how distribution services have been treated by the economics and marketing literature in the context of channel issues. The aim of this section is to illustrate rather than to provide a comprehensive or exhaustive review.

8.1 ECONOMIC POWER IN A CHANNEL[1]

In general economic power is the ability to influence an economic agent's choices in terms of levels and/or margins of outcome variables. In the context of channel activities, for example, one agent has power over another if any decision variable under the control of the former affects the profit levels and/or the profit margins of the latter. Since the choice of a level of distribution service affects the levels of costs and demand of any firm, it follows that control of distribution services by a channel member should in general affect the levels of profits and/or margins experienced by other channel members and, thus, implies the exercise of economic power. If one views distribution services as essential components of marketing strategy, this definition of the exercise of economic power coincides with what the marketing literature labels as channel power. For instance, Stern and El-Ansary (1992) define channel power as 'the ability to control the decision variables in the marketing strategy of another member in a given channel at a different level of distribution. For this control to qualify as power, it should be different from the influenced member's original level of control over his own marketing strategy'.

To illustrate in the simplest possible setting let's assume the standard leader–follower model in a situation of bilateral monopoly. That is, the manufacturer chooses the wholesale price, w, to maximize profits knowing that the retailer is also a profit maximizer who faces a demand function and a cost function. The main difference with the standard model is that the manufacturer knows that the retailer faces a demand function, $Q(p,D)$, and a cost function, $C(Q, D)$, that depend not only on the retail price, p, but also on a distribution service, D. Furthermore, the retail price and the level of the distribution service are both assumed to be under the control of the retailer. The manufacturer's problem is choosing w to maximize profits, π_M, given by

$$\pi_M = w\, Q(p, D) - \psi[Q(p, D)], \qquad (8.1)$$

where $\psi[Q(p, D)]$ is the manufacturer's cost function.

Under the usual assumption of the standard leader–follower model, the manufacturer has full information on the retailer's choices. Therefore, demand can be written as a composite function of the wholesale price and (8.1) becomes

$$\pi_M = w\, Q\{p\,(w), D(w)\} - \psi[Q\{p(w), D(w)\}]. \qquad (8.2)$$

Hence, the value of w that maximizes (8.2) follows from the first-order condition that yields, after some manipulation, the following expression for the manufacturer's price–cost margin

$$w - \psi_Q = -Q/Q_p\{(\partial p^*/\partial w) + (Q_D/Q_p)(\partial D^*/\partial w)\}.^2 \qquad (8.3)$$

The retailer's problem can be written as

$$\pi_R = (p - w)\, Q\,(p, D) - C[Q(p, D), D], \qquad (8.4)$$

which is the special case of (2.9) that applies to a monopolist, that is, when $\mu = 0$ in (2.9). From the first-order conditions we obtain the retailer's price–cost margin as

$$p - w - C_Q = -Q/Q_p. \qquad (8.5)$$

Finally, at each optimum, the ratio of retailer's to manufacturer's price–cost margins is

$$\rho = (p - w - C_Q)/(w - \psi_Q) = (\partial p^*/\partial w) + (Q_D/Q_p)(\partial D^*/\partial w). \quad (8.6)$$

Not surprisingly, the first point to make is that if distribution services are constant, $(\partial D^*/\partial w)$ is identically zero and this ratio collapses to $\rho = (\partial p^*/\partial w)$. That is, it collapses to the standard result in the literature for bilateral monopoly without distribution services. A more subtle result is contained in the second point to be made. Namely, if distribution services are subject to choice but under the control of the manufacturer, Betancourt and Gautschi (1998) show, using the same analysis as above, that this ratio also collapses to $\rho = (\partial p^*/\partial w)$. The reason is simple. In the standard leader–follower bilateral monopoly model the manufacturer already has the maximum amount of relative power available in the channel. Thus, in contrast to the retailer's case, giving the manufacturer additional power through the control of the distribution service is redundant with respect to affecting relative power in the channel.

In the standard leader–follower bilateral monopoly model without distribution services the ratio of profit margins depends on the nature of retail demand and retailer's costs (for example Tirole, 1988). The same is true in the more general case underlying expression (8.6) here. For instance, if we let demand be linear and additive as in $Q = a + bp + cD$, where $a > 0$, $b < 0$, and $c > 0$, and costs be linear and constant in output, Q, but convex in distribution services, D, (8.6) becomes

$$\rho = 1/\{2 + [c^2/C_{DD}\, b]\} > 1/2. \quad (8.7)$$

If distribution services are constant, do not exist, or are not valued by consumers, $c = 0$ and (8.7) becomes equal to 1/2. Thus, the existence of a distribution service controlled by a retailer increases the monopoly power of the retailer relative to the manufacturer compared to a situation where the distribution service does not exist, is constant or is controlled by the manufacturer. Moreover, the example illustrates that the more the consumer values distribution services (higher c), the greater the relative power of the retailer in terms of profit margins.

Similarly if we let demand be concave in prices and convex in distribution services, as in $Q = a\, p^b D^c$ where $a > 0$, $b < -1$, and $0 < c < 1$, while assuming constant marginal costs in both dimensions, (Q, D), (8.6) becomes

$$\rho = \partial p^*/\partial w + (cp/bD)(\partial D^*/\partial w), \quad (8.8)$$

where $\partial p^*/\partial w = [1/H][-Q^2 c(c-1)/s^2] > 0$ and $\partial D^*/\partial w = [1/H][Q^2 c(b+1)/pD] < 0.$[3] Once again if distributions services are constant, do not exist or are not valued by consumers, $c = 0$ and the second term in (8.8) becomes zero instead of taking a positive value. Thus, in this case it will also be true that the existence of a distribution service controlled by the retailer increases the power of the retailer relative to the manufacturer compared to situations in which these services do not exist, are constant or are controlled by the manufacturer. Furthermore, it is also the case here that the more the consumer values distribution services (higher c), the greater the relative power of the retailer in terms of profit margins.

One question frequently asked of bilateral monopoly models is what happens to the levels of the variables relative to the vertically integrated solution. It is easy to show that profits will always be at least as high in the vertically integrated solution as in bilateral monopoly. For the vertically integrated firm can choose whatever values of retail prices and distribution services it wants to operate at, including the ones chosen by the retailer and manufacturer in the bilateral monopoly. The retailer and the manufacturer, on the other hand, are always constrained in their choices because they either don't control both variables or must use a suboptimal decision (from their point of view) by the other one as an input in their own decision making.

What happens to the level of prices and distribution services relative to the integrated solution, however, is less easy to ascertain. It turns out that one can obtain definite results by assuming functional forms for demand and costs. Assuming the same functional forms for demand as above, that is, either linear or a power function, and similarly simple forms for costs, leads to higher levels of retail prices and higher levels of distributions services under bilateral monopoly than in the vertically integrated solution.[4] While producers always benefit from the vertically integrated structure, consumers receive mixed benefits in some circumstances due to lower prices, which increase welfare, and lower levels of distributions services, which decrease welfare, prevailing in the integrated structure. Thus, the introduction of distribution services into the analysis can be shown to lower the benefits of vertical integration for consumers.[5]

To conclude this section, mention should be made of an insightful paper by Lal and Narasimhan (1996). In that paper the model underlying Lal and Matutes (1994), which was discussed in Chapter 5, section 6, is augmented by introducing explicitly a monopolist manufacturer for one of the two goods, namely the one for which retailers must advertise to attract customers to the store. In one equilibrium, where a Stackelberg leader monopolist manufacturer provides information through advertising to consumers, Lal and Narasimhan show that the margin for the manufacturer increases, while the margin for the retailers decreases. That is, this result illustrates how the provision of a distribution service by the manufacturer clearly shifts the distribution of economic power in his/her favor.

Of course the result does not hold under all circumstances. For instance, it applies only to the margins of the good being advertised by the retailer; similarly, it requires the existence of another good so that there is an incentive for one-stop shopping; finally, the information provided by the manufacturer must increase consumers' demand for the product advertised. But it is robust to some extensions, for example the introduction of competition among manufacturers. More generally, their results show that Stackelberg leadership by a manufacturer is not sufficient for control of distribution services by manufacturers to have no impact on the channel's distribution of economic power. Lal and Narasimhan's finding implies that this result requires the absence of multiproduct retailers.

8.2   EMPIRICAL EVIDENCE ON CHANNEL POWER

Equation (8.6) can be used as an initial starting point for the design of empirical work or the interpretation of empirical results addressing the issue of relative economic power in the channel. Note that one would expect from the first equality on the RHS of (8.6) that the ratio of margins would be affected by the level of competition among retailers (negatively) and by the level of competition among manufacturers (positively). Similarly, factors that decrease the marginal costs of retailing relative to manufacturing, for example scanners, should affect this ratio positively. If we impose the structure of the bilateral monopoly model captured in the second equality on the RHS of (8.6), one would expect, in addition, that an increase in distribution services controlled by the retailers, for example information or assurance, should affect this ratio (positively). If these services are controlled by manufacturers, however, they should have no effect on this ratio for single-product retailers, or perhaps lower it for multiproduct retailers in view of the results discussed at the end of the previous section.

At least three very different approaches have been employed to investigate empirically the issue of economic power in a channel. One approach has concentrated on the food industry or the grocery channel and has relied on regression analysis of time series data. For example, Messinger and Narasimhan (1995) use as dependent variables operating return on assets of retailers, of manufacturers and the ratio of manufacturers' prices to retailers' prices over the period 1961–87. Each of these dependent variables is explained in terms of measures of manufacturer and retailer concentration, scanner adoption, new product introduction and number of items carried per store. Their best equation (in terms of variables with statistically significant coefficients) is the one explaining the operating return on assets of manufacturers. It is the only one where manufacturers' (retailers') concentration ratios are positive (negative) and statistically significant at the 5 per cent level. The only other statistically significant variable in any equation is the adoption of scanners, which is negative and statistically significant at the 5 per cent level in this equation and in the price ratios equation.

Based on these results the authors conclude that there is no evidence of power in the channel shifting in favor of retailers, which has been a frequent assertion in the popular press over the last 20 years.[6] These results also suggest, from our point of view, that the model underlying the second equality in (8.6) with the manufacturer as a Stackelberg leader is consistent with the data, since the number of new products, which generates a dimension of distribution services (assortment) controlled by manufacturers, has no effect on operating returns on assets. These results also suggest, however, that the model underlying the second equality in (8.6) is not consistent with the data, for the number of items per store is a measure of a dimension of assortment controlled by the retailer and it has no effect on the operating returns on assets of either retailers or manufacturers.[7]

More recently Kapinos (2002) has revisited the issue of economic power in the grocery channel. He points out that the data on operating returns on assets of retailers used by Messinger and Narasimhan was compiled by Robert Morris Associates and included accounting data only from companies with total assets below 100 million dollars, which excluded large grocery chains. To correct for this problem, Kapinos' calculates his profitability measures from data collected by the Food Marketing Institute Operations Review. Kapinos' other contribution is to use a somewhat clever procedure to calculate the retailer's profit (RP) as a share (RSP) of channel profits, that is, $RSP = RP/CP$, in terms of operating margins and retail margins expressed as a percentage of sales.[8]

RSP is Kapinos' dependent variable. He explains this variable in terms of manufacturers' concentration, retailers' concentration, shares of private labels in total sales, number of new products and products per selling area. His preferred results come from considering all retailers and all manufacturers of food products. He estimates this relationship with data from 1980 to 2000 and finds statistically significant relationships (at the 1 per cent level) for manufacturers' concentration (negative), share of private labels (positive), and number of new products (positive). He also finds a statistically significant relationship at the 10 per cent level for products per selling area (positive) and no relationship at any reasonable level for retailers' concentration.[9]

Kapinos also runs a regression in which his dependent variable is the share of profits of the small retailers (that is the ones used by Messinger and Narasimhan (1995)). Manufacturer concentration and share of private labels continue to be statistically significant at the 1 per cent level and with the same signs, number of products and products per selling area no longer matter but retailer concentration becomes statistically significant (at the 1 per cent level) with a negative sign. He uses this last result to argue that power has shifted to the big retailers and that the retailers' concentration measure in this second regression is capturing the lack of power of the small retailers.[10]

From our point of view, his results are consistent with what we expect to find from (8.6) for manufacturers' concentration, and the share of private labels. The latter can be viewed as an increase in a distribution service by a retailer, namely the depth of assortment, and thus it has the expected positive sign. We would have expected the number of products introduced to either have a negative effect or to have no effect if the manufacturer is a Stackelberg leader.[11] This is consistent with Kapinos' result for the second equation but not for the first one. Similarly, we would have expected the number of products per selling area to have a positive effect since it represents an increase in a dimension of a distributions service controlled by the retailer. This is consistent with Kapinos' result for the first equation but not with the result for the second one.

Incidentally, one difficult problem with implementing (8.6) is that it refers to profits at the margin and the latter require measures of marginal costs, which are notoriously difficult to obtain. Both Messinger and Narasimhan and Kapinos rely on measuring average profits rather than marginal profits.[12] The same problem would seem to affect the next empirical approach to the issue of power in the channel, but we argue below that in the context of their performance measures it becomes irrelevant. Ailawadi, Borin and Farris (1995) extend the empirical analysis in two different ways: first, by including industries other than the food industry and, second, by introducing new measures of profits.

One of these measures is what the business press calls economic value added (EVA) and corresponds to what academics call abnormal or economic profits. In practice it is measured as $EVA = S - C(R) - C(GS) - C(\text{Capital})$. It can be expressed as a proportion of sales, in which case $EVA/S = ROM - C(\text{Capital})/S$. The practical difficulty here is to measure the cost of capital ($C(\text{Capital})$), which the authors do as the sum of interest expense adjusted for its tax deductibility and the estimated cost of equity. The latter is defined as the book value of equity times a risk adjusted rate, which is calculated based on the Capital Asset Pricing Model. The other measure is closely related to this one, namely, Market Value Added or MVA which is defined as the discounted value of the sum of expected EVA from the present period to the end of the planning horizon. In practice, it is measured as the difference between the market value of the firm and its book value in any particular period. Conceptually, EVA aims to capture exercised economic power and MVA aims to capture potential economic power.

In so far as fixed costs play an important and differential role in determining profits for manufacturers and retailers, these new measures provide information on power in the channel that is not contained in the marginal measures that define equation (8.6). Thereby they should be viewed as complements to earlier measures rather than as substitutes. Just like the measures used in previous studies, they are not designed to capture marginal costs; but in contrast to these measures they should not be viewed as approximations to the price–cost margin. Just as illustrated in section 8.1, the exercise of power in a channel affects decisions in terms of margins and in terms of levels.[13] These last two measures are particularly suited to capture effects on levels of profits.

In any event the authors' calculations for 14 consumer goods industries over the period 1982 to 1992 generate a number of interesting findings.[14] By and large EVA for manufacturers exhibits a positive trend while EVA for retailers does not. This is true and statistically significant (at the 5 per cent level) for the aggregate of all retailers, for the food industry by itself and for five of the other consumer goods industries in the sample. Furthermore in the remaining eight industries the trend in EVA for manufacturers is negative and statistically significant in only one (computers). There is no positive and statistically significant trend in EVA for any retailers. The results for MVA, however, are quite different. While the trend for manufacturers is positive and statistically significant for 12 of 14 industries, the trend for retailers is also positive and statistically significant in 14 of 14 industries. Moreover, in a substantial number of industries (nine) retailers seem to be better off relative to manufacturers in terms of the magnitude of their trend in MVA. Once Wal-Mart is eliminated from the sample, however, this number is reduced to three.

To sum up, in terms of actual power there is no evidence of a shift in power toward retailers at the industry level; in terms of potential power there is not much of a shift once Wal-Mart is excluded.[15] Furthermore, the logic underlying the actual measurement of MVA relies on the efficient capital markets hypothesis which is a controversial hypothesis. Therefore, this suggests caution in interpreting results based on this measure.

A third empirical approach to the issue of economic power in a channel is best exemplified by Kadiyali, Chintagunta and Vilcassim (2000) (hereafter KCV). This study differs from previous ones in that it looks at firm-level data rather than industry-level data, it focuses on estimating the profit margins of retailers and manufacturers, and it imposes far more economic structure on the estimation than the previous approaches. While it can say nothing about shifts in economic power, it does find convincing evidence of substantial retailer power, judging by their estimated share of marginal channel profits. One potential extension, pointed out by the authors, is to include strategic variables besides prices in the analysis, for example, some distribution services such as information provided through advertising.

Their analysis focuses on two case studies. It looks at the interactions between Dominick's Finer Foods as the retailer and three manufacturers of canned tuna (where the private label has no significant market share) and two manufacturers of refrigerated juices (where the private label has a significant market share). One way to think of their study in relation to previous ones is as follows. While equation (8.6) represents a reduced form (the first equality) or a semi-reduced form (the second equality), KCV set out to estimate two types of structural forms in each market: one for the retail mark-up, $r_i = [p_i - w_i - C_Q]$ for each brand and one for the manufacturer's mark-up for each brand $[w_i - \psi_{Q(i)}]$. These forms are derived from the first-order conditions for profit maximization with the latter restricted to include only within-category considerations. This estimation was undertaken under the assumption that the marginal costs of retailing (C_Q) were zero. It also required specification of the demand functions for each brand. In all eight equations were estimated for refrigerated juice and nine for tuna (no need to estimate a manufacturer's mark-up equation for the private label).

An ingenious feature of the estimation was the specification of response functions in the mark-up equations. Since p_i can be written as $r_i + w_i$, the authors define $\partial p_j / \partial w_i$ as $1 + \partial r_i / \partial w_i = 1 + \theta (r_i, w_i)$ for same brand and $\theta (p_j, w_i)$ for other brands in the manufacturers' equations. Similarly, they define $\partial p_j / \partial r_i$ as $1 + \partial w_i / \partial r_i = 1 + \theta (r_i, w_i)$ for same brand and $\theta (w_j, r_i)$ for other brands in the retailer's equation. These parameters can capture a wide range of interactions between retailers and manufacturers, corresponding to different pricing games.[16]

In any event their main results are that the retailer's share of channel profits relative to each manufacturer is well above 50 per cent in both markets and for all manufacturers. These results suggest substantial retailer power in that all estimates of ρ are greater than unity. The theoretical analysis underlying section 8.1 suggests that for single product retailers with linear demand curves, linear or convex costs, no distribution services and bilateral monopoly interactions ρ would be less than or equal to 1/2!

To conclude, empirical research on the distribution of power in a channel is at an early stage of development. Continued progress requires that clear distinctions be made on whether one is focusing on margins or levels of outcome variables. Distribution services affect outcomes whenever they are included in the analysis. Hence, regardless of the empirical approach, a systematic effort at introducing these services offers a promising avenue for future research.

8.3   RETAILER LOCK-OUT? VHS VERSUS BETAMAX

One dramatic way of exercising power is by driving a product out of existence. If Goldsmith (2002) is correct in his arguments, it was the exercise of economic power by retailers through their control of a distribution service, the level of assortment, that led to the demise of the Betamax video cassette recorder. He quotes a Walt Disney spokesman to this effect 'As long as there is a market we'll provide (the movies). A lot of stores only carry VHS, but it's not for a lack of us providing the product.' Before providing the details of the argument it is useful to note the broader context in which this issue arises.[17]

The disappearance of the Betamax recorder has become one of the two most famous examples of lock-in the economics literature. It is also quite controversial. Supporters of lock-in are said to argue that VHS ended up as the only player in the market, despite its technological inferiority, due to the incompatibility of tapes for the two recorders and the existence of network effects. Opponents of lock-in argue that the inferiority of VHS was a 'fable', since the VHS recorder was able to tape longer than the Betamax, even if its image was not as good in terms of quality.[18] Furthermore, the network effects in the case of VHS versus Betamax occur through the extent of adoptions of a complementary product, the movie cassette, and, thus, are indirect network effects.[19] A small empirical literature has tried to measure indirect network effects in other settings and the effects they find are too weak to generate lock-in. In view of these arguments, Goldsmith (2002) sets out to find an alternative explanation for the disappearance of the Betamax recorder.

Goldsmith (2002, Chapter 3) develops a simple profit maximizing model of assortment choice by a video store and extends it to account for competition, the existence of multiple platforms or cassette recorder types, platform fixed costs and capacity constraints. Consumers are of two types: those who own type A of video cassette recorder and those who own type B.[20] Type A consumers, for example, derive utility from increases in the variety or assortment, S, of movies of type A that are available to them at the store, but they don't care about the variety of type B movies. Similarly for type B. Consumers of both types are uniformly distributed along a line of unit length which has one store (1, 2) located at each end. The stores carry both platforms or types of video rentals.

For a type A consumer at x to patronize store 1, $U_{1A} > U_{2A}$, where $U_{1A} = (S_{1A})^{\sigma} - tx - p$ and $U_{2A} = (S_{2A})^{\sigma} - t(1 - x) - p$. U^* is the consumer's reservation utility so that if both U_{1A} and U_{2A} are less that U^*, the consumer will not go to either video store. σ is a parameter between zero and unity that introduces diminishing returns to variety. t is the per unit travel cost and p is the price of the video rental. The value of x that makes the consumer of type A indifferent between the assortment and travel choices implied by the patronage of either store is $x_{1A} = [(S_{1A})^\sigma - (S_{2A})^\sigma + t]/2t$. Assuming that all consumers will choose a video store in equilibrium, this is also the share of consumers of type A choosing retailer 1.

On the retailers' side the choices are the assortments or variety levels provided for each platform as a result of maximizing profits,[21] which are given for store 1 by $\Pi_1 = M_{1A} N_A x_{1A} + M_{1B} N_B x_{1B} - C(S_{1A} + S_{1B})$, where M is the profit margin $(p - c)$ per transaction and c is the marginal cost of a transaction. N is the density of types and C is the cost per item of carrying inventory. Goldsmith obtains optimal expressions for assortment for each type of platform and for each store, assuming the levels of assortments of the other store are fixed. The important point in our context is that if one assumes platforms have fixed costs, for example F_{1A}, F_{1B}, the profit function for store 1, for example, can be evaluated at its optimal values for each platform and it yields (a similar expression will hold for the other store in equilibrium due to symmetry):

$$\Pi_1{}^* = \Pi_{1A}{}^* + \Pi_{1B}{}^* = [M_{1A} N_A x_{1A}{}^* - CS_{1A}{}^* - F_{1A}]$$
$$+ [M_{1B} N_B x_{1B}{}^* - CS_{1B}{}^* - F_{1B}]. \tag{8.9}$$

If a store cannot make profits on a platform, it will abandon this platform. This will be more likely the higher the fixed costs of a platform due to the need for different layouts and displays as well as additional dividers and identifiers. It will also be more likely the smaller the number of consumers supporting a type or platform, the lower the margin and the higher the carrying costs. Nonetheless, the argument thus far would suggest lock-out to be a rare event. Goldsmith, however, adds capacity constraints to this model. This is reasonable since empty shelf space is not a frequent sight in video stores.[22] He then shows that in addition to the need to cover the fixed costs of the platform you also have to cover the opportunity costs of the profits lost from selling items through the other platform. This consideration makes lock-out of one of the two platforms by a retailer far more likely to happen.

8.4   INCENTIVES FOR EXPANSION: BACKWARD INTEGRATION, WAL-MART AND PRIVATE LABELS[23]

A retail enterprise has a profit incentive for backward integration. This can be shown using the simple monopolistic competition model developed in Chapter 2, section 4. Equations (2.4) to (2.6) can be rewritten, respectively, as

$$\pi = pQ - C(V, Q, D) - wQ \tag{8.10}$$
$$p - w - p\mathbb{E} - C_Q = 0 \tag{8.11}$$
$$p\delta_j - S_j\, C/Q = 0, \qquad j = 1, \ldots J, \tag{8.12}$$

where (8.12) allows for more than one distribution service in the profit maximization. Note that $S_j = C_j\, D_j/C$ or the elasticity of costs with respect to the jth distribution service, $\delta_j = \partial p/\partial D_j\, (D_j/p)$ or the reciprocal of the elasticity of demand with respect to distribution services and $\mathbb{E} = - \partial p/\partial Q\, (Q/p)$ is the absolute value of the reciprocal of the price elasticity of demand $(0 < \mathbb{E} < 1)$.

Activities that lower w, the price at which the retailer obtains the explicit product from either wholesalers or manufacturers, will increase the retailer's profit. This follows directly from (8.10), which always increases as a result of a decrease in w. This is a direct and powerful profit incentive for backward integration by a retailer. For instance, if there is any type of double marginalization in a channel, a retailer that has the ability to supply to herself the explicit product at marginal cost can always improve her profit situation relative to the existing channel.[24]

In addition there are indirect profit incentives for backward integration as a result of the adjustments the firm can make after the change in w. Whatever adjustments the firm makes afterwards must increase profits, because the firm always has the option of continuing operations at previous levels of the decision variables. Suppose distribution services are given ((8.12) is irrelevant) after a decrease in the wholesale price, the retail firm can increase profits further by adjusting to a lower w through an increase in Q and, thus, lowering price until (8.11) holds again in the new situation. What has been ignored in the literature is that the existence of distribution services also provides indirect profit incentives for backward integration. Suppose now that the quantity of the explicit product (Q) is given ((8.11) is irrelevant); after a change in w (8.12) is unlikely to hold at the original optimal levels of distribution services (before the change in w). Therefore, the retail firm will be able to increase profits further by adjusting distribution services until (8.12) holds again in the new situation, namely with the lower w. In practice, of course, the retail firm will use both instruments, the quantity of the explicit product (Q) and the quantity of distribution services (D_j), to adjust to a change in w.

Can we say anything about the strength of these indirect profit incentives for backward integration as a result of the existence of distribution services? With a bit of additional effort, the answer is, yes. By adding up the marginal conditions for distribution services and using the long-run equilibrium condition in monopolistic competition, $p - w = C/Q$, we obtain

$$[p\Sigma\delta_j - (C/Q)\Sigma S_j] = \{p[\Sigma\delta_j - \Sigma S_j] + w\Sigma S_j\} = 0. \tag{8.13}$$

It follows from the second equality that $dp/dw = -\Sigma S_j/[\Sigma\delta_j - \Sigma S_j] > 0$. Thus, the process of entry and exit of firms after backward integration, if successful in lowering w, leads to a lowering of price in equilibrium. Furthermore, the size of the potential profits from backward integration that can be eliminated by the entry and exit process will be larger, other things being equal, the greater are economies of scale in the provision of distribution services (the smaller is ΣS_j), which is a common phenomenon,[25] and the greater the consumers' valuation of the distribution services (the greater $\Sigma\delta_j$). That is, $\partial[dp/dw]/\partial[\Sigma S_j] < 0$ and $\partial[dp/dw]/\partial[\Sigma\delta_j] > 0$. Thus, economies of scale in the provision of distribution services and high valuation of these services by consumers provide additional profit incentives for backward integration by retailers.

Similar forces are at work in providing profit opportunities for moves into new geographical markets. That is, profits from operating in two markets will be given by

$$\pi = p_1 Q_1 + p_2 Q_2 - C(V, Q_1, Q_2, D) - w_1 Q_1 - w_2 Q_2, \qquad (8.14)$$

and the profits from moving into the second market will be given by

$$[p_2 - w_2]Q_2 - \{C^T(V, Q_1, Q_2, D) - C(V, Q, D)\}. \qquad (8.15)$$

As long as the increase in net revenues $(p - w)$ from the second market is larger than the increase in costs from operating a second market, the retail firm has a direct profit incentive to move into new markets. Indeed, if the two markets are identical with respect to demand and cost conditions and there are constant returns to scale with respect to turnover, $C^T(V, Q_1, Q_2, D) = 2C(V, Q, D)$. Hence, if it pays the firm to operate in the first market it will always pay the firm to operate in the second market.

Furthermore there will also be indirect profit incentives to operate in the second market once the firm is allowed to adjust to the new equilibrium by choosing optimal levels of the quantities of explicit products and distribution services under its control. The first-order conditions become

$$p_i - w_i - p_i \in_{ii} - C_i = 0, \qquad i,k = 1,2, \text{ and} \qquad (8.16)$$

$$p_1 \delta_{1j} + p_2 \delta_{2j}(Q_2/Q_1) - S_j C^T(V, Q_1, Q_2, D)/Q_1 = 0, \qquad j = 1, \ldots J, \qquad (8.17)$$

Since we are assuming geographically separate markets, $\in_{ki} = 0$, that is, there are no demand interdependencies between the markets. Suppose one adds the first-order conditions with respect to distribution services, assumes constant returns to scale with respect to turnover ($C^T = 2C$) and $Q_2 = Q_1$. Then, if one imposes the long-run equilibrium condition in each market $\{[p_i - w_i] = C(V, Q_i, D)/Q_i\}$, one gets

$$[p_1 \Sigma \delta_{1j} + (p_2 \Sigma \delta_{2j})(Q_2/Q_1) - (C^T/Q_1)\Sigma S_j] = 2\{p_i[\Sigma \delta_j - \Sigma S_j] + w_i \Sigma S_j\} = 0. \qquad (8.18)$$

Hence, whatever indirect profit incentives the firm has in the first market, it will experience the same incentives in the second market.

Last but not least, the same forces provide profit incentives for retail firms to expand their assortments by adding additional product lines and additional varieties within their product lines. For simplicity of exposition let us consider first adding different product lines or categories. Our analysis of demand in Chapter 3 suggests that gross complementarities prevail in this case or at best categories are gross independent so we are justified in continuing to assume that $\in_{ki} = 0$.[26] In this case, the analysis goes through as in the case of two markets. First, as long as the increase in net revenues from the second product line is larger than the increase in costs from adding the second product line, the retail firm has a direct profit incentive to add the second product line just as before. That is (8.15) holds and we simply interpret the second market as a second product. Second, the indirect profit incentive will be similar to what we found with respect to the second geographical market in (8.18), which in turn resembled what we found with respect to backward integration in (8.13). Nonetheless, there will be a difference in practice.

According to (8.13) economies of scale in the provision of distribution services lead to additional profit incentives for backward integration and the same would be the case with respect to adding an additional product or market. The practical difference stems from the fact that, up to this point, we have made no argument on behalf of the existence of economies of scale in the provision of distribution services as a result of backward integration or moving into a new geographical area. When we come to adding a new product, however, the existence of fixed costs in the provision of many distribution services makes it obvious that there are likely to be considerable returns to scale as a result of unused cash registers or cashiers, storage space, parking lots, and so on.

Basic but powerful incentives for expansion in three different dimensions (backward integration, new markets and new products) highlight the pressures on retail firms to become complex organizations. Furthermore these three dimensions lie at the heart of one of the most important phenomena illustrating this process in twentieth century retailing, namely the evolution of Wal-Mart into the biggest retailer in the world. Let's consider the incentive to add more product categories just discussed in more detail. We saw in Chapter 5 that expansions of breadth of assortment (Proposition 5.4) lead to the expansions of other common distribution services (for example accessibility of location) and lower prices.[27] These associations explain two fundamental characteristics underlying Wal-Mart's expansion. One of them, the incentive to add new product categories and offer lower prices, is captured succinctly in a recent somewhat uncomplimentary book on Sam Walton, Wal-Mart's founder. Ortega (1998) writes 'But really, the fundamental credo was simpler: Offer the lowest price. . . . Make your profit by selling more goods, instead of selling goods for more.'

Low prices and broad assortments have been a feature of Wal-Mart from its inception in the 1960s. Similarly, other common distribution services have been emphasized since the beginning, for example, extended hours and accessibility of location through expansion into geographically separate but nearby markets.[28] In particular, expansion into geographically separate but almost contiguous markets was the result of strategy not of random events. Indeed, in 1981 Walton is quoted as saying 'We have more retail stores in a tighter geographical area than any other retail chain' (Vance and Scott, 1994, Chapter 4). Part of the reason for emphasizing nearby markets was saving money while meeting the need to resupply stores quickly and to keep inventory levels down. The expansion process into new markets, while preserving the basic business format, was the main mechanism in creating a national discount chain (Vance and Scott, 1994, Chapter 5) and the addition of new product categories in the 1980s was the main mechanism in creating the world's largest retailer by the early 1990s (Vance and Scott, 1994, Chapters 6 and 8).

Finally, one of four factors cited recently for Wal-Mart's advantages over other large scale retailers is cost-conscious 'corporate culture' (Basker, 2002). This is not a new phenomenon. In 1984 an officer in a supplier firm remarked (Vance and Scott, 1994, Chapter 4), about Wal-Mart buyers 'They'll drive as hard a deal as anyone anywhere.' Not surprisingly, a recent study of the employment effects of Wal-Mart expansion over the period 1977–98 finds that wholesale employment in a county declines by 35 jobs over the long run after a Wal-Mart store enters a county (Basker, 2002). Wal-Mart substitutes for wholesalers in two different ways. First, part of its advantage over competitors is the use of superior logistics, distribution and inventory control, but these are all functions that are performed by wholesalers in other settings. Second, Wal-Mart has engaged in sufficient backward integration that Basker (2002) offers as one explanation of the decline in wholesale employment that it is a vertically integrated firm. This aspect of Wal-Mart's experience illustrates the third dimension of our profit incentives for expansion by retail firms.

Consider now expansion by a retail firm through the addition of new varieties within a product category. Even in this case empirical work often finds relationships of gross complementarity or independence (just as indicated in note 26), in which case the same analysis as in the addition of product categories applies.

Nevertheless, what is unique to this situation is that a relation gross substitutability may apply that diminishes, but is far from eliminating, the profit incentives to add new varieties relative to the profit incentives to add new product categories.

Profits in the new situation are given by (8.14) and the change in profits is given by a new version of (8.15), namely

$$[p_2 - w_2]Q_2 + [p_1 - w_1]\Delta Q_1 - \{C^T(V, Q_1, Q_2, D) - C(V, Q, D)\}. \quad (8.15)'$$

The new term, $[p_1 - w_1]\Delta Q_1$, captures the change in profits generated by the old variety as a result of the introduction of the new variety, evaluated at the new retail and wholesale prices for the old variety. It will be zero if the new and existing varieties are gross independents, negative if gross substitutes, and positive if gross complements. It will also be zero if we assume that there is no quantity adjustment to the introduction of the new variety. More generally, however, (8.15)' captures the direct profit incentive of introducing a new variety given no change in the profit margin of the existing variety.

Once again there will be indirect profit incentives to add the new variety once the firm is allowed to adjust by choosing optimal levels of the quantity of explicit products and distribution services under its control. The first-order condition for the explicit product is adjusted as follows

$$p_i - w_i - p_i \in_{ii} + p_k \in_{ki} (Q_2/Q_1) - C_i = 0, \qquad i, k = 1, 2, \text{ and } i \neq k. \quad (8.16)'$$

Note that if $\in_{ki} > 0$ the goods are gross substitutes. The first-order condition for distribution services remains the same as in the case of adding a product category or a new market (8.17). Therefore, compared to adding a product category, adding a new variety that is a gross substitute for an existing variety lowers the direct profit incentive to expand, because less of the old variety will be sold at the initial retail price. In addition, it will also lower the indirect profit incentive to expand because there will be a lowering of the retail price of the existing variety. Furthermore, with respect to the indirect profit incentive provided by the existence of distribution services this will also be attenuated, relative to adding a product category, because the impact on demand of distribution services is likely to be smaller and the scale economies in adding a variety are also likely to be smaller.

By the way of a conclusion, it is useful to illustrate the application of these ideas to the analysis of private labels or store brands. Conceptually, the introduction of private labels or store brands is a response to two of the three incentives for expansion faced by retail firms. First, it is a response to the incentive for backward integration. Suppose that the private label were to replace a national brand completely. Then (8.15)' and (8.14) collapse to (8.10) and the incentives to introduce the private label are the same as the incentives toward backward integration.[29] In particular, the greater the mark-up or profits embedded in the wholesale price, w, the greater the direct profit incentive to integrate backwards through the use of a store brand. Similarly, the greater the consumer's valuation of distribution services and the greater the degree of economies of scale in their provision, the greater the indirect profit incentives to introduce the private label.

Second, it is a response to the incentive to expand by adding an additional variety within a product category. Suppose the private label is an addition to existing national brands in a category. In this case, the direct profit incentive is attenuated by the diminished retailer profit from the existing brands. By how much will depend on whether demand increases as a result of the additional variety.[30] On the other hand, the increase in retailing costs from the introduction of the additional variety is likely to be small. In particular, the existence of fixed costs that can be spread over additional varieties in a product category makes it more profitable to introduce additional varieties, including the store brand. Furthermore, even in the case of gross substitutes the indirect profit incentive is likely to be greater the greater the valuation of distribution services, especially those specific to the category, and the greater the degree of economies of scale in providing these services.

Private labels have been around for a long time. Indeed, a standard reference on the subject, Fitzell (1998), convincingly argues (Chapter 1) that they existed prior to the creation of national brands in the late 19th century. Yet, this source also argues (Chapter 12) that private labels emerge as an industry in the late 1970s with the creation of a trade association, Private Labels Manufacturers Association (PLMA), and the launching of a trade magazine. In any event, Sayman, Hoch and Raju (2002) note that private labels and store brands have been ignored in the literature until recently and that they are quantitatively important, for example 20 per cent of unit sales in supermarkets.

These authors (SHR) go on to do a theoretical and empirical analysis of the positioning of store brands. In one empirical study they find that, if the store brand targets an existing brand, the targeted brand is the leading national brand.[31] Our analysis of the direct incentive for backward integration would lead to this conclusion if the leading national brand has the greater profit mark-up in the wholesale price it offers the retailer. Furthermore, if consumers' valuation of the distribution services associated with this brand (information about product characteristics for example) are higher than for other brands, the indirect incentive for backward integration would also lead the retailer to have the store brand target the leading national brand. In a second empirical study, they estimated cross-price elasticities (and cross-price effects) within a category for 19 product categories where store brands were classified as high quality on the basis of prior research and expert opinion. They found higher values for the cross terms involving store brands and national brands than for any of the other comparisons in the categories where the store brands were classified as high quality. This can be explained in terms of the same incentives for backward integration as before.

On the other hand, their lack of similar robust results for the low-quality store brands can be interpreted in terms of our analysis as indicative of the existence of an alternative profit incentive for expansion, namely, the addition of product varieties that appeal to different consumer segments or that are not very costly to produce and retail given the existing ones and the distribution services necessary to offer them. Incidentally, one would expect distribution services to play a role, probably a different one, in determining outcomes in both cases, but the authors don't incorporate variables that can be viewed as proxy for these services in their analysis.

8.5   DISTRIBUTION SERVICES AND THE ECONOMICS AND MARKETING LITERATURE ON CHANNEL ISSUES

There are two related strands of literature in industrial organization where the dimensions we have identified as distribution services have received some attention either directly, indirectly or both.[32] The first of these strands is the vertical integration literature. For instance, in Perry's (1989) survey of this topic for the Handbook of Industrial Organization, subsets of what we have identified as distribution services show up as an incentive for vertical integration in at least two distinct ways. First, some distribution services, for example accessibility of location and depth of assortment, can be thought of as generating product diversity and vertical integration internalizes the choice of product diversity. Second, some distribution services, for example information and assurance of product delivery in the desired form, can generate externalities in their provision that can be internalized by vertical integration.

Perry (1989) notes that ease of access or what we called accessibility of location, as captured in spatial models based on Salop's circular spatial model (for example, Dixit (1983) or Mathewson and Winter (1983)), generates consumer demands in which competition is localized and new retailers 'crowd' the market because entry does not increase total demand in the spatial model. Each consumer demands at most one unit of a good from a retailer. In our framework, the general situation is one where increased accessibility of location either increases the consumer's willingness to pay a higher price for each unit of the good sold by a retailer (for example, the inverse demand function case in Chapter 2, section 4) or induces the consumer to buy more units of the good at a given price (for example, the standard demand function in Chapter 2, section 5, that was derived from 'primitives' in Chapter 3).

Similarly, Perry (1989) notes that non-spatial models of product differentiation based on the CES specification of Spence (1976) or Dixit and Stiglitz (1977), for example Perry and Groff (1985), generate consumer demands in which competition is generalized (each firm competes with all others) and entry increases total demand. While Perry seems to view these two specifications as alternative ways of modeling the impact of product diversity on vertical integration, our analysis of distribution services suggests that they apply to two very different economic phenomena. The CES demand specification in Perry and Groff, for example, can be viewed as a sensible specification of depth of assortment, since it imposes the restriction that the elasticity of substitution between the different varieties is greater than unity, that is, $0 < \beta < 1$ in their notation. But this restriction makes no sense to describe breadth of assortment or accessibility of location. For instance, there is not much substitutability in demand between product categories such as shirts and detergents, nor does the restriction seem that useful as a description of substitutability in demand across locations.[33]

Perry (1989) goes on to note that other non-price dimensions of the retail stage may affect the evaluation of the welfare effects of vertical integration. He explicitly identifies the role of advertising as a mechanism for providing information to consumers and the externalities that can arise in this process, which were incorporated into extensions of the spatial model by Mathewson and Winter (1984, 1986). He also identifies the role of service, which he defines as presale non-appropriable information. The latter was introduced by Perry and Porter (1990) as an extension of the CES model of Perry and Groff. This extension also allowed for externalities in service provision. From our point of view advertising is one of the means of providing information to consumers, and service, as defined by Perry, can be viewed as another means of doing so. Service, however, can also be defined more broadly to include not only the provision of information at the store similar to what you may receive in an advertisement but also assurance of product delivery to the consumer in the desired form, for example, consumer-specific illustrations of how well a product fits particular needs. In any event, Perry's conclusion on these issues (p. 205) is that 'a complete welfare evaluation of vertical integration requires an examination of the relevant non-price dimensions of competition. The problem is that such models become very cumbersome'.

Not surprisingly in light of this conclusion, the literature has moved on to explore other aspects of vertical integration. For example, demand uncertainty has led to the development of a theory of buyer–seller networks (Kranton and Minehart, 2001), in which 'networks are equilibrium outcomes and yield greater welfare than vertical integration', Kranton and Minehart (2000, p. 572). Similarly, interest in the make or buy decision has led to, for example, a model explaining the emergence of outsourcing or vertical integration in an industry equilibrium (Grossman and Helpman, 2002). Finally, old hypotheses on the determinants of vertical integration have been revisited empirically (Elberfeld, 2002). In these other aspects of vertical integration, however, distribution services play no explicit role in the analysis.[34]

The second related strand of literature in industrial organization where distribution services have received some attention is in the vertical contractual relations literature. For instance, while evaluating welfare consequences in an early survey of this literature, Katz (1989) discusses promotional efforts and product variety, which correspond to information and depth of assortment in our terminology, as specific determinants of welfare that need to be evaluated with respect to a given contractual practice of vertical control. He concludes (p.714) that 'there is no widespread agreement on whether a particular practice is socially beneficial or harmful'. More recent contributions in this strand of literature, however, have been more direct and conclusive in addressing the role of distribution services.

Winter (1993) develops a model that highlights as one of its three basic features the role of retailers' services as a mechanism for reducing consumers' shopping costs. This feature in Winter's model is exactly the same as what we have called earlier in the book assurance of product delivery at the desired time. Moreover, it is modeled by Winter to have the two basic properties of a distribution service, namely, providing more of the service is costly for the retailer and providing a higher level of the service reduces the cost to the consumer of patronizing the store by lowering the full price of acquiring the product. Winter adds two other features to the model: retailers differentiated on location, which is exogenously given by the use of spatial model with a retailer at each end of a line (consumers are uniformly distributed along the line); and heterogeneous consumers, who are identically distributed with respect to the opportunity cost of their time at each location. Also, consumers buy at most one unit of the good from retailers; they have a reservation price at or above which they will not purchase.

In this setting, the optimal complete contract between a manufacturer of the physical product and the two retailers providing services involves identical prices and service levels at both outlets. This solution maximizes joint profits and it eliminates two distortions: the vertical externality that arises from retailers ignoring double marginalization and the horizontal externality that arises from retailers trying to compete with each other on price. The decentralized solution, however, will differ as a result of the existence of both externalities. Retailers will try to attract the low shopping costs customers by offering low prices. Winter shows that a contract in which the manufacturer can extract a fixed fee from retailers allows the manufacturer to charge a wholesale price that differs from marginal cost to elicit the optimal amount of service provision while using a price floor set at the optimal level of the joint profit maximization. This contract, thus, replicates the first best solution. A fixed fee, exclusive territories and a wholesale price equal to marginal cost would also do so. Substantively, this result provides an economic rationale for resale price maintenance in the form of a price floor without resorting to the assumption of service externalities in the provision of a distribution service. The latter assumption is typical of earlier literature, for example Perry and Porter (1990).

A key condition for the price floor to be part of the optimal contract is the following $\in_p (R)/\in_p (I) > \in_D (R)/\in_D (I)$, where $\in_p (R)$ is the retailer's elasticity of demand with respect to her price and $\in_p (I)$ is the market elasticity of demand with respect to her price and, similarly, $\in_D (R)$ is the retailer's elasticity of demand with respect to her level of distribution services and $\in_D (I)$ is the market's elasticity of demand with respect to her distribution service. This condition implies that the cross elasticities of demand are higher in price than in service, that is, competition is stronger in price than in services. An alternative way to view this condition is to note that a necessary and sufficient condition for a uniform wholesale price contract to generate the first best optimum is that the following holds, $\in_p (R)/\in_p (I) = \in_D (R)/\in_D (I)$. This also implies $\in_D (R)/\in_p (R) = \in_D (I)/\in_p (I)$.[35]

Another contribution to the contractual vertical relations literature that addresses the role of distribution services explicitly is Romano (1994). In his introduction he identifies local advertising and sales effort as examples of variables controlled by the downstream firm that affect demand and national promotion as an example of a variable controlled by the upstream firm that also affects demand.[36] These examples are means of providing distribution services that we have identified as information or assurance of product delivery in the desired form. More importantly, Romano models them with the two features stressed throughout the book. That is, providing a higher level of each of these variables increases costs for the provider, and higher levels of each of these services increase consumer demand. He labels the non-price variable controlled by the producer, y and the one controlled by the retailer, x.

His model is one of successive monopolies. Thus, there are three possible sources of distortions that arise in any contract arrangement with respect to the integrated solution: the double marginalization problem, a vertical externality with respect to promotion at the retail stage, and another vertical externality with respect to promotion at the manufacturer's level. If contracts can be written on y and x, Romano shows that the first best or integrated solution can be attained in three different ways: by setting the wholesale price equal to marginal cost and using a fixed fee to capture the rents upstream, by quantity forcing and the fixed fee, and by resale price maintenance (RPM) via a price ceiling at the first-best final good price and a uniform wholesale price above marginal cost that transfers the rents upstream. If y can be contracted but x can not be, then the first two solutions can still generate the first-best outcome but the third one can not do so because the vertical externality with respect to promotion at the retail stage remains.

If y is also non-contractible, however, the first two solutions can't generate the first best outcome. Indeed, under these conditions Romano shows that the first best outcome is unattainable, Proposition 2, and that, in general, there are strict gains from RPM, Proposition 3, when y and x are chosen non-cooperatively in a simultaneous move Nash equilibrium. That is the case unless the change in quantity demanded as a result of the direct price effects and indirect price effects (through equilibrium changes in promotions at both levels) is zero. Whether a price ceiling or a price floor is the appropriate contract restriction depends on whether the quantity demanded increases (floor) or decreases (ceiling) as a result of the direct and indirect effects of a price change. Romano also shows that a similar result holds under the assumption of Stackelberg leadership by the retailer.

In sum, Winter's and Romano's work extends the analysis of the model of section 8.1 by introducing, respectively, competition at the retail stage and the choice of a level of a distribution service at the upstream stage. Furthermore, on the substantive side their work demonstrates that distribution services provide a fundamental economic rationale for resale price maintenance.

Other contributions to this strand of literature lead to the analysis of franchises, including the role of private information in vertical contractual relations. Franchises are the sole topic of the next chapter and we discuss additional economic and marketing literature in that context. To conclude our discussion of the economics literature here I will briefly point out one broad area where distribution services as such have played no explicit role but where they may do so in the future: namely, the impact of financial variables on real ones in the context of retailing. A seminal article on the topic is Chevalier's (1995) study of the impact of leveraged buyouts on supermarket product competition. She concludes that it softens product competition, but she also asserts (p.421) 'the methodology in this paper cannot separate changes in price competition from changes in quality competition'. While she does not explicitly indicate what she means by quality competition, the standard interpretation is competition on the non-price variables which I call distribution services.

In the marketing literature on channel issues, just as in the economics one, some writers have incorporated distribution services into their analyses, with or without using our specific terminology, and others have ignored them completely. In order to keep the size of this chapter manageable, I limit the discussion to two basic contributions in marketing that capture how distribution services are treated in this area's literature on channel issues. Jeuland and Shugan's (1983) work defines the management of channel profits as a coordination problem, has become a standard reference on channels in marketing and, thus, has affected the approach adopted by subsequent literature to the analysis of distribution services. Their basic model relies on four simple assumptions, some of which are relaxed subsequently: a two-member channel, a downward sloping retail demand function, full information on all variables except channel member behavior and symmetry in what channel members control.[37]

Their first extension of this basic model is to introduce non-price variables for the manufacturer (y) and for the retailer (x). In substantive terms they characterize the first one as quality and the second one as selling effort. Since they assume that costs are increasing in y and x and that the demand function depends positively on y and x, however, for practical purposes these variables act as distribution services in both cases. Their first result is to show that perfect coordination, which is what one would have under joint ownership of the channel, would lead to lower prices and higher levels of both distribution services than lack of coordination under separate ownership of each of the two channel members. The authors view their contribution as seeking how full channel cooperation can be achieved, where full implies 'involving other marketing mix variables than price'.[38]

Several solutions to this coordination problem are considered, vertical integration, simple contracts and implicit understandings, and discarded on the grounds, respectively, of lack of efficiency due to scale or scope economies and legal constraints, non-contractability and lack of assurance of the existence of a rational expectations equilibrium. The solution preferred by the authors is the sharing of total channel profits by the manufacturer and the retailer on the basis of a share k ($0 < k < 1$) to the manufacturer and ($1 - k$) to the retailer and a fixed payment F ($-\infty < F < +\infty$) to the manufacturer and $-F$ to the retailer. The authors argue that quantity discounts[39] are an excellent mechanism for implementing profit sharing in this context.

Of course, not all schedules of quantity discounts generate the profit sharing solution. A discount schedule that does in their model when non-price variables are included is given by

$$t = kp + (1 - k)(C(y) + y/Q) - k(C(x) + x/Q) + F/Q, \qquad (8.19)$$

where p is the retail price, Q is the quantity demanded, C is a cost function for producing distribution services at either level of the channel and t is the discounted price. Discount schedules can run into problems similar to those attributed to the other solutions of the coordination problem and may also be illegal in some cases. Nevertheless, the authors point out that many marketing procedures, for example promotional allowances, cooperative advertising and price rebates, are de facto mechanisms in which the retailer and the manufacturer can participate in profit sharing without running into the same legal difficulties as they could with quantity discounts. Finally, they argue that the actual values of k and F will be determined as the outcome of a bargaining process between retailers and manufacturers. In the end, this part of their analysis illustrates that non-linear schedules in contracts can be, at least in theory, as applicable to distribution services as they are to prices.

Given the set-up in the previous paper, it is not surprising that, substantively, the marketing literature on channels concentrates on only two of the distribution services that we emphasize in the book, that is, information of some type that can be provided by the retailer or the manufacturer and assurance of product delivery in the desired form, which again can be provided by the retailer or the manufacturer. Either one of these services is often viewed as quality when provided by the manufacturer. In general the multiproduct aspect of retailing and the provision of even these two services as common[40] distribution services are difficult to capture due to the analytical complexities that arise in doing so. To conclude I look at a recent contribution by two active researchers in the marketing literature on channels which allows us to highlight some of these issues.

Coughlan and Ingene (2002)'s paper is in a tradition similar to Jeuland and Shugan's in that they ask a question particularly relevant from a marketing perspective and proceed to find answers that are quite relevant from an economic perspective. They consider a service that adds value to a channel and that can be provided either by the manufacturer or the retailer and ask the question, who should bear the cost of providing the service?

An obvious answer is whoever finds it less costly to do so. Indeed, there are some practical circumstances in which the cost differences are so large that only the upstream or the downstream member is able to do so. For instance, if the service is some form of final fitting of an item, for example a dress or a window, to a consumer or his home environment, the costs of doing so by a manufacturer are likely to be extremely high due to the transportation costs involved. Similarly if the service to be provided is a finishing of the item that is closely associated with the original production process, the provision of a cloth or a leather interior for an automobile for example, the costs of doing so for the retailer are likely to be prohibitive.

Coughlan and Ingene (2002) assume there are no cost reasons for making the choice, so they can focus on strategic ones. This means their analysis is applicable to distribution services such as information on the characteristics of an item or assurance of product delivery in the desired form provided through mechanisms such as credit and perhaps warranties. On the other hand, it is difficult to conceive how it could apply to assortment, accessibility of location or ambiance. Assuming Stackelberg leadership by the manufacturer, they consider the effects of assigning the service provision to one or the other level of the channel on retailer, manufacturer and channel profits as well as on the equilibrium level of service provision. They look at these effects under four alternative assumptions about channel structure, alternative assumptions about the relative strength of competition in the channel, which is similar to comparing $\in_p (R)/\in_p (I)$ in Winter's analysis, and the relative valuation of service provision to price.

In the bilateral monopoly case everyone's profits are higher if the retailer bears the cost of service provision and the equilibrium level of service provision is higher if provided by the retailer. This is not surprising because under Stackelberg leadership by the manufacturer, the latter takes into consideration the retailer's decisions on price and service. The introduction of competition at the retail level by having two retailers and one manufacturer, however, makes some of the results conditional. While manufacturer and channel profits continue to be highest if the retailer does the service, this is the case for the retailer only if competition is not strong and the relative valuation of service to price is high. Equilibrium service provision by the retailer is always higher than if the manufacturer provides the service. If instead the introduction of competition takes place at the manufacturer's level, the retailer and channel profits are highest when the retailer does the service and the manufacturer's profits are highest when they do the service if competition is strong and the relative valuation of service is high. Equilibrium service provision by the retailer is higher than if manufacturers provide the service only for very high valuations of the service and low levels of competition by the manufacturers.

Finally if there is competition at both the retail (two retailers) and the manufacturing level (two manufacturers), the determination of outcomes becomes quite complex.[41] For instance, retailers' profits are higher when they do the service only if the relative service valuation is high and competition is low; manufacturers' profits are highest when they do the service if competition is high and the relative valuation of the service is also high; total channel profit is higher if the retailer does the service but only when competition is low and the relative valuation of the service is also low. Equilibrium levels of service are higher when the retailer does the service except when competition is high and relative service valuation is low.

By and large competitive channel structures lead to greater service provision with one exception, that is, when the retailer provides the service and there is competition among manufacturers the equilibrium level of service is lower than under bilateral monopoly. Analytically, Coughlan and Ingene extend the model of section 8.1 by allowing for competition at the retailing as well as at the manufacturing stage. Substantively their results imply that control of distribution services entails the exercise of economic power under alternative channel structures, because this allocation affects important outcomes such as profits of channel members and equilibrium levels of distribution services themselves.

NOTES

1. This section draws heavily on earlier work (Betancourt and Gautschi, 1998).
2. Recall that the properties of retail demand (Chapter 3) imply $Q_D > 0$ and $Q_p < 0$. Also note that the price–cost margin is the standard measure of monopoly power in economics and it captures one of the dimensions of economic power identified at the beginning of this chapter.
3. H is the principal minor of the determinant of the coefficients of the endogenous variables in the differentials of the first-order conditions. It can be shown to be positive by the second-order conditions.
4. See Betancourt and Gautschi (1998) for the detailed results.
5. This result, in contrast to the previous one on relative power, obtains regardless of who controls the distribution service. In both cases, that is, regardless of manufacturer or retailer control of the service, the decentralized solution is a second-best one and the decision maker adjusts by choosing a higher level of the distribution service than in the first-best solution, since the price is higher than in the first-best solution.
6. It should be noted that the authors discussed a wide-ranging set of issues related to this topic and our summary focuses on only one aspect.
7. Of course these results could also be spurious due to other shortcomings of the empirical analysis such as omitted variables; Here we are taking them at face value.
8. That is, $RSP = RP/CP = [S - C(R) - C(GS)]/[S - C(R) - C(M)]$, where S is retail sales, $C(R)$ represents the costs of retailing, $C(GS)$ identifies the costs of goods sold, which equal manufacturers' sales, and $C(M)$ are the costs of manufacturing the products But RSP can be calculated as $RSP = ROM/[ROM + (1 - R) * MOM]$. Note that $ROM = [S - C(R) - C(GS)]/S$, $R = [S - C(GS)]/S$ and $MOM = [C(GS) - C(M)]/C(GS)$.
9. The last result is to be expected since retail competition is usually a local phenomenon and Kapinos's retail concentration measures have difficulty capturing this feature.
10. Kapinos does not include the adoption of scanners in his analysis. Both the result of Messinger and Narasimhan and the logic of equation (8.6) suggest that he should have. Hence, our interpretations are conditional on either no bias from leaving this variable out or a sufficiently small one not to reverse the results.
11. This expectation is based on the assumption that manufacturers introduce the new products. One could argue, however, that it is in fact retailers who make the choice, in which case this interpretation would not be valid.
12. Of course, this is not a problem if marginal costs are constant and equal to average costs, but this is a rather strong assumption.
13. Interestingly, Horowitz (2000) has shown recently that, in the presence of fixed costs, the equilibrium prices generated through a Bertrand/Nash duopoly model of manufacturer's competition at the horizontal level can yield negative profits for a common retailer downstream who is a Stackelberg follower. The results are likely to generalize to any channel structure where the price reaction functions of retailers are increasing in manufacturers' prices. Hence, he argues that in the analysis of channel issues one should include fixed costs explicitly.
14. Their basic data are annual means of 909 manufacturers and 274 retailers grouped into 14 SIC codes.
15. Other category killers (Toys 'R' Us and Home Depot) also perform well in terms of MVA but nothing comparable to Wal-Mart.
16. Ironically, they can not capture as special cases leader–follower relationships.
17. It is also useful to note how this study fits in as a channel issue. The choices of a distribution service by retailers (video rental stores) in the context of their interactions with their suppliers (movie studios) has a dramatic effect on a third type of economic agent (the manufacturers of video cassette recorders) who are *adjacent* members of the channel, to use Wernerfelt's (1994) terminology.
18. For an easy-to-read one-sided view of this aspect of the issue that, nonetheless, contains all the relevant references, see Liebowitz (2002, Chapter 3).

19. Direct network effects would exist in the case of, for example, telephones or fax machines.
20. Goldsmith provides no explanation of the decision to purchase the recorder because the video rental use of the recorder occurred later than the other two uses (time shifting of TV programs and running of home made movies).
21. Mortimer (2002) undertakes an empirical analysis of contractual choice in the current video rental industry. The basic model underlying her investigation is quite similar to Goldsmith's in that the key choice variable of the retailer is the level of depth of assortment or variety of titles, which she calls inventory. Of course, there is only one type of cassette for rent since she is looking at a phenomenon that takes place after the disappearance of Betamax recorders.
22. It is noteworthy in this context that capacity plays an important role in the theoretical analysis of revenue sharing contracts in the video rental industry by Dana and Spier (2001).
23. The first part of this section draws heavily from the discussion of Proposition 7 in Betancourt and Gautschi (1988).
24. Furthermore there can be, of course, more complex reasons for backward integration such as foreclosure or hold-up problems but we are not addressing those here.
25. The argument underlying this assertion was put forward in Chapter 4.
26. For instance, the results of Mulhern and Leone (1991) suggest gross complementarity or gross independence between their two categories. Even within category they found only one relationship of gross substitutability. Similarly, Hoch, Kim, Montgomery and Rossi (1995) assume gross independence between categories in their estimation procedure and we showed that even their within-categories estimates imply that gross complementarities prevail in five of their 18 categories.
27. In Chapter 5 the retailer was a price setter in the explicit product market. Here, we have been treating the retailer as a quantity setter in the explicit product market.
28. Vance and Scott (1994, Chapter 3) provide an insightful, detailed historical account of the birth of Wal-Mart and the basis for these assertions.
29. Interestingly, Neff writing in Advertising Age (10/29/2001) estimates that Wal-Mart accounted for 3/4 of the growth in private label sales in non-food categories in 2001.
30. The store brand could have features different from the national brands in terms of size, for example.
31. Targeting was determined through the evaluation of extrinsic characteristics of the brands by two independent observers.
32. Of course, the literature does not necessarily refer to these dimensions as distribution services.
33. West (2000) reports a move from vertical integration to decentralization as a result of privatization in liquor retailing in Canada. Consequently prices and the number of stores increased, which is consistent with the predictions of both spatial and non-spatial models, just as he notes. If depth of assortment increased, however, this would support the non-spatial models. Unfortunately, West's study did not address this issue.
34. With respect to the analysis of Grossman and Helpman one can argue that some distribution services play a role implicitly, because in their outsourcing equilibrium the need to search for a specialized supplier is equivalent to the need to acquire information in any exchange and the need to prove quality of an input is equivalent to the need to provide assurance of product delivery in the desired form in any exchange.
35. These conditions can also be expressed in terms of the slopes. Similar conditions will play a role later in our discussion of the marketing literature.
36. He also uses the quality of the product generated by the production process as equivalent to national promotion but I find it preferable to keep characteristics of production separate from those of distribution whenever possible. The main reason will be discussed in Chapter 10.
37. Symmetry means to them, for example, that if one channel member controls a non-price variable and a price one, the other channel member will also control a (different) non-price variable and a price one.

38. This version of their model is the same as Romano's under the assumption that y and x are contractible.
39. These quantity discounts are conceptually the same as those defined in Chapter 6. That is, a quantity discount implies that the larger the quantity, the lower the price.
40. See Chapter 2, section 2, for a definition of the concept and Chapter 5, section 5, for some of its implications.
41. This complexity arises despite the assumption of Stackelberg leadership by the manufacturer. In the marketing literature on channels ignoring distribution services, other alternatives are usually considered in addition to Stackelberg leadership by the manufacturer and they do affect outcomes (see for example Lee and Staelin, 1997).

9. Franchises

Franchises are organizational forms that lie in-between vertically integrated firms and arm's length market exchange. Firms exist to internalize transaction costs, according to Coase (1937) and Williamson (1985), and they satisfy a need for long-run contracts to facilitate exchange. Hence, at this most elementary level one can view franchises as an alternative to both vertical integration and arm's length market exchange due to the existence of substantial transaction costs that are difficult to internalize and the need for long-run contracts to facilitate exchange.

As an organizational form, franchising encompasses two very different types of franchise systems: product trade name or authorized franchise systems, and business format franchises. In the former a physical good is always one of the basic products transacted at all levels of the channel structure and the franchisees are primarily a distribution system. In the latter a process or way of doing things is always one of the basic products transacted between the franchiser and the franchisee, and a service is often one of the basic products transacted between the franchisee and the consumer. While the franchisees in this case also provide a distribution system, they often have to do much more than distribute because production and distribution are frequently inseparable in business format franchising. Finally, product trade name franchising can be traced back to the late nineteenth century whereas business format franchising becomes a significant activity after World War II. While the former type still dominates the latter in terms of actual economic size, business format franchising is the more dynamic and fastest-growing type (Khan, 1999, Chapter 1).

In the next section, some quantitative information on franchising is provided. This type of information is very difficult to obtain on a comprehensive and consistent basis because government agencies don't collect systematic information on this organizational form. In section 9.2 the main economic characteristics of one of the two most important product trade name retail franchises, gas stations, are identified and discussed in detail. In particular, I stress their relation to the provision of distribution services by the franchiser directly to consumers. Similarly, in section 9.3 the main economic characteristics of the other main type of product trade name retail franchises, new automobile dealers, are identified and analysed, together with their relationship to the provision of distribution services by the franchisees to consumers. Finally, in section 9.4 the main economic characteristics of business format franchising are also identified and analysed together with their relationship to the provision of distribution services by both the franchiser and the franchisee. In general our aim is to bring out the role of distribution services in determining important features of franchise arrangements. In identifying the latter we rely heavily on the existing literature.

9.1   QUANTITATIVE INFORMATION ON FRANCHISES

According to Stern and El-Ansary (1992, pp.343–44) sales of goods and services by franchising companies totalled about $680 billion in 1989. Most of these sales are retail sales.[1] They constituted about 33 per cent of all retail sales in 1989, according to the same source. The following figures, which are taken from Table 7.1 in the above source, indicate the principal retail sectors in which these organizational forms have taken hold. These five sectors represent about 80 per cent of outlets and sales of franchising companies and a greater proportion of outlets and sales of retail franchises. Furthermore, product trade name franchises, that is, the first two categories in Table 9.1, represent at least 68 per cent of sales. Unfortunately, the latest edition of this text doesn't update these figures.

Data on retail franchises are next to impossible to obtain from standard official government statistics for two reasons. First and foremost, the Census typically does not gather data on the basis of this organizational form. Second, while franchised establishments dominate sectors such as the above five they are not, in general, the only form of operation in these sectors. Hence, looking at the behavior of the aggregate of the sectors can be misleading with respect to what is going on in the franchised part.

Perhaps the only exception to the first reason is the category 'automobile and truck dealers'. The US Statistical Abstract publishes one table every year on Franchised New Car Dealerships. For instance, the 2000 issue (Table 1278) shows that the number of dealerships declined steadily between 1980, when

Table 9.1   Distribution of sales and outlets of franchise companies, 1989

Sector	% of establishments	% of sales
Automobile and truck dealers	5.5	52
Gasoline service stations	22.5	16
Restaurants (all types)	18.9	10.2
Convenience grocery stores	3.5	2.1
Hotels, motels, camps	2.0	3.1

there were 27 900 of them, and 1999, when there were 22 400 of them. Interestingly, the number of new cars sold went from 8.98 million to 8.70 million during the same period. Even in this case, however, the source of most of the data in Table 1278 is the National Automobile Dealers Association.

Despite these difficulties, it is useful to report some data on two of the above categories published by the Census. Convenience grocery stores in the Census are part of food stores, but they consist of two types: convenience food stores and convenience food stores with gas stations. Gasoline sales must be less than 49 per cent for the latter category or it would be classified as a gas station. Similarly, gasoline stations in the Census are of two types: gas stations with convenience store or gas stations/other, usually with a repair shop. Why does this matter? The entities in these different classifications are evolving in very different fashions.

In Table 9.2 we show what has happened to the number of outlets in these four different categories between 1987 and 1997.[2] Similar trends affect sales. While convenience stores have grown during this period, the growth is entirely due to the growth in the sub-category that has expanded the assortment to include gasoline sales. Along similar lines, the decline in the number of outlets classified as gasoline stations obscures two dramatically opposite trends, namely, a rapid decline in what used to be the standard format, that is, with a repair shop associated with the station, and an even more rapid increase in a new format, that is, with a convenience store associated with the station.[3]

Convenience stores are normally classified as business format franchises and gasoline stations are normally classified as product trade name or authorized dealership franchises. Hence, these trends suggest the possibility of direct competition between the two types of franchises in the current economy.[4] These trends also cast some doubt on Oi's (1992) interpretation of the evolution of the gasoline station industry as one in which assortments have narrowed. While the repair function has been declining, as he demonstrates and the above data confirm, the addition of a convenience store represents a move to broader assortments.

Last but not least is the information from a recent study of franchising sponsored by the International Franchise Association (IFA), namely *The*

Table 9.2   Outlets of gas stations and convenience stores

Sector	Outlets 1987	Outlets 1997
Gasoline/convenience store	15,625	53,641
Gasoline/other	99,123	45,205
Convenience stores	30,864	27,081
Convenience food/gasoline	18,650	28,043

Profile of Franchising: A Statistical Abstract of 1998 UFOC Data. It was
released in 2000 and is available on IFA's website. It is not comprehensive,
since it is limited to franchise systems that are offering franchises in a particular year in one of 12 states requiring annual registration. All of the data comes
from the Uniform Franchise Offering Circular (UFOC) required by the FTC for
those companies that meet its definition of a franchise. Nonetheless, it is the
most comprehensive source that exists at the moment. It covers 1226 franchise
systems operating in 1998. All of the data refer to business format franchises.

This source breaks down the franchise population in its data base into 18
'industry' categories deemed relevant by the data collection organization.[5] It
finds that four food-related industries account for 34 per cent of the population
of franchise systems in its data base. These industries are: Baked Goods, Fast
Food Industry, Restaurants and Retail Food Industry. Indeed, the Fast Food
category contains the largest percentage of franchise systems in the data base
(18 per cent). It is followed by General Retail (11 per cent), which comprises
beauty-related products, computer products and services and clothing and
accessories and party-related goods and services. This is then followed by a tie
between Restaurants (9 per cent) and Service Businesses (9 per cent). The
latter comprise health and fitness, publications, security-related services and
general services. Automotive Products and Services comes in next at 8 per
cent and these five categories account for 55 per cent of the franchise systems
in the data base.

Limited but useful information is provided on several fundamental characteristics of franchise operations. For instance, 44 per cent of the franchise
systems in this data base have over 90 per cent of their units as franchises. At
the other end, 9 per cent of the systems have only company-owned stores.
Presumably the latter observations correspond to franchise systems in the
early stages of development. About 53 per cent of the systems have less than
50 units and 47 per cent have more than 50 units. Incidentally most of these
systems have been in operation for a while, since 62 per cent of them have
been in business over 12 years and 41 per cent of them have been in franchising over 12 years.

With respect to the basic economic characteristics of a franchise contract,
these data offer interesting insights. The initial franchise fee for 82 per cent of
these systems is over $10 000 and for 7 per cent of them it is over $50 000.
The average initial fee is greater than $20 000 in 17 of the 18 industry cate-
gories identified in the data. These fees seem substantial, especially when one
takes into account that large companies are unlikely to be in the data base. For
instance, 95 per cent of the systems are listed as privately held companies.

A related item is initial investment in the franchise. For 43 per cent of the
systems it is less than $100 000 and for 34 per cent of them it is between $100
000 and $249 999. The average initial investment is less than $100 000 in five

of the 18 'industry' categories in the data set. The lodging industry is an outlier where the average initial investment is over \$2 million. While this initial investment is supposed to exclude real estate costs, it is not certain that respondents always did so in their answers.

Data on royalty fees reveal that 84 per cent of these systems charge a royalty fee in percentage terms,[6] 6 per cent charge a flat royalty fee in dollar terms and 4 per cent charge no royalty fee.[7] Of the 84 per cent that charge a royalty fee in percentage terms, 93 per cent do so as a percentage of sales or revenues and this percentage of sales lies between 3 and 6 per cent for 71 per cent of them. Most of these systems require frequent payments of the royalty fee, for example 72 per cent of them require the royalty fee to be paid on a weekly or monthly basis.

To conclude, this report provides data on three other interesting aspects of the franchise contract: advertising fees, territorial exclusivity, and contract length. Fifty-two per cent of the systems charge a national advertising fee as a percentage of sales, 5 per cent charge a flat rate, 28 per cent charge no advertising fee and 12 per cent charge only a regional or local advertising fee. Among those charging a national advertising fee as a percentage of sales, 83 per cent charge between 0.01 per cent and 3 per cent. Seventy-one per cent of the systems offer grants of territorial exclusivity. Finally, 91 per cent of the contracts offer the possibility of renewal and the average contract length for original contracts is 10.3 years and for renewals it is 8.2 years. Thus, franchise contracts are long-term contracts.

9.2 RETAIL PRODUCT TRADE NAME FRANCHISES: GAS STATIONS

For simplicity we begin the analysis by focusing on gasoline stations. A useful starting point is Shepard's (1993) seminal article on contractual form in this industry. She characterizes refiners of branded gasoline as having three basic choices of contract form to distribute their product through gas stations. One is company-owned stations where the manager is hired by the refiner, which corresponds to the vertically integrated channel. Another is a lessee–dealer arrangement where the land and the immobile capital are owned by the refiner and the manager is self-employed, which corresponds to a franchise contract. The two main features of this contract are that the refiner sets the wholesale price and the annual rental or royalty fee, which is aimed at being proportional to the net income that the station generates. Finally, the last one is an open dealer contract where the refiner has no investment in the station and controls only the wholesale price, except for restrictions on product purity and labeling and minimum purchase requirement.[8]

An interesting aspect of the franchise contract for lessee–dealer stations is that it does not rely on most of the incentive devices that we saw in section 9.1, such as franchise fees, initial investment, advertising fees or territorial agreements. The only incentive device used from the list in section 9.1 is a royalty fee as a percentage of net income or profits. The Appendix to this chapter presents a simple model that shows how royalty fees as a percentage of sales or profits (and a wholesale price set by the manufacturer) are sufficient to replicate the vertically integrated solution when the manufacturer provides a distribution service to the consumer. An essential feature of the interaction between refiners and their distributors is the provision by the refiner of a distribution service to consumers through the brand name.

More generally, an insightful paper on channel coordination by Lal (1990) shows that royalty fees are not necessary for channel coordination when the retailer provides a distribution service to the consumer or when franchisee retailers can free-ride on each other. But Lal (1990) also shows that when the franchiser affects the demand of its franchisee retailers by providing a distribution service to the consumer, royalty fees are necessary as a mechanism for channel coordination. The distribution service can be provided, for example, through investments that maintain or expand a brand name. One way Lal motivates this result is by noting that the royalty payments assure the franchisee of profits by providing incentives for the franchiser to invest in the brand name.

One of the arguments established in Chapter 8, section 4, was that retailers have profit incentives to expand into new products that are accentuated by the existence of distribution services. Thus, it is not surprising that one sees retail gas stations adding new product lines such as repair services or convenience stores, depending on the judgment of which local markets support one or the other profitably. What is of interest in the setting of choice of contractual form by refiners considered by Shepard is that repair services are far more difficult to monitor than convenience stores, in terms of revenues generated and a level of effort that produces an outcome for consumers with the appropriate level of assurance of product delivery in the desired form. This feature of repair services creates or enhances a principal–agent problem for the refiner in his/her choice of contractual form.

An implication of this characteristic is that the principal–agent problem favors the choice of a lessee–dealer contractual form or an open dealer form relative to a company owned form for gas stations that operate a repair shop. This is what Shepard finds in fitting a multinomial logit to data on the choice of contractual form by refiners for gas stations in Massachusetts. In each of three different specifications (Shepard, 1993, Tables 4 and 5), the presence of a repair shop substantially lowers the probability of choosing a company-owned contract form relative to a lessee–dealer form and this result is statistically significant at the 1 per cent level in all three empirical specifications reported. Similarly, the presence of a repair shop substantially lowers the probability of choosing a company-owned form relative to an open dealer form, but not by as much as with respect to the lessee–dealer form.[9] The opposite result holds for the presence of a convenience store at a gas station: it increases the probability of choosing a company-owned contractual form relative to the other two forms.[10]

A more recent study by Blass and Carlton (2001) uses nationwide data, limits the choice of contractual form to company-owned and lessee–dealer forms, and finds similar results. The probability of having a lessee–dealer contract form in 1988 for 513 new stations built by refiners between 1984 and 1987 is larger, the greater the number of service bays the gas station operates. The result is statistically significant at the 1 per cent level and robust to limiting the sample to the 204 stations built in 1984–85. These authors go on to estimate the implications of these results for the costs of extending the divorcement laws introduced in some states to the whole country.[11] Finally, a recent analysis based on a quasi-experiment in California, provided by ARCO's acquisition of over 260 independent gas stations from Thrifty in 1997, supports the case against divorcement. In this study Hastings (2004) found that the elimination of an independent (Thrifty) gas station increases prices in its local market, but these increases were unrelated to the choice of contractual form. That is, they were unrelated to whether the gas station was converted by ARCO into a company-operated station or a dealer-operated station.

9.3 RETAIL PRODUCT TRADE NAME FRANCHISES: NEW AND USED AUTOMOBILE DEALERS

A useful starting point to discuss this type of franchise is the set of incentive features characterizing the franchise contract in this retail sector. On the negative side one finds that, just as in gas station franchises, there are no explicit franchise fees or advertising fees. For instance, Dnes (1992) reports this to be the case for the two auto dealer franchises (Austin Rover and Ford) in his analysis of 19 case studies of franchise systems in England. In contrast to gas stations operated under lessee–dealer contracts, however, Dnes (1992) reports no royalty fees for the two car dealerships in his case studies of franchises. Similarly, Smith (1982) in his classic study of state restrictions on automobile distribution in the US makes no mention of franchise fees or royalty fees. He does discuss an end to cooperative advertising by GM in 1949 as an attempt to prevent passage of a nationwide act protecting dealers and subsequently as one of the restrictions imposed by state regulations. In the two English case studies, there are restrictions imposed by the manufacturer on local advertising but they refer to territory in which the dealer can advertise.

On the positive side the two main incentive features of franchise contracts for automobile dealerships are a significant initial investment by the franchisee in showroom, inventory and repair facilities, and various forms of territorial restrictions. In the US Smith (1982) notes that an initial investment to the satisfaction of the manufacturer is an explicit feature of franchise agreements. Indeed, Pashigian's (1961) early study of automobile distribution in the US shows how sizable these investments are. For example dealerships marketing a low-price make in the late 1950s had an investment requirement of over $200 000 for city dealerships or dealerships expected to sell over 700 new cars annually (Table 30, p.126). These figures are exclusive of investments in real estate and buildings. Similarly, in England the two auto dealers studied by Dnes (1992) make specific investment in signs, tools and service facilities and have special provisions for financing stock of inventories.

Territorial restrictions are intrinsic to the functioning of automobile dealerships in the US. According to Smith (1982, p.130) 'The franchisee was expected to provide display and repair facilities in exchange for which he was granted exclusive territory'. And this characterized the system from 1903 to 1940. Since the manufacturer could terminate the agreement with some ease, this situation appears to have favored the manufacturer. The thrust of the rest of the Smith article is an attempt to show how the balance of power has shifted towards the dealer as a result of legislation, especially by the states, limiting the manufacturer's ability to terminate the agreement, violate territorial restrictions or impose other costs on the dealer. Dnes (1992) also reports the existence of territorial restrictions for the two auto dealerships in his case studies of franchises in England. In these cases, however, the restrictions are with respect to location and marketing activities and the exclusivity restrictions are relaxed for small dealerships.

What are the main operating characteristics of auto dealerships? A differentiated durable good produced by a manufacturer is distributed by a retailer. The distribution process is difficult to monitor and control, and requires a fair amount of effort in order to provide a high level of distribution service through the repair and service facilities. That is, the retailer has to provide a high level of assurance of product delivery in the desired form in terms of a properly functioning vehicle in both the short run and the long run. The dealer also provides information through his or her showroom and demonstration cars. This information is easily appropriable by third parties who can acquire it by visiting one dealer while purchasing from another. Dealers have specialized knowledge of the local market, not easily available to manufacturers, in the form of prices to offer for trade-ins. Most of the time, new car dealers also sell used cars and the latter are not subject to the franchise agreement.

In general, manufacturers are attracted to a franchise agreement relative to company ownership because of the incentive features of residual ownership rights for the dealers under a franchise agreement. Dnes (1992) states (p.304) 'The answer typically given by franchisers emphasizes that franchisees are more committed to their local business success due to having their own capital tied up in the enterprise'. In this particular case manufacturers are also attracted to a franchise agreement relative to an arm's length relationship because of the existence of a principal–agent problem induced by the need to operate at a high level of 'quality' in providing a distribution service downstream. The large initial investment in the franchise agreement acts as the posting of a bond by the franchisee, which makes him or her a hostage to the franchiser, in that it is a 'highly firm-specific productive investment which will have only a low salvage value' (Klein, 1980, p.358), if the franchise agreement is terminated. This provides an incentive to provide the right level of distribution service by the franchisee that is absent in the arm's length relationship.[12]

Dealers are attracted to the franchise agreement for several reasons. Dnes (1992) reports that several of the franchisees of Austin Rover and Ford mention that the manufacturer's brand name provides legitimacy to their used car business.[13] The territorial restrictions in the franchise agreements generate monopoly profits. Indeed, Bresnahan and Reiss (1985) model this industry in terms of the double marginalization problem and the use of exclusive territories, that is, independently of franchise and service considerations, and they show that the main implication of double marginalization is consistent with their data. Finally, territorial restrictions limit the extent of free-riding by other dealers.

By the way of a conclusion we note that this type of franchise arrangement has provided the basis for automobile distribution for over one hundred years. Hence, it has passed the market test for durability. Perhaps the most important reason it has done so is its ability to reconcile the interests of the manufacturers and the dealers. This has taken place despite the basic incompatibility of incentives presented by the double marginalization problem inherent in a differentiated durable product distributed through a system of spatial monopolies.

Some insight into this reconciliation is provided by Mathewson and Winter's (1994) analysis of territorial restrictions in franchise contracts. They develop a model based on maximizing the joint profits of franchisee and franchiser from the business. On this basis, they show that territorial restrictions should be positively associated with other restrictions in the contract designed to 'constrain upwards the retailer's efforts by fixing minimum quantities to be sold or inventories to be maintained'. This is certainly the case for automobile dealers who must post the suggested retail price by the manufacturer and, thus, usually sell for a lower price; meet the franchise agreement's restrictions associated with the initial investment in repair inventories and parts; and face sales quotas or sales targets or sales bonuses that are restrictions or inducements designed to increase output.[14]

9.4   BUSINESS FORMAT FRANCHISES

Once again a useful starting point for the analysis of this type of franchise is the set of characteristics of the franchise contract. Just as reported in section 9.1, a typical business format franchise contract entails payments of an initial franchise fee, percentage royalty fees and a substantial initial investment by the franchisee. Two features of these payments by the franchisee are noteworthy. First, the differences in magnitude between the initial franchise fee and the initial investment are quite substantial, for example (as noted in section 9.1) in 17 out of 18 industries the average initial franchise fee is greater than $20 000 but in 13 of these 18 industries the average initial investment is greater than $100 000. Second, over 80 per cent of business format franchise systems have all three kinds of payments by the franchisees specified in the franchise contract.

Interestingly, one of the fundamental theoretical articles on franchise contracts, Mathewson and Winter (1985), does not mention explicitly the initial investment in the franchise, but concentrates instead on the initial franchise fee as part of a non-linear royalty fee. This article focuses on explaining the essentials that give rise to the existence of franchise contracts where profits are shared. Their conclusion can be summarized as follows (p.525): 'some form of binding franchisee wealth constraint or limitations on commitments and the incompleteness of contracts are both necessary and sufficient for franchise contracts. Vertical externalities are essential for franchises; horizontal externalities are not'.

Dnes (1992) builds on the following Mathewson and Winter's formulation of the principal–agent problem. The franchiser's profits, π_F, are given by

$$\pi_F = FF + \alpha \left\{ \Sigma t_i \, Q_i \, [D_i \, (dn), D(up)] \right\} - C(p) - D(up) - G, \qquad (9.1)$$

where FF is the initial franchise fee, α is the royalty fee as a percentage of sales in both demand states (Q_i). Since prices are set at unity, sales (X_i) and output coincide and both depend on efforts provided by the franchisee (which can be interpreted as distribution services provided downstream), $D_i \, (dn)$, during the low $(i = 1)$ and the high demand $(i = 2)$ period. t_i is the probability that state i occurs, $i = 1, 2$. Sales also depend on the efforts of the franchiser (which can be interpreted as distribution services provided upstream), $D(up)$. The level of these services is assumed to equal the franchiser's investment in the brand. $C(p)$ are the franchiser's monitoring costs and p is the probability of detecting chiseling or reporting falsely the state of nature by the franchisee. G are the franchiser's sunk costs.

Profits of the franchisee, given by π_E below, must be non-negative.

$$\pi_E = \Sigma t_i \{(1 - \alpha)Q_i [D_i (dn), D(up)] - D_i (dn)\} - FF \geq 0. \qquad (9.2)$$

Maximization of (9.1) subject to (9.2) yields the first-best solution ignoring that the franchisee may chisel about the state of demand or that the franchiser may abscond with the franchise fee. Here is where the Dnes formulation differs from Mathewson and Winter. Dnes (1992) adds two constraints to capture these issues in the form given below.

$$(1 - \alpha)Q_2 [D_2 (dn), D(up)] - D_2(dn) \geq (1 - p)\{(1 - \alpha)Q_1$$
$$[D_1 (dn), D(up)] - D_1 (dn)y\} \qquad (9.3)$$

$$\pi_F + G \geq rFF. \qquad (9.4)$$

That is, (9.3) requires that profits of the franchisee in the good state of demand be greater than or equal to profits that result from presenting the good state as the bad one when chiseling takes place $(1 - p)$ and the franchisee's effort is adjusted when chiseling (y). Mathewson and Winter also include the franchise fee in this constraint. Similarly, (9.4) requires that sunk costs plus the profits from franchising to the franchiser exceed the expected value of absconding with the franchise fee, where r is the probability that the franchiser absconds with the franchise fee. If we assume the worst about franchisers, $r = 1$, (9.4) implies that when franchisers make normal profits, $(\pi_F = 0)$, the franchise fee will cover the franchiser's sunk costs. Mathewson and Winter's formulation of this constraint implies in the same extreme case that the franchise fee will cover half of the sunk cost, that is, $2FF \geq G$.

It is interesting that in Dnes' (1992) case studies initial franchise fees were viewed by most franchisers as covering set-up costs and by most franchisees as spent in covering initial set-up costs. These results are generally consistent with the view that the initial franchise fee provides the franchiser with some modest income to cover sunk costs and perhaps a small profit, but it can not act as performance bond or hostage for the franchisee in the way the initial investment acts. In general this suggests that the insights derived from our previous two sections continue to be valid in this one. Namely, royalty fees as a percentage of sales are intimately related to the provision of a distribution service to consumers by the franchiser or upstream firm,[15] large initial investments are a mechanism to ensure adequate provision of distribution services to the consumer by the franchisee or downstream firm, and initial franchise fees are neither necessary nor sufficient to address these two issues.

Initial franchise fees are too low to act as a mechanism for capturing rents by the franchiser. In a definitive study of this issue in the context of McDonald's franchises, Kaufman and Lafontaine (1994) note that the existence of ex-post rents that they observe for McDonald's (Table 1) is consistent with most incentive theories of franchising. That is, the costs to the franchisee of reducing effort and having termination clauses applied to them by the franchiser as a result are made higher by the existence of these ex-post rents. What these authors find surprising in the case of McDonald's is that there also appear to be substantial ex-ante rents (Table 2). They explain these ex-ante rents in terms of the existence of liquidity constraints among the potential franchisees that McDonald's would like to recruit, which is consistent with one of the explanations for franchising stressed by Mathewson and Winter. While McDonald's has no territorial restrictions, 71 per cent of the franchise systems considered in the IFA study of section 9.1 offer territorial exclusivity to their franchisees. Given low initial franchise fees, these territorial restrictions are an explicit source of ex-post rents and a potential source of ex-ante rents for the franchisees.

Are there easy-to-identify operating characteristics of business format franchises, and what effect do they have on outcomes? Most of the discussion, thus far, implicitly assumes that the product of the business format franchise is a service where production and distribution are not separated explicitly. This setting is usually described as brand franchising. It certainly applies to the equations defining the principal–agent problem, (9.1) to (9.4), above. It is also appropriate as a description of the business of restaurants, including fast food ones such as McDonald's. Nonetheless there are business format franchise systems covered, for example, by the data in section 9.1 or in Dnes's (1992) case studies, that are not services.

For instance Dnes (1992) identifies three systems that sell a good to consumers other than cars: namely Apollo blinds, Bally shoes and Yves Rocher beauty products. While these systems are classified as business format franchises and rely on initial franchise fees and/or on percentage royalty fees, they have one feature that differentiates them from the pure service ones. The franchiser has an additional instrument to attain optimal levels of operation for the system in the wholesale price of the product.[16] Interestingly enough, Rao and Srinivasan (1995) find that royalty rates are higher in franchise systems that sell services to consumers than in franchise systems that sell goods to consumers. Furthermore, they explain this empirical regularity as a consequence of the franchiser having two instruments (royalty rate and wholesale price) to induce franchisees to set output and service levels consistent with the system's optimum in the case of products, but only one in the case of services.

More generally, in a careful paper integrating theory and data on agency theory and business format franchising Lafontaine's (1992) main conclusion is that 'the empirical results are broadly consistent with two sided hidden-action or moral hazard explanation of franchising, suggesting that there really are incentive issues on both sides'. Our emphasis on the provision of distributions services by both the franchiser and the franchisee is quite consistent with this conclusion. Moreover, it may provide the basis for better empirical measurements of the independent variables than available in the existing literature.[17]

A wide-ranging survey of the empirical literature by Lafontaine and Slade (1997) summarizes several empirical regularities with respect to the choice of dependent variables, explanatory factors and inconsistencies with theoretical models. I will argue that a critical factor in interpreting these regularities is that the literature tends to ignore the importance of the initial investments in the franchise by the franchisee as an aspect of the contract design.

First, Lafontaine and Slade (1997) note that most of the empirical studies end up focusing on explaining the extent of franchising, or proportion of company owned outlets, rather than dimensions of the franchise contract in terms of initial franchise fees or royalty fees. They also note that the three exceptions that consider these two contract dimensions find results similar to the ones found for the proportion of company-owned stores and, thus, restrict their attention in the survey to the latter studies.[18] For all three choices of dependent variables, however, it is customary to include as an explanatory variable some measure of the capital required to open an outlet. This introduces a serious simultaneity problem into the analysis of all three dependent variables if initial investments by the franchisee are an important aspect of the implicit or explicit contract design. To my knowledge, no empirical study has acknowledged, let alone addressed this econometric problem. The information in section 9.1 suggests that the initial investment is as important or a more important dimension of the franchise contract than the franchise fee.[19]

Second, Lafontaine and Slade (1997) identified nine empirical regularities in the studies they reviewed and argued that six of them are consistent with theoretical models of franchising. The validity of this consistency between the theoretical predictions and the six empirical regularities is contingent on assuming that the simultaneity bias from ignoring the endogeneity of the initial investment by the franchisee is immaterial to these results; the initial investment by the franchisee or variables highly correlated with this initial investment, for example size of outlet measured by capital or sales, are often used as explanatory variables in these studies.

Third, at least two of the three empirical regularities that Lafontaine and Slade (1997) find that are supposedly inconsistent with theoretical models of franchising can be made consistent with these models once one acknowledges the importance of initial investments by the franchisee as part of the design of the franchise contract.[20] For instance, they argue that outlet size should be inversely related to the proportion of company-owned outlets, because it measures the importance of the agent's input into the final outcome of the business activity and the more important is this input the more one should observe franchise operations. Three of the six studies listed by them measure outlet size by the initial investment. All three find a positive effect on the proportion of company-owned establishments. Instead of contradicting theoretical predictions, this is exactly what one would expect if initial investment is part of the bond or hostage dimension that the franchisee must contribute to the business in the contract design (and the simultaneity bias does not lead to a change in the theoretically expected sign).

Along similar lines, they list low, within-firm (franchise system) contract uniformity as one of the empirical findings predicted by the theory that is contradicted by the data. Since they find that most franchise systems offer uniform contract terms to their franchisees in terms of initial franchise fee and percentage royalty fees, this is viewed as a contradiction of the theoretical prediction of high variability. Nevertheless, if one views the initial investment as part of the franchise contract design it is not clear that there is low, within-firm contract uniformity in the first place. The empirical regularity that one finds is that the franchise fee is not used as an important instrument to drive the system toward optimal values by capturing downstream rents, but Lafontaine's explanation for this phenomenon in her earlier work (1992) is quite sensible and consistent with the principal–agent model in, for example, Dnes (1992) or Mathewson and Winter (1985). Namely, (p.281) 'if the franchise fee is chosen simply as a way to remunerate the franchiser for services offered in starting out the franchise, there would be no need for any relationship between the franchise fee and the royalty rate'.

More recent work also ignores the importance and endogeneity of the initial investment by the franchisee.[21] For example, Affuso (2002) provides some evidence that, in addition to double-sided moral hazard, there is an adverse selection or hidden information problem in the decision to franchise. She finds at the outlet level that the wages of the agent in a prior job are positively related to the probability of franchising, but one of her control variables treated as exogenous is the initial investment by the franchisee.

A similar neglect arises in a recent paper by Blair and Lafontaine (2003). In section 9.3 we saw how franchising in the new and used car dealers sector revolved around the requirements of significant initial investment by the franchisee in exchange for grants of territorial exclusivity by the franchiser, which in turn led to a substantial amount of legislation by states. Blair and Lafontaine's (2003) paper analyses conflicts between franchisers and franchisees in the context of business format franchises, since similar legislation has been undertaken recently in this context. While they devote substantial attention to the use of territorial restrictions as an ex-ante solution to these conflicts, their analysis pays no attention to the role of initial investments by the franchisee in generating these conflicts. For instance, it is not explicit in their illustrative model (fixed investment by the franchisee is the same every year) and it is not directly discussed. Indeed, the topic appears only indirectly in a footnote citing Lutz' (1995) work on the differential incentives, relative to managers, provided by asset ownership to franchisees.

To conclude, I discuss briefly the last two dimensions of business format franchise contracts identified in the IFA study: advertising fees and contract length. Advertising fees as a percentage of sales have been treated in the literature as simply another form of royalty fees as a percentage of sales. This is true of both the theoretical literature, for example, Mathewson and Winter (1985), and the empirical literature, for example, Lafontaine (1992) and Sen (1993). Such treatment seems warranted for the 52 per cent of franchise systems that charge a national advertising fee as a percentage of sales and unnecessary for the 28 per cent that charge no advertising fee. Similarly, not much attention has been paid in the literature to contract length. One exception is Thompson (1994) who found little evidence for a life cycle effect where franchise systems revert to an increasing proportion of company-owned outlets.

APPENDIX: THE BASIC ROLE OF ROYALTY FEES

A manufacturer that provides a distribution service to the consumer in a vertically integrated channel can be characterized as follows in the simplest possible setting.

$$\pi(I) = pQ - cQ - aD, \qquad (9.A1)$$

where c is a constant marginal cost with respect to Q and a is a constant marginal cost with respect to D. Q is the consumer's demand function, which is specified as usual, that is, $Q = f(p, D)$. D is a distribution service. It can be thought of as information provided through advertising or through the development of a brand name, or more generally as any distribution service provided directly to the consumer by the manufacturer.

The manufacturer maximizes (9.A1) through his choice of p and D. The first-order conditions will be given by

$$\partial\pi/\partial p = p\,[1 - (1/\in)] - c = 0. \qquad (9.A2)$$

$$\partial\pi/\partial D = (p - c)\partial Q/\partial D - a = 0. \qquad (9.A3)$$

The retail price is chosen so that marginal revenue equals marginal cost and the level of the distribution service is chosen so that the marginal revenue it generates also equals marginal cost. Thus, this is just a special case of the model in Chapter 2, section 2.5, and the variables are defined in exactly the same way. Maximum profits will be given by $\Pi^*(I) = p(I)Q(I) - cQ(I) - aD(I)$, or profits at the vertically integrated solution.

Under a decentralized arrangement, we can characterize the problem of the retailer as follows:

$$\pi\ (R) = pQ - wQ - \alpha pQ, \tag{9.A4}$$

assuming a royalty fee based on a percentage of sales. The symbols have the same meaning as before, w is the wholesale price charged by the manufacturer and α, $0 \leq \alpha < 1$, is the royalty fee charged by the manufacturer. Profit maximization by the retailer entails choosing p, given w, α and the market demand function $Q = f(p, D)$. The first-order condition will be

$$\partial\pi/\partial p = p[1 - (1/\in)] - w/(1 - \alpha) = 0. \tag{9.A5}$$

If the royalty fee is zero, so that we have an arm's length relationship between manufacturer and retailer, any wholesale price higher than marginal cost will lead the retailer to charge a higher retail price and the double marginalization problem arises. If the wholesale price charged equals marginal cost, c, the retailer will charge the same retail price as under vertical integration, assuming the manufacturer provides the same level of service. Of course, in this case the retailer obtains all the monopoly profits as well as the revenues the manufacturer would have used to cover the costs of providing the distribution service under vertical integration. In this setting the manufacturer will go out of business or provide zero levels of the distribution service and make zero profits.

Instead of going out of business or making zero profits, however, the manufacturer can obtain the vertically integrated solution by charging the retailer a non-zero royalty fee and a wholesale price, w, that differs from the marginal cost of an additional unit of output, c. Any combination of w and α such that (9.A6) below holds,

$$w/(1 - \alpha) = c, \tag{9.A6}$$

will lead the retailer to charge the same price as in the vertically integrated solution given that the manufacturer is providing the same level of distribution services to the consumer. Thus the higher the royalty rate, the lower the wholesale price will be (below marginal cost) so that (9.A6) holds.

How should the royalty rate be set? The manufacturer wants to extract all the monopoly profit by replicating the vertically integrated solution. It will set the royalty rate so that the retailer bears the cost of providing the level of distribution services the manufacturer would have chosen and the maximum profits the manufacturer would have obtained under vertical integration, that is,

$$\alpha = aD(I)/p(I)Q(I) + \Pi^*(I)/p(I)Q(I). \tag{9.A7}$$

Given the level of α implied by (9.A7), the wholesale price must be chosen according to (9.A6) so that the consumer faces the same level of prices and distribution services as under the vertically integrated solution. All of the retailer's monopoly profits are extracted through the royalty fee and part is used to cover the costs of providing the distribution services by the manufacturer, who enjoys the same level of profits as under complete vertical integration.

If the royalty fee is based on a percentage of profits, then the retailer's optimal choice of price will be independent of the royalty fee. The manufacturer can set the wholesale price, w, equal to marginal cost, c, and replicate the integrated solution by providing the same level of services as under the integrated solution and setting the royalty fee according to (9.A8), so the retailer bears the cost of providing the service and the manufacturer enjoys the same monopoly profits as under vertical integration.

$$\alpha = a \, D(I)/[p(I) - c]Q(I) + \Pi^*(I)/[p(I) - c]Q(I). \tag{9.A8}$$

NOTES

1. These sales figures include, for example, sales to soft drink bottlers (3.6 per cent of the total) who are wholesalers. They also include some categories that are difficult to classify such as business aids and services or maintenance and cleaning. In any event, over 90 per cent of the sales of these franchising companies are clearly retail sales.
2. Due to the change in classification from SIC to NAICS, 1997 is the last year for which this comparison can be made, based on the publicly available data.
3. Incidentally, these stores usually sell a narrower line of convenience products than the traditional convenience store.
4. Furthermore these trends have given rise to a new term, 'dual concept franchising' (Khan, 1999, Chapter 1), which describes arrangements where two different franchise systems, for example a gas station and a restaurant or convenience store, share the same location.
5. This classification of industries does not correspond necessarily to standard classifications such as SIC or NAICS.
6. If a percentage fee had a dollar cap, it was still counted as a percentage fee in these data.
7. The remaining 6 per cent would be royalty fees related to the categories: inventories, transactions or other.
8. While Shepard does not discuss this option, there are also independent stations that sell gasoline under their own name even if it is branded gasoline, for example see Hastings (2004). This latter category fits more closely the notion of arm's length contracts than the open dealer contracts.

9. Given the form in which the results are presented it is impossible to ascertain the statistical significance of this second result, but if one is willing to assume orthogonal regressors these results are also statistically significant at standard levels.

10. Shepard explains the choice between lessee–dealer contracts and open dealer contracts in terms of capacity volume being sufficiently high under lessee–dealer contracts to justify the royalty payments. Her empirical results are consistent with this explanation. In turn this implies that the vertically integrated solution was not feasible in the markets served by open dealers. Open dealer contracts can't replicate the vertically integrated solution due to double marginalization.

11. These divorcement laws ban or restrict refiners from having company-owned stations.

12. Of course, the degree of asset specificity, and thus the strength of this argument, can vary a great deal from one industry to the next.

13. The website of the National Association of Automobile Dealers (NADA Data) reports that in the US 17 per cent of operating profits of car dealers in 2002 came from sales of used vehicles (28.6 per cent of sales), 48 per cent of operating profits came from sales of parts and service (11.8 per cent of sales) and 35 per cent of operating profits came from new vehicle sales (59.6 per cent of sales).

14. Recently, Marx and Shaffer (2001) have shown that non-discrimination clauses in the original contract lead to maximizing the joint profit from the business if sunk costs are sufficiently low. In this case, they provide an alternative to territorial restrictions.

15. The fact that 93 per cent of percentage royalty fees are based on sales rather than profits is most likely due to the fact that sales are far easier to monitor than profits, for example Dnes (1992, p.236).

16. Incidentally, Dnes (1992) also identifies five systems that rely on a specialized input provided by the franchiser, for example Midas, which raise similar considerations. That is, the transfer price of the specialized input plays a similar role to the wholesale price in giving the franchiser an additional instrument to attain optimal levels of the system.

17. This may be one of the reasons Lafontaine (1992) was able to explain the proportion of outlets franchised far better than the percentage of royalty rates or the franchise fees, for example see Tables 5 and 6 in her study.

18. One of these studies is the one by Lafontaine (1992) previously discussed. A second one is Sen's (1993) analysis of franchise fees and royalty fees, which concludes that channel control is the main factor influencing payment design. Two of the main determinants of channel control in his view are the franchiser's commitment to the brand name and malfeasance by the franchisee, which correspond to the double moral hazard view stressed by Lafontaine (1992). The third study is Lafontaine's (1993) analysis (and rejection) of signaling models as an explanation of these dimensions of contract design in franchising.

19. An interesting study by Lafontaine and Shaw (1999) is the first one to look at dynamic issues empirically. It attempts to explain variations in the royalty rate and the franchise fee and it instruments for each of them in the relevant equation, but it does not include as an explanatory variable in these regressions the initial investment (with or without instrumenting for it). One wonders if the large amount of explanatory power generated by the firm-specific fixed effects is partly due to the omission of this variable from the regressions explaining royalty rates and franchise fees.

20. The third supposed inconsistency is that there is a positive empirical association between risk and franchising, but this is an inconsistency with the theory only if one assumes that franchisees are risk averse and franchisers are risk neutral. In any event, the analysis here has nothing to add on this issue.

21. Some of the more recent work considers new issues where this consideration may be less relevant, for example the determinants of multi-unit ownership as in Kalnins and Lafontaine (2003).

10. Retailing of services and concluding issues

In the previous nine chapters I have emphasized the role of distribution services in determining economic outcomes. Furthermore, in Chapter 1, I stressed that most of the results derived here for the retailing of goods also apply to the retailing of services. This applicability is eminently desirable from an economic viewpoint, because about 70 per cent of GDP in advanced economies is associated with activities that can be described as the production and distribution of services.[1] In view of this economic importance, it is desirable to provide additional support for our claim of applicability. A useful starting point in this endeavor is identifying explicitly the inherent characteristics of services, if any, and of distribution services in particular. Thus, in section 10.1, I consider the question, what are the 'fundamental' or defining characteristics of services, including those of the distribution services emphasized in this book?

Throughout the book I have also made reference to and even discussed in some detail situations that involve the retailing of services rather than of goods.[2] This has been done, however, without addressing consistently systematic differences that may arise between the retailing of services and the retailing of goods. Thus, in section 10.2, I consider two related questions, are there implications of these 'fundamental' characteristics of services identified in section 10.1 for their retailing? Or, more generally, are there 'fundamental' ways in which the retailing of services differs from the retailing of goods? Section 10.3 illustrates the relevance of the economic role of distribution services with respect to financial services by summarizing applications of our approach to two different segments of this industry, households and firms. Finally, section 10.4 concludes by offering a brief perspective on what the book accomplishes.

10.1 'FUNDAMENTAL' CHARACTERISTICS OF SERVICES

One way of examining this issue is through the definition of services in the economics and marketing literature. For instance, in a recent marketing text on services, Lovelock (2001, p.3) presents as one of two definitions that capture the essence of services 'A service is an act or performance offered by one party to another. Although the process may be tied to a physical product, the performance is essentially intangible and does not normally result in the ownership of any of the factors of production'. Similarly, in the economics literature Betancourt and Gautschi (2001) have suggested the following definition: 'From the perspective of a "consumer", a service can be viewed as the dual of work that the "consumer" might otherwise conduct'.[3]

The five distribution services identified in Chapter 2, section 1, satisfy both definitions. One can view each of them as tied to the physical products or goods that a retailer wants to distribute, but this is not a necessity. One can also view them as associated or tied to a service, for example restaurant meals, doctor services, the showing of films at movie theatres, and so on.[4] Finally, in some cases they can also be viewed as stand-alone services of their own, for example in some instances the provision of accessibility of location for a good or service is simply the provision of transportation services. The latter is one of the standard service categories in the national income accounts. The performance of each of these five distribution services, or the levels at which they are offered, is normally intangible. Finally, each of these five distribution services operates as a mechanism that reduces potential work for a 'consumer'. That is the essence of cost shifting stressed in Chapter 2. Needless to say many other economic activities also satisfy these two definitions, ranging from personal and government services to financial services to communication services. Definitions, however, don't take us very far in understanding the 'fundamental' characteristics of services.[5]

One of the potential 'fundamental' characteristics of services that emerges from this discussion of definitions is 'intangibility'. Unfortunately, this characteristic is not satisfied by all services. For instance, Griliches (1992, p.6) pointed out that electricity is an example of a tangible service. Electricity generation and distribution are part of the activities classified as services in the national income accounts.[6] Similarly, the provision of entertainment services through rentals of movie videos or DVDs takes place by distributing a tangible object to consumers. Hence, we were able to analyse important aspects of this process in Chapter 8, section 3, without appealing to any inherent feature of services.

Textbooks on marketing services, for example Zeithaml and Bitner (1996), usually add three more characteristics as 'fundamental': simultaneity of production and consumption, perishability or a non-storable product and heterogeneity. Notwithstanding, Lovelock's (2001) recent textbook notes these four characteristics and points out that any one of them need not apply to all services. Betancourt and Gautschi (2001) have developed a framework for the analysis of service institutions that sheds light on some of these 'fundamental' characteristics of services, their interactions with economic activities and why they may or may not apply to a particular service activity. Thus, it is useful to proceed by presenting some details of their framework and analysis.

Betancourt and Gautschi's (2001) analysis identifies three primitive or basic types of activities: production, distribution and consumption. In any particular circumstance associated with the performance of an economic activity, all three primitive types have to be involved. Nevertheless, how they are connected to each other can vary in two essential dimensions: space and time.[7] This variation then generates the possibility of performing economic activities in 25 intrinsically different ways, according to the tableau in Table 10.1.

Many commonplace economic activities that involve the retailing of goods will end up assigned to cell 25, where the primitive economic activities of production, distribution and consumption take place separately in space and time. Any economic activity involving purchases of a good produced away from a store and consumed or used away from the store premises at a later time can in principle be assigned to this cell. Yet, it is easy to think of exceptions that suggest alternative assignments. For instance, one can go to a 7/11 convenience store and buy milk that is consumed later at home but one can also patronize a 7/11 by consuming a bottled soft drink on the premises. While the former activity can be assigned to cell 25, the latter can not, since distribution and consumption are at least joint in space and perhaps also on time, in which case cell 19 would be the correct assignment.

Similarly, a non-trivial number of activities that involve the retailing of services will end up assigned to cell 1, where the primitive economic activities of production, distribution and consumption take place jointly in space and time. Any economic activity involving the purchase of a service that is primarily produced and consumed on the premises can in principle be assigned to this cell. For instance meals away from home in restaurants where the meal is

Table 10.1   Tableau of primitive economic activities

Time	{P, D, C}	D|{P, C}	C|{P, D}	P|{C, D}	P|D|C
Space					
{P, D, C}	1	2	3	4	5
D|{P, C}	6	7	8	9	10
C|{P, D}	11	12	13	14	15
P|{C, D}	16	17	18	19	20
P|D|C	21	22	23	24	25

Note: | denotes separation; { } denotes joint activities; P, D and C denote production, distribution and consumption, respectively.

produced, served (or distributed) and consumed within the relevant calendar period of time, let us say an evening, should in principle be assigned to this cell. Yet, it is again easy to think of exceptions that suggest alternative assignments. Suppose you make reservations the day before. An essential element of distribution, assurance of product delivery at the desired time, is being separated in time from other aspects of distribution of the meal as well as from production and consumption. Thus, this argues for assignment of this economic activity to cell 2.

More generally, there is a variety of forms in which services can be delivered in terms of the connections between primitive economic activities across space and time. Indeed, Betancourt and Gautschi (2001) offer as major propositions arising from this framework that 1) jointness in production, distribution and consumption is neither necessary nor sufficient to distinguish a service product from other market products and 2) one of the primary economic functions of service institutions is to separate at least some aspects of production distribution and consumption across space and time. Thus jointness of consumption and production is another 'fundamental' characteristic of service activities that need not apply to all services.[8]

The tableau also provides a convenient mechanism for discussing a third 'fundamental' characteristic of services, perishability or lack of storage possibilities. Modern technology renders perishability or lack of storage possibilities irrelevant as a defining characteristic of services in the communications and information industries. For instance teleconferencing allows separation in space between the production, distribution and consumption of visual communications, making the last row of the tableau feasible in principle for this industry. When coupled with video tapes it also allows the separation of production distribution and consumption of visual communications in time, thus rendering perishability or lack of storage possibilities irrelevant as a fundamental characteristic in this area of the communications industry.[9] Similarly, voice mail and e-mail render irrelevant perishability or lack of storage possibilities as fundamental characteristics of other areas of the communications and information industries. Indeed, it seems that one of the main purposes of these technological innovations is precisely to allow the separation of production, distribution and consumption of messages across time which makes this characteristic irrelevant.[10]

In order to prevent misunderstandings, Betancourt and Gautschi (2001) point out that the tableau is not meant to be used as a classification scheme for service institutions because the assignment of activities to cells in the tableau is sensitive to the purpose of analysis or level of aggregation. For instance, if one focuses on a trip as the consumption activity, one can think of production and consumption of the trip taking place simultaneously in space and time while distribution, if it involves the services of a travel agent at a different time and location, is occurring separately in space and time, cell 7. On the other hand, if one focuses on production and consumption of a *claim* (the airline ticket) to a trip at a travel agent's office as the consumption activity, then the producer of the claim (the airline) is separate in space from the distributor (the travel agent) and the consumer, who are joint in space while all three are joint in time when producing the claim, cell 16. This also illustrates how a distribution service (assurance of product delivery at the desired time) in the form of the claim to the trip can be viewed as jointly provided with the core service (namely the trip), as in cell 7, or as a stand-alone service or the core service itself, as in cell 16, by the choice of a level of aggregation for the definition of the service activity.

What about heterogeneity as a fourth 'fundamental' characteristic of services? There are at least two different sources of heterogeneity stressed in the literature, for example, Zeithaml and Bitner (1996, p.20). One source is that the recipient of the service is a human being and, therefore, different human beings will experience even the same service in different ways. While this is true, it is not specific to services. Human beings will experience goods such as books or flowers in different ways as well. The other source of heterogeneity is that the provider of the service is a human being and as such may not deliver the same performance all the time. While this is also true, the range of variability may be quite limited and it may not matter. For instance, in the case of aeroplane trips we don't worry about the pilot's performance unless the range of variability affects the probability of a crash or violent oscillations during a trip. While a barber's mood may be quite variable, unless one's haircut is visibly affected as a result, one rarely drops patronage. Finally some services are provided by machines; for instance, neither the mood nor the range of variability of an ATM machine leads to wide oscillations in its provision of a means of payment at the desired time and in the desired place.

In sum, the so-called four 'fundamental' characteristics of services are not that fundamental in that they don't necessarily apply to all services. Of course, a more directly relevant question is, what are their implications for the retailing of services in those settings where they do apply? To this question we now turn.

10.2   IMPLICATIONS FOR RETAILING

Perhaps the most important economic implication for retailing of any of these characteristics is the implication of jointness in production, distribution and consumption across space and time for the specification or definition of profits. Jointness in these basic coordinates for all three primitive economic activities usually implies that the costs of production and distribution of a product can not be separately identified. When this happens, distribution is subsumed under production and, instead of writing the profit equation as in equation 2.4 of section 2.4, one writes the profit equation as

$$\pi = pQ - C(Q, D, v, r),\qquad(10.1)$$

where Q is the level of output or turnover of the core product, which would normally be a service; D is a vector capturing the level of each of the distribution services we have emphasized throughout; v are the prices of the inputs used to generate distribution services; r are the prices of the inputs used to generate the core service product; and C is a cost function that now captures the costs of production and distribution of the core service product, Q, as well as the costs of producing the distribution services, D.[11]

A way of thinking about this distinction is that the specification in equation (2.4) is the one normally applied to the retailing of goods and of those services where the costs of production and distribution of a product can be identified separately. By contrast, the specification in equation (10.1) is the one normally applied to the retailing of most services, where the costs of production and distribution of a product can not be identified separately. It is also tempting to conjecture that the services to which (2.4) can be applied will be tangible services or services distributed through the use of a tangible physical product. That is certainly the case for our examples of electricity, and rentals of videos and DVDs.

In any event, for our purposes, the most important implication that comes from comparing equation (10.1) with equation (2.4) is that the economic role of distribution services in both equations is the same for all practical purposes.[12] These distribution services are outputs of the retailer and as such have the same properties in the cost function as they did in Chapter 4. Since on the demand side nothing has changed and the demand for items in Chapter 3 applied to goods as well as to services, the analysis in subsequent chapters that did not involve explicitly the cost of goods sold, or their wholesale prices, goes through exactly as before.

One practical consequence of this distinction between the retailing of goods and the retailing of services has been mentioned in the introduction, namely the classification of eating and drinking establishments with respect to the retail sector. This distinction helps explain why the US Census Bureau, in switching from the SIC classification to the NAICS classification system for industries in 1997, drops eating and drinking establishments from the retail sector classification and puts them with hotels and restaurants in the new classification. One of the basic principles of NAICS is that economic activities should be classified together, in so far as possible, according to their use of the same production function.[13]

Just as noted in Chapter 2, the inability to separate clearly production from distribution which differentiates the retailing of meals in restaurants from the retailing of goods in the retail sector has other consequences. For instance, this difference is also reflected in the very large retail gross margins of restaurants (around 60 per cent) relative to other retail sub-sectors. These large differences between sales and costs of goods sold for restaurants are mainly due to the considerable amount of production (of the meal) that takes place in the restaurant.

What are the main economic implications of non-storage for the retailing of services in those service areas where it applies? One of the dimensions of assurance of product delivery in the desired form is goods that work and services that are satisfactory. In the case of goods, they can be returned, so return policies, including warranties for example, are the institutional devices used for dealing with failure to achieve the desired form. In the case of services, they can't be returned but most can be repeated, whether or not they are storable. Hence 'return' policies often take other forms, for example refunds or future considerations. For instance, hotels and airlines provide complimentary future services when they fail to provide a satisfactory service at a point in time. Thus, the main difference introduced by this characteristic in the retailing of services is that it requires a bit more ingenuity in the design of mechanisms for providing restitution to the consumer for failure to achieve the desired form in providing the (service) product.

What are the main economic implications of lack of tangibility for the retailing of services? Intangibility of services is one of the main reasons quality is difficult to observe with precision and assess properly in the case of services. For instance, Holmstrom (1985) in a substantial early contribution writes, 'The most important one [feature of services] is the difficulty with which quality of a service can be observed or assessed.' He then goes on to discuss how contingent contracts, reputation and certification and monitoring provide institutional mechanisms in service markets that mitigate this difficulty in providing quality assurance. Indeed in Chapter 9 we already saw one of these mechanisms in operation in the retailing of gasoline. Gas stations that also provide repair services require more monitoring, due to the difficulty of assuring quality of this output dimension, and as a result they are more frequently operated as franchises than as company-owned establishments. When the core product is a good, it is possible to differentiate between the quality of the core product and the quality of the distribution services associated with its retailing; when the core product is a service, this distinction often becomes impossible with respect to at least some of the distribution services.[14]

What are the economic implications of heterogeneity, when it matters, for the retailing of services? Both sources of heterogeneity, the variability in human beings to whom the service is provided as well as the variability in the human beings providing the service, have the same consequence in that they are the other main reason quality is difficult to observe with precision and assess properly. Hence, they have the same economic implication as intangibility for the retailing of services. When the core product is a service, it becomes difficult to differentiate between the quality of the core product and the quality of some of the distribution services. If a lawyer loses a case, for example, is it because of lack of quality in the lawyer's services (the core service product), or failure to deliver these services to a particular customer (assurance of product delivery in the desired form), or even inadvertent failure of the customer to provide relevant information, or a lousy case?

Generalizations with respect to services are difficult, but it seems that these four 'fundamental' characteristics of services lead to two systematic differences between the retailing of goods and the retailing of services. First, there is use of a different specification of the profit equation for the retailing of goods and tangible services than for the retailing of most services. Second, there is greater difficulty in measuring quality when retailing services than when retailing goods. While the first difference does not affect the economic role of distribution services in retailing very much, the second difference can make it impossible to distinguish between the quality of the core service product and the quality of some of our five distribution services depending on the context.

Are there other systematic differences between the retailing of services and of goods? Perhaps, in any event there are two places to look if one wants to pursue this question. First, there is the role of the consumer in the process. In the case of the retailing of goods and tangible services, I think standard tools appropriately modified allow one to conduct the analysis effectively as demonstrated in Chapter 4, section 4. In the case of intangible services, when quality issues are important and it is difficult to separate quality in the core service from quality in assurance of product delivery in the desired form, the role of the consumer in the analysis may not be as easily reduced to demand and supply considerations within the standard economic treatments of uncertainty.

Second, there is the definition of quality. Interestingly enough, there is a literature in marketing that differentiates between two types of quality: customization quality and standardization quality. One of the differences relevant here is that the latter concept of quality is viewed as more likely to be relevant for goods and the former is viewed as more likely to be relevant for services, for example, Anderson, Fornell and Rust (1997). These authors also assert that *total* costs decrease with increases in standardization quality while they increase with increases in customization quality. Most economists would find the first part of the assertion unlikely to be true in practice, because it is difficult to think of *total* costs decreasing with any desirable dimension of output. Nevertheless, the general idea of a distinction between concepts of quality with different implications for goods and for services is promising.

10.3 APPLICATIONS TO FINANCIAL SERVICES

To complete the effort of establishing the applicability of our approach to the retailing of services, we provide details of two applications to financial services. We start with Hanak's (1992a) analysis of banking services retailing already mentioned in the introduction. She defines the function of banks (p.183) as, 'Specifically, banks provide the explicit service of intermediating a loan or deposit account, in conjunction with a host of implicit services that enhance the quality of that account, such as accessibility, information and availability of an assortment of other explicit services'. Hanak goes on to discuss in detail the distribution costs that are relevant to this intermediation process and the distribution services into which they map. Of special relevance to our present context, she notes that, in contrast to the retailing of merchandise, the explicit product in the case of banking is a distribution service itself, assurance of product delivery in the desired form with respect to liquidity services and insulation against interest rate and default risk. Moreover, it is provided through the choice of assortment of financial products available in terms of deposit and loan products. It also implies that both loans and deposits can be viewed as outputs of banks.

Hanak (1992a) derives the demand for financial services from a simple extension of the household production model to a two-period setting. She obtains price elasticities and distribution service elasticities for deposits and loans analogous to those derived in Chapter 3. Furthermore, she finds the same tendency toward gross complementarity in the demand for financial products of banks that we found in Chapter 3 with respect to items. One difference generated by this model on the demand side is that Hanak (1992a) defines the prices of the financial products in terms of discounted interest margins. For instance in the case of loans, $I^* = (i - r^m + h)/(1 + r^m)$ where I^* is the discounted interest margin on a particular loan product, i is the interest rate charged by the bank on that loan product, r^m is the market rate of interest and h is any non-interest fee charged on this loan product. Similarly in the case of deposits, $R^* = (r^m - r + h)/(1 + r^m)$ where r is the interest rate paid by the bank on the particular deposit product.

Hanak (1992a) also investigates in detail the technology for producing financial services. From her perspective two features stand out because they have been previously ignored in the banking literature. First, some implicit services such as the accessibility of location provided by bank branches are common to all or most of the financial products provided by a bank whereas other implicit services such as the accessibility of location provided by an automatic teller machine are specific and available only to a narrow range of highly liquid deposit accounts. Second, some distribution services are jointly produced in the sense that an increase in one automatically raises the level of the other. For instance, an expansion of the assortment of financial products also increases assurance of product delivery in the desired form (the desired amount of liquidity for example). One consequence of these features is that, just as in the general discussion of services in the previous section, in this application to financial services one can not use specifications of profits based on a well-defined separation of the costs of distribution and the costs of production.

Profits to be maximized in Hanak's banking firm are defined as the sum of the products of the discounted interest margins from deposit and loan products and the respective quantities of deposits and loans minus the costs of producing the deposit and loan products as well as the accompanying distribution services, plus the difference between the interest value of net worth and the interest costs of reserve requirements.[15] Several implications of the model are stressed by Hanak (1992a). Increases in the opportunity cost of time generate powerful incentives for one-stop financial shopping, including lower average prices for financial products. The pricing policy for deposits is not separable from the pricing policy for loans. Retail banking is, at best, monopolistically competitive and likely to allow for the coexistence of banking institutions providing very different levels of distribution services in the absence of regulation.

Two other implications follow from this analysis. One of them is that the demand for money by households will be affected by the levels of distribution services provided, just as any other financial product. In subsequent work using aggregate data, Hanak (1992b) shows how innovations in the provision of distribution services have affected the stability of the demand for money in the US (they are the source of the instability). While the importance of financial innovation in determining the stability of the demand for money is widely acknowledged, a typical approach to the problem is by modeling financial innovation as a deterministic trend or a random walk (Arrau et al., 1995). Yet, these same authors acknowledge that the main disadvantage of this approach 'is that it is too general to be helpful in tracing the origin of the innovation process'.

A second implication of this analysis, which Hanak (1992a) suggests as a possibility for future research, is that similar considerations should prevail in determining the demand for money by firms. Bakhache (1999) takes up the suggestion and extends Hanak's analysis to the demand for liquidity services by firms. Some of his results are similar to Hanak's in that Bakhache shows that the demand for liquidity services by firms depends on interest margins for financial products, $I = I^* (1 + r^m)$ and $R = R^* (1 + r^m)$,[16] as well as on distribution services. Nonetheless there is a major difference with respect to the demand for money by households: namely the critical role of trade credit as an alternative source of liquidity services in the demand for money by firms.

Using flow of funds aggregate data, Bakhache (1999) establishes three important and robust empirical results with respect to the demand for money by firms: first, while real money demand by firms and output need not be co-integrated, real money demand plus real trade credit is co-integrated with output. Second, there is a co-integrating vector between real money demand by firms, real trade credit, interest rates and output as predicted by the theoretical analysis. Indeed, the null hypothesis that real trade credit and real money demand by business firms are substitutes on a one-to-one basis in this relationship can't be rejected by the data. Finally, an error correction model of money demand by firms, incorporating the previously established long-run relationship, shows that increases in distribution services, measured either in terms of the number of bank branches (accessibility of location) or in terms of the number of electronic transfers (assurance of product delivery at the desired time), decrease real money demand by firms. Thus, by increasing the liquidity services provided by financial products these distribution services decrease the need for firms to hold real money balances. This result is what would be expected from his theoretical analysis.

8.4   CONCLUDING REMARKS

Just as indicated in the preface, the book integrates earlier material on the economic role of distribution services with new material that has been developed in the literature. By doing so in a systematic and rigorous way that brings together research in marketing and economics, a sound foundation is provided for a much easier continuation of this process in the future. While the integration takes place throughout the book, Chapters 2, 3 and 4 are particularly useful in this regard. Thus, they are a foundation for the analysis of topics in retailing other than the ones explicitly included here.[17] The latter is a task and a challenge for future research that one hopes is taken up by professionals in marketing, who increasingly have the necessary training in economics, and by economists, who increasingly seem to have the equally necessary interest in retailing topics.

Investigating the economic role of distribution services systematically in the book leads to a number of novel insights with respect to a wide variety of topics throughout the book, but especially in Chapters 5–7. These include, for example, the benefits for consumers of the Internet as a retail channel and the fundamental role of gross complementarity in 'loss leading', the welfare consequences of packaging, and the role of assortment in determining modern retail formats. Indeed, one of my aims has been that everyone who reads a chapter of the book should learn something new as a result. I expect some of these novel insights to become part of the conventional wisdom about retailing in due time.

Finally, whenever the choice has arisen, I have opted for covering a topic thoroughly at the expense of leaving other topics completely uncovered. Once again this strategy has been followed throughout the book, but it affects especially the last three chapters (8–10). With respect to the earlier parts, one broad area stands out as potentially fruitful for further research. Namely, the integration of the ideas developed here with the models and techniques for decision support systems presented in, for example, Leeflang et al. (2000) or Wierenga and van Bruggen (2000). With respect to the last three chapters, the possibilities are too numerous to identify individually. Yet it is worth mentioning one issue that cuts across all three chapters and that we have largely ignored throughout the book. That is, the economic role of distribution services in the development of new market forms through contract enforcement mechanisms that arise as a result of the evolution of institutions or technology, or both.

To conclude, we note that this last chapter can be viewed as providing the underpinnings for a variety of research projects, or perhaps beginnings for a new book. In particular, the previous section demonstrates how the economic role of distribution services in individual service industries can be captured and analysed. This was accomplished despite the difficulties posited by the inability to separate production from distribution in generating the core service and the fact that the core service itself is a distribution service in the case of financial services. With equivalent diligence and imagination similar difficulties can be overcome in the analysis of other service industries, where the additional difficulty of identifying quality with precision may arise.

Measuring quality with precision is not an insurmountable difficulty in service industries. This is well illustrated by Jin and Leslie's (2003) recent paper on restaurants in Los Angeles County. Despite the intangibility of the core service, by introducing the practice of publicly posting hygiene grade cards, a key dimension of product quality becomes observable by customers. Also, the authors show that it leads to a decrease in the number of food-related digestive disorders in the affected area as well as increased revenues for the relatively best performing restaurants.

NOTES

1. Incidentally, just as noted in chapter 1, this 70 per cent of GDP in advanced economies

    includes about 10–15 per cent of GDP due to the production and distribution of retail services associated mainly with the distribution of goods.

2. In particular this has been the case in the introduction, Chapter 2 and in the last two chapters.

3. It should be understood that the 'consumer' in this quotation is any economic agent occupying the demand side of a market, for example, it could be a business firm.

4. Of course, in this setting we would view them as retaining their two essential features as outputs of a firm and inputs into the household production function of 'consumers'.

5. In this particular case there are too many of them. For example, just as noted by Griliches (1992), the 1946 edition of Webster's Collegiate Dictionary has 20 different definitions of the word 'service'.

6. They are included in the US Statistical Abstract (2000), for example, under energy, gas and sanitary services.

7. The particular circumstance defining the economic activity can occur at any level of a channel, of course.

8. Since we have mentioned electricity generation and distribution as an example of a tangible service, for the sake of completeness it is useful to relate it to the tableau. The production or generation of residential electricity, for example, can take place separately from its distribution in terms of space but not in terms of time, whereas consumption is usually separate from production and distribution in space and time. Thus, it can be assigned to cell 23.

9. In terms of the tableau, it allows for the actual existence of cells 21, 23, 24 and 25 in this industry. When an activity, for example, a sporting event or a lecture, takes place and is simultaneously transmitted to other areas where it is received by the attendees to the teleconference site, cell 21 arises; if the activity is videoed and transmitted to be experienced at a later date, cell 23 arises; if the activity is videoed but not transmitted until the date at which it is to be experienced, cell 24 arises; finally, if it is videoed, transmitted and experienced at different dates, cell 25 arises.

10. In terms of the discussion in this book, voice mail, for example, is an innovation designed to provide, among other things, the maximum level of one of our distribution services: namely, assurance of product delivery at the desired time for messages.

11. Incidentally, in the analysis of business format franchises in Chapter 9 the specification of the profit equation for both franchiser, equation (9.1), and franchisee, equation (9.2), corresponds to the specification in equation (10.1), after adjustment for the existence of uncertainty.

12. One minor difference is that it is now even more difficult than before to identify in practice the outputs of a retail entity as having a quantity dimension or turnover and a service dimension or value added. Since this was not feasible before, as we saw in Chapter 4 (section 1), it merely accentuates an existing problem.

13. Another practical consequence of this distinction has been indicated in Chapter 9, where it was noted that Rao and Srinivasan (1995) use it to explain why royalty rates are higher in franchise systems that sell services to consumers than in the ones that sell goods. The nonexistence of a wholesale price in the former situation eliminates one of the two instruments needed by the franchiser to arrive at a choice of output and services consistent with the system optimum.

14. For instance, if the core product is watching a play in a theatre, it becomes impossible to disentangle whether a persistently coughing customer diminishes the quality of the core service, or the quality of the ambiance in which the service is experienced. Of course, it is also not clear how the distinction in this example matters from an economic point of view.

15. That is, this firm maximizes the discounted profits to be earned in the second period subject to the standard balance sheet constraint for models that allow banks to produce both loans and deposits, for example, Klein (1971).

16. Bakhache's model is a single-period one where the need for liquidity arises out of the need to synchronize receipts and payments. Hence, the interest margins are not discounted.

17. Parenthetically, one such topic that easily comes to mind is an extension to discrete choices of the household production model of Chapter 3.

References

Aalto-Setälä, V. (1999), *Economies of Scale, Product Differentiation and Market Power*, Ph.D. dissertation, Helsinki: Helsinski School of Economics.

Adams, W. J. and J. L.Yellen (1976), 'Commodity bundling and the burden of monopoly', *Quarterly Journal of Economics*, **90**, 475–98.

Affuso, L. (2002), 'An empirical study on contractual heterogeneity within the firm: the vertical integration–franchise contracts' mix', *Applied Economics*, **34**, 931–44.

Agrawal, J., P. E. Grimm and N. Srinivasan (1993), 'Quantity surcharges in groceries' *Journal of Consumer Affairs*, **27**, 335–56.

Ailawadi, K., N. Borin and P. Farris (1995), 'Market power and performance: a cross-industry analysis of manufacturers and retailers', *Journal of Retailing*, **3**, 211–48.

Albion, M. S. (1983), *Advertising's Hidden Effects: Manufacturer's Advertising and Retail Pricing*, Boston: Auburn House Publishing Company.

Anderson, E.W., C. Fornell and R. Rust (1997), 'Customer satisfaction, productivity and profitability: differences between goods and services', *Marketing Science*, **16**, 129–45.

Anderson, J. H. and R.R. Betancourt (2002), 'The distribution sector and the development process: are there patterns? Yes', *Economic Inquiry*, **40**, 66–76.

Arrau, P., J. De Gregorio, C. Reinhart and P. Wickham (1995), 'The demand for money in developing countries: the role of financial innovations', *Journal of Development Economics*, **46**, 317–40.

Bagwell, K. and G. Ramey, (1994), 'Coordination economies, advertising and search behavior in retail markets', *American Economic Review*, **84**, 498–517.

Baily, M. N. (1993), 'Competition, regulation and efficiency in service industries', *Brookings Papers on Economic Activity: Microeconomics*, **2**, 71–159.

Bakhache, S. (1999), *Essays on the Demand for Money by Firms*, Ph.D. dissertation, College Pk., MD: University of Maryland.

Bandyopadhyay, U. (1998), 'Distribution costs and services in the continuum of goods model', *Review of International Economics*, **6**, 164–78.

Bandyopadhyay, U. (1999), 'Trade and the distribution sector: some evidence for the OECD countries', *Canadian Journal of Economics*, **32**, 1299–312.

Barber, C. and B. Tietje (2004), 'A distribution services approach for developing effective competitive strategies against "big box" retailers', *Journal of Retailing and Consumer Services*, **11**, 98–107.

Barger, H. (1955), *Distribution's Place in the American Economy Since 1869*, Princeton: Princeton University Press.

Basker, E. (2002), 'Job creation or destruction? Labor market effects of Wal-Mart expansion', forthcoming in *Review of Economics and Statistics*.

Baumol, W. and Y. Braunstein (1977), 'Empirical study of scale economies and production complementarities: the case of journal publications' *Journal of Political Economy*, **85**, 1037–48.

Baumol, W., J. Panzar and R. Willig (1982), *Contestable Markets and the Theory of Industry Structure*, New York: Harcourt, Brace, Jovanovich, Inc.

Becker, G. S. (1965), 'A theory of the allocation of time', *Economic Journal*, **75**, 493–517.

Berné, C., J. M. Múgica and M. J. Yagüe (1999), 'Una evaluación de los modelos de regresión switching para la medición de la productividad en el comercio minorista', *Economia Industrial*, (326), 159–72.

Betancourt, R.R. (1993), *An Analysis of the US Distribution System*, Paris: OECD.

Betancourt, R.R. and D. A. Gautschi (1986), 'The evolution of retailing: a suggested economic interpretation', *International Journal of Research in Marketing*, **3**, 217–32.

Betancourt, R.R. and D.A. Gautschi (1988), 'The economics of retail firms', *Managerial and Decision Economics*, **9**, 133–44.

Betancourt, R.R. and D.A. Gautschi (1990), 'Demand complementarities, household production and retail assortments', *Marketing Science*, **9**, 146–61.

Betancourt, R.R. and D.A. Gautschi (1992a), 'The output of retail activities: French evidence', *Applied Economics*, **24**, 1043–52.

Betancourt, R.R. and D.A. Gautschi (1992b), 'The demand for retail products and the household production model: new views on complementarity and substitutability', *Journal of Economic Behavior and Organization*, **17**, 257–75.

Betancourt, R.R. and D.A. Gautschi (1993a), 'Two essential characteristics of retail markets and their economic consequences', *Journal of Economic Behavior and Organization*, **21**, 277–94.

Betancourt, R.R. and D.A. Gautschi (1993b), 'The outputs of retail activities: concepts, measurement and evidence from US census data' *Review of Economics and Statistics*, **75**, 294–301.

Betancourt, R.R. and D.A. Gautschi (1996), 'An international comparison of the determinants of retail gross margins', *Empirica*, **23**, 173–89.

Betancourt, R.R. and D.A. Gautschi (1998), 'Distribution services and economic power in a channel', *Journal of Retailing*, **74**, 37–60.

Betancourt, R.R. and D.A. Gautschi (2001), 'Product innovation in services: a framework for analysis', in M. R. Baye and J. P. Nelson (eds), *Advances in Applied Microeconomics: Advertising and Differentiated Products* (Volume 10), Amsterdam and Greenwich, CT: JAI Press.

Betancourt, R. R. and M. Malanoski (1999), 'An estimable model of super-market behavior: prices, distribution services and some effects of competition', *Empirica*, **26**, 55–73.

Bhatnagar, A. and B. Ratchford (2000), 'A theory of retail margins and assortments', mimeo, R.H. Smith School of Business, University of Maryland.

Biglaiser, G. and J. W. Friedman (1999), 'Adverse selection with competitive inspection', *Journal of Economics and Management Strategy*, **8**, 1–32.

Blair R. and F. Lafontaine (2003), 'Legislating exclusive territories: encroachment in franchising and proposed solutions', mimeo, University of Michigan Business School.

Blass, A.A. and D.W Carlton (2001), 'The choice of organizational form in gasoline retailing and the cost of laws that limit that choice', *Journal of Law and Economics*, **44**, 511–24.

Blattberg, R., R. Briesch and E. Fox (1995),'How promotions work', *Marketing Science*, **14**, 122–32.

Bliss, C. (1988), 'A theory of retail pricing', *Journal of Industrial Economics*, **36**, 372–91.

Bloch, P.H., N.M. Ridgeway and S.A. Dawson (1994), 'The shopping mall as consumer habitat', *Journal of Retailing*, **71**, 23–42.

Boskin, M. J., E. R. Dulberger, Z. Griliches, R. J. Gordon and D. Jorgensen (1996), 'Toward a more accurate measure of the cost of living', Final Report to the US Senate Finance Committee.

Bresnahan, T.F. and P.C. Reiss (1985), 'Dealer and manufacturer margins', *Rand Journal of Economics*, **16**, 253–68.

Brynjolfsson, E. and M. D. Smith (2000), 'Frictionless commerce? A comparison of internet and conventional retailers', *Management Science*, **46**, 563–85.

Brynjolfsson, E. and M. D. Smith and Y. Hu (2003), 'Customer surplus in the digital economy: estimating the value of increased product variety', forthcoming, *Management Science*.

Bucklin, L. (1973), *Productivity in Marketing*, Chicago, Illinois: American Marketing Association.

Bultez, A. and P. Naert (1988), 'S.H.A.R.P.: Shelf-Allocation for Retailers' Profit', *Marketing Science*, **7**, 211–31.

Burstein, A.T., J.C. Neves and S. Rebelo (2003), 'Distribution costs and real exchange rate dynamics during exchange rate based stabilizations', *Journal of Monetary Economics*, **50**, 1189–214.

Carbajo, J., D. de Meza and D. J. Seidman (1990), 'A strategic motivation for commodity bundling', *Journal of Industrial Economics*, **38**, 283–98.

Carroll, K. and D. Coates (1999), 'Teaching price discrimination', *Southern Economic Journal*, **66**, 466–80.

Caves, D., L. Christensen and E. Diewert (1982), 'The economic theory of index numbers and the measurement of input output and productivity', *Econometrica*, **50**, 1393–1404.

Chae, S. (1992), 'Bundling subscription TV channels: a case of natural bundling', *International Journal of Industrial Organization*, **10**, 213–30.

Chandler, A.D. (1977), *The Visible Hand: The Managerial Revolution in American Business*, Cambridge, MA: Harvard University Press.

Chevalier, J. A. (1995), 'Capital structure and product-market competition: empirical evidence from the supermarket industry', *American Economic Review*, **85**, 415–35.

Chevalier, J. A., A. K. Kashyap and P. E. Rossi (2003), 'Why don't prices rise during periods of peak demand? Evidence from scanner data', *American Economic Review*, **93**, 15–37.

Christensen, L. and W. Greene (1976), 'Economies of scale in US electric power generation', *Journal of Political Economy*, **84**, 655–76.

Coase, R.H. (1937), 'The nature of the firm', *Economica*, **4**, 386–405.

Coughlan, A. and C. Ingene (2002), 'A theory of functional shifting in distribution channels', mimeo, Department of Marketing, Northwestern University.

Dana, J. and K. Spier (2001), 'Revenue sharing and vertical control in the video rental industry', *Journal of Industrial Economics*, **49**, 223–45.

Dawson, J. (1993), *The Distribution Sector in the UK*, Paris: OECD.

De Palma, A., R. Lindsey, B. von Hohenbalken and D. West (1994), 'Spatial price and variety competition in an urban retail market' *International Journal of Industrial Organization*, **12**, 331–57.

Deacon, R. and J. Sonstelie (1991), 'Price controls and rent dissipation with endogenous transaction costs', *American Economic Review*, **81**, 1361–73.

Dean, E. and K. Kunze (1992), 'Productivity measurement in the service industries', in Z. Griliches (ed.), *Output Measurement in the Service Sector*, Chicago: University of Chicago Press, pp. 73–107.

Deaton, A. and J. Muellbauer (1980), *Economics and Consumer Behavior*, Cambridge, UK and New York, US: Cambridge University Press.

Divakar, S. and B. Ratchford (1995), 'Estimating the demand and supply for retail services', mimeo, Department of Marketing, SUNY at Buffalo.

Dixit, A. (1983), 'Vertical integration in a monopolistically competitive industry', *International Journal of Industrial Organization*, **1**, 63–78.

Dixit, A. and J. Stiglitz (1977), 'Monopolistic competition and optimum product diversity', *American Economic Review*, **67**, 297–308.

Dnes, A.W. (1992), *Franchising: A Case-study Approach*, Aldershot, England and Brookfield, Vermont: Avebury Ashgate Publishing Limited.

Dudey, M. (1990), 'Competition by choice: the effect of consumer search on firm location decisions', *American Economic Review*, **80**, 1092–104.

Ehrlich, I. and L. Fisher (1982), 'The derived demand for advertising: a theoretical and empirical investigation', *American Economic Review*, **72**, 366–88.

Elberfeld, W. (2002), 'Market size and vertical integration: Stigler's hypothesis reconsidered', *Journal of Industrial Economics*, **50**, 23–42.

Eppli, M. and J. Shilling (1995), 'Large-scale shopping centers development opportunities', *Land Economics*, **71**, 35–41.

Feenstra, R. and M. Shapiro (2003), 'High frequency substitution and the measurement of price indexes', in R. Feenstra and M. Shapiro (eds), *Scanner Data and Price Indexes*, Chicago: University of Chicago Press, pp. 123–46.

Fitzell, P. (1998), *The Explosive Growth of Private Labels in North America: Past, Present and Future, A Flickinger Family Private Label Study*, New York: Global Books.

Foster, L., J. Haltiwanger and C. Krizan (2002), 'The link between aggregate and micro productivity growth: evidence from retail trade', mimeo, Center for Economic Studies, US Bureau of the Census.

Fuchs, V. (1968), *The Service Economy*, New York, NY: Columbia University Press.

Furubotn, E. and R. Richter (1997), *Institutions and Economic Theory*, Ann Arbour, Michigan: University of Michigan Press.

Fuss, M. and D. McFadden (1978), *Production Economics: A Dual Approach to Theory and Applications*, Amsterdam: North Holland Press.

Geithman, F. E. and B. W. Marion (1993), 'Testing for market power in supermarket prices: a review of the Kaufman-Handy/ERS study', in R.W. Cotterill (ed.), *Competitive Strategy Analysis in the Food System*, Boulder: Westview Press, pp. 253–91.

Gerstner, E. and J. D. Hess (1987), 'Why do hot dogs come in packs of 10 and buns in 8s and 12s: a demand side investigation' *Journal of Business*, **60**, 491–517.

Gleason, S. and D. Hosken (1998), 'An example of economic analysis in antitrust litigation', mimeo, Washington, DC: Federal Trade Commission.

Goldsmith, J. V. (2002), *Essays on Consumer Access to new Products and Technologies*, Ph.D. dissertation, College Pk., MD: University of Maryland.

Gong, B. and R. Sickles (1992), 'Finite sample evidence on the performance of stochastic frontiers and data envelopment analysis', *Journal of Econometrics*, **51**, 259–84.

Griliches, Z. (1992), *Output Measurement in the Service Sector*, Chicago: University of Chicago Press.

Grossman, G. and E. Helpman (2002), 'Integration versus outsourcing in industry equilibrium', *Quarterly Journal of Economics*, **117**, 85–120.

Hanak, E. (1992a), 'A service based theory of retail banking', *Managerial and Decision Economics*, **13**, 183–200.

Hanak, E. (1992b), *A Service Based Theory of Retail Banking, with an Application to the Estimation of Money Demand*, Ph.D. dissertation, College Park, MD: University of Maryland.

Hastings, J. (2004), 'Vertical relationships and competition in retail gasoline markets', *American Economic Review*, **94**, 317–28.

Henderson, J. M. and R. Quandt (1980), *Microeconomic Theory: A Mathematical Approach*, New York, NY: McGraw-Hill.

Hoch, S.J., B. Kim, A.L. Montgomery and P. E. Rossi (1995), 'Determinants of store-level price elasticity', *Journal of Marketing Research*, **32**, 17–29.

Holmstrom, B. (1985), 'The provision of services in a market economy', in R. P. Inman (ed.), *Managing the Service Economy: Prospects and Problems*, London: Cambridge University Press, pp. 183–213.

Horowitz, A. (2000), 'Pricing in a vertical channel with fixed costs: a sticky price equilibrium with e-commerce implications', mimeo, Department of Economics, University of Arkansas.

Hosken, D. and D. Reiffen (2004), 'Patterns of retail price variation', forthcoming, *Rand Journal of Economics*.

Hosken, D., D. Matsa and D. Reiffen (2001), 'Pricing dynamics of multiproduct retailers', in M. R. Baye and J. P. Nelson (eds), *Advances in Applied Microeconomics: Advertising and Differentiated Products* (Volume 10), Amsterdam: JAI Press, pp. 129–53.

Hotelling, H. (1929), 'Stability in competition', *Economic Journal*, **39**, 41–57.

Ingene, C. (1984a), 'Productivity and functional shifting in spatial retailing' *Journal of Retailing*, **60**, 15–36.

Ingene, C. (1984b), 'Scale economies in American retailing: a cross industry comparison', *Journal of Macromarketing*, **4**, 49–63.

International Franchise Association (2000), *The Profile of Franchising: A Statistical Abstract of 1998 UFOC Data*, www.franchise.org/edufound/profile/profile.asp.

Ito, T. and M. Maruyama (1991), 'Is the Japanese distribution system really efficient?', in P. Krugman (ed.), *Trade With Japan*, Chicago: University of Chicago Press, pp. 149–73.

Jarmin, R., S. Klimek and J. Miranda (2002), 'Firm entry and exit in the US retail sector, 1977–1997', mimeo, Center for Economic Studies, US Bureau of the Census.

Jeuland, A. and S. Shugan (1983), 'Managing channel profits', *Marketing Science*, **2**, 237–72.

Jin, G.J. and P. Leslie (2003), 'The effects of information on product quality: the evidence from restaurant hygiene grade cards', *Quarterly Journal of Economics*, **118**, 409–51.

Johnson, A., D. Porter, T. Cobolla and R. Dolamore (2000), *Productivity in Australia's Retail and Wholesale Trade*, Canberra: Productivity Commission Staff Research Paper.

Kadiyali, V., P. Chintagunta and N. Vilcassim (2000), 'Manufacturer retailer channel interactions and implications for channel power: an empirical investigation of pricing in a local market', *Marketing Science*, **19**, 127–48.

Kalnins, A. and F. Lafontaine (2003), 'Multi-unit ownership in franchising: evidence from fast-food restaurants in Texas', forthcoming, *Rand Journal of Economics*.

Kapinos, A. (2002), 'Two decades of the grocery channel: division of profits and changes in performance', mimeo, Department of Marketing, University of California (Berkeley).

Katz, M. (1989), 'Vertical contractual relationships', in R. Schmalensee and R.D. Willig (eds), *The Handbook of Industrial Organization*, Amsterdam: North Holland and New York, US: Elsevier Science Publishers, pp. 655–721.

Kaufman, P. J. and F. Lafontaine (1994), 'Costs of control: source of economic rents for McDonald's franchises', *Journal of Law and Economics*, **37**, 417–53.

Kaufman, P.R. and C. R. Handy (1993), 'The Geithman-Marion review of the ERS supermarket pricing study: a response', in R.W. Cotterill (ed.), *Competitive Strategy Analysis in the Food System*, Boulder: Westview Press, pp. 293–310.

Khan, M.A. (1999), *Restaurant Franchising* (second edn), New York: Van Nostrand Reinhold Publishing Company.

Klein, B. (1980), 'Transaction cost determinants of 'unfair' contract arrangements', *American Economic Review*, **70**, 356–62.

Klein, M. A. (1971), 'A theory of the banking firm', *Journal of Money Credit and Banking*, **3**, 205–18.

Koelemeijer, K. and H. Oppewal (1999), 'Assessing the effects of assortment and ambiance: a choice experimental approach', *Journal of Retailing*, **75**, 295–318.

Kranton, R.E. and D. Minehart (2000), 'Network versus vertical integration', *Rand Journal of Economics*, **31**, 570–601.

Kranton, R.E. and D. Minehart (2001), 'A theory of buyer–seller networks', *American Economic Review*, **91**, 485–504.

Lach, S. and D. Tsiddon (1996), 'Staggering and synchronization in price-setting: evidence from multiproduct firms', *American Economic Review*, **86**, 1175–96.

Lachner, J., U. Tager and G. Weitzel (1993), *A Country Study of Distribution Systems: Contribution for the Federal Republic of Germany*, Paris: OECD.

Lafontaine, F. (1992), 'Agency theory and franchising: some empirical results', *Rand Journal of Economics*, **23**, 263–83.

Lafontaine, F. (1993), 'Contractual arrangements as signaling devices: evidence from franchising', *Journal of Law, Economics and Organization*, **9**, 256–89.

Lafontaine, F. and K.L. Shaw (1999), 'The dynamics of franchise contracting: evidence from panel data', *Journal of Political Economy*, **107**, 1041–80.

Lafontaine, F. and M.E. Slade (1997), 'Retail contracting: theory and practice', *Journal of Industrial Economics*, **45**, 1–25.

Laitinen, K. and H. Theil (1978), 'Supply and demand of the multiproduct firm', *European Economic Review*, **11**, 107–54.

Lal, R. (1990), 'Improving channel coordination through franchising', *Marketing Science*, **10**, 299–318.

Lal, R. and C. Matutes (1989), 'Price competition in multimarket duopolies', *Rand Journal of Economics*, **20**, 516–37.

Lal, R. and C. Matutes (1994), 'Retail pricing and advertising strategies', *Journal of Business*, **67**, 345–70.

Lal, R. and C. Narasimhan (1996), 'The inverse relationship between manufacturer and retail margin: a theory', *Marketing Science*, **15**, 132–51.

Lal, R. and R. Rao (1997), 'Supermarket competition: the case of everyday low pricing', *Marketing Science*, **16**, 60–80.

Lancaster, K. J. (1966), 'A new approach of consumer theory', *Journal of Political Economy*, **74**, 132–57.

Lee, E. and R. Staelin (1997), 'Vertical strategic interaction: implications for channel pricing strategy', *Marketing Science*, **16**, 185–207.

Leeflang, P.S.H., D.R. Wittink, M. Wedel and P.A. Naert (2000), *Building Models for Marketing Decisions*, Norwell, MA and Dordrecht, the Netherlands: Kluwer Academic Publishers.

Leibtag, E.S. (2002), *Determinants of Retail Price Margins and Quality Adjustment of Price Indices in Retail Food Stores*, Ph.D. dissertation, University of Maryland.

Lewbel, A. (1985), 'Bundling of substitutes or complements', *International Journal of Industrial Organization*, **3**, 101–07.

Liebowitz, S.J. (2002), *Re-Thinking the Network Economy: The True Forces that Drive the Digital Marketplace*, New York: AMACOM.

Lovelock, C. (2001), *Services Marketing: People, Technology, Strategy*, (fourth edn), New Jersey: Prentice Hall.

Lutz, N. (1995), 'Ownership rights and incentives in franchising', *Journal of Corporate Finance*, **2**, 103–31.

McAfee, P. R., J. McMillan and M. D. Whinston (1989), 'Multiproduct monopoly, commodity bundling and correlation of values', *Quarterly Journal of Economics*, **104**, 371–83.

MacGee, J. (2002), 'Distribution, trade and relative prices', mimeo, Department of Economics, University of Western Ontario.

McKeever, J. R. and N. Griffin (1977), *Shopping Center Development Handbook*, Washington, DC: Urban Land Institute.

Maruyama, M. (1993), *A Country Study of the Distribution System in Japan*, Paris: OECD.

Marx, L.M. and G. Shaffer (2001), 'Opportunism and nondiscrimination clauses', mimeo, Simon School of Business, University of Rochester.

Mathewson, G.F. and R.A. Winter (1983), 'Vertical integration by contractual restraints in spatial markets', *Journal of Business*, **56**, 497–517.

Mathewson, G.F. and R.A. Winter (1984), 'An economic theory of vertical restraints', *Rand Journal of Economics*, **15**, 27–38.

Mathewson, G.F. and R.A. Winter (1985), 'The economics of franchise contracts', *Journal of Law and Economics*, **28**, 503–26.

Mathewson, G.F. and R.A. Winter (1986), 'The economics of vertical restraints in distribution', in F. Mathewson and J. Stiglitz (eds), *New Development in the Analysis of Market Structure*, Cambridge, MA: MIT Press, pp. 211–36.

Mathewson, G.F. and R.A. Winter (1994), 'Territorial rights in franchising contracts', *Economic Inquiry*, **32**, 181–92.

Matutes, C. and P. Regibeau (1992), 'Compatibility and bundling of complementary goods in duopoly', *Journal of Industrial Economics*, **40**, 37–54.

Messerlin, P. (1993), *The French Distribution Industry and the Openness of the French Economy*, Paris: OECD.

Messinger, P. and C. Narasimhan (1995), 'Has power shifted in the grocery channel?', *Marketing Science*, **14**, 189–223.

Messinger, P. and C. Narasimhan (1997), 'A model of retail formats based on consumers economizing on shopping time', *Marketing Science*, **16**, 1–23.

Michael, S.C. (1994), 'Competition in organizational form: mail order versus retail stores, 1910–1940', *Journal of Economic Behavior and Organization*, **23**, 269–86.

Moorthy, K. (1988), 'Product and price competition in a duopoly', *Marketing Science*, 7, 141–68.

Moorthy, K., B.T. Ratchford and D. Talukdar (1997), 'Consumer information search revisited', *Journal of Consumer Research*, **23**, 263–77.

Mortimer, J.H. (2002), 'The effects of revenue-sharing contracts on welfare in vertically separated markets: evidence from the video rental industry', Harvard Institute of Economic Research, Discussion Paper 1964.

Mulhern, F. J. and R. P. Leone (1991), 'Implicit price bundling of retail products: a multi-product approach to maximizing store profitability', *Journal of Marketing*, **7**, 63–76.

Mundlak, Y. (1996), 'Production function estimation: reviving the primal', *Econometrica*, **64**, 431–38.

Muth, R.F. (1966), 'Household production and consumer demand functions', *Econometrica*, **34**, 699–708.

Nooteboom, B. (1983), 'Productivity growth in the grocery trade', *Applied Economics*, **15**, 649–64.

Nooteboom, B. (1985), 'A mark-up model of retail margins', *Applied Economics*, **17**, 647–67.

Nooteboom, B., A. Kleijweg and R. Thurik (1988), 'Normal costs and demand effects in price setting', *European Economic Review*, **32**, 999–1011.

Ofer, G. (1973), 'Returns to scale in retail trade', *Review of Income and Wealth*, **19**, 363–84.

Oi, W. (1992), 'Productivity in the distributive trades: The shopper and the economics of massed reserves', in Z. Griliches (ed.) *Output Measurement in the Service Sector*, Chicago: University of Chicago Press.

Ortega, B. (1998), *In Sam We Trust: The Untold Story of Sam Walton and How Wal-Mart is Devouring America*, New York: Times Books.

Palmer, J.W. (1997), 'Electronic commerce in retailing: differences across retailing formats', *The Information Society*, **13**, 97–108.

Pan, X., B. Ratchford and V. Shankar (2002), 'Can price dispersion in online markets be explained by differences in e-tailer service quality?', *The Journal of Academy of Marketing Science*, **30**, 433–45.

Parsons, L. (1994), 'Productivity versus relative efficiency in marketing: past and present', in G. Lillien, L. Gilles and B. Pras (eds), *Research Traditions in Marketing*, New York: Kluwer Academic Publishers, pp. 169–96.

Pashigian, B.P. (1961), *The Distribution of Automobiles, An Economic Analysis of the Franchise System*, Englewood Cliffs, NJ: Prentice Hall.

Pashigian, B.P. and E. D. Gould (1998), 'Internalizing externalities: the pricing of space in shopping malls', *Journal of Law and Economics*, **41**, 115–42.

Pellegrini, L. and L. Cardani (1993), *The Italian Distribution System*, Paris: OECD.

Pepall, L., D.J. Richards and G. Norman (1999), *Industrial Organization: Contemporary Theory and Practice*, Cincinnati: South Western College Publishing.

Perry, M.K. (1989), 'Vertical integration: determinants and effects', in R. Schmalensee and R. Willig (eds), *Handbook of Industrial Organization*, Amsterdam: North Holland and New York, US: Elsevier Science Publishers, pp 183–255.

Perry, M.K. and R.H. Groff, (1985), 'Resale price maintenance and forward integration into a monopolistically Competitive Industry', *Quarterly Journal of Economics*, **100**, 1293–311.

Perry, M.K. and R. Porter (1990), 'Can resale price maintenance or franchise fees correct sub-optimal levels of retail services?', *International Journal of Industrial Organization*, **8**, 115–41.

Pesendorfer, M. (2002), 'Retail sales. A study of pricing behavior in supermarkets', *Journal of Business*, **75**, 33–66.

Preston, L. (1962), 'Markups, leaders and discrimination in retail pricing', *Journal of Farm Economics*, **444**, 291–306.

Rao, R.C. and S. Srinivasan (1995), 'Why are royalty rates higher in service-type franchises?', *Journal of Economics and Management Strategy*, **4**, 7–31.

Ratchford, B. (2003), 'Has the productivity of retail food stores really declined,'*Journal of Retailing*, **79**, 171–82.

Ratchford, B. and G. Stoops (1992), 'An econometric model of a retail firm', *Managerial and Decision Economics*, **13**, 223–32.

Ratchford, B., X. Pan and V. Shankar (2003), 'On the efficiency of internet markets for consumer goods', *Journal of Public Policy and Marketing*, **22**, 4–16.

Ray, D. (1998) *Development Economics*, Princeton: Princeton University Press.

Reinsdorf, M. (1992), 'Changes in comparative price and changes in market share: evidence from the BLS point of purchase survey', *Managerial and Decision Economics*, **13**, 233–45.

Richards, T. J. (1999), 'A dynamic model of fresh fruit promotion: a household production approach', *American Journal of Agricultural Economics*, **81**, 195–211.

Robinson, E. (1958), *The Structure of Competitive Industry*, Chicago: University of Chicago Press.

Romano, R. (1994), 'Double moral hazard and resale price maintenance', *Rand Journal of Economics*, **25**, 455–66.

Rotemberg, J. and G. Saloner (1986), 'A supergame-theoretic model of business cycle and price wars during booms', *American Economic Review*, **76**, 390–407.

Salinger, M. A. (1995), 'A graphical analysis of bundling', *Journal of Business*, **68**, 85–98.

Salop, S. and J. Stiglitz (1977), 'Bargains and rip-offs: a model of monopolistically competitive price dispersion', *Review of Economic Studies*, **44**, 493–510.

Santos-Requejo, L. (1996), *Factores Determinantes del Margen de las Empresas Minoristas en España*, Ph.D. dissertation, Salamanca: University of Salamanca.

Sayman, S., S.J. Hoch and J.S. Raju (2002), 'Positioning of store brands', *Marketing Science*, **21**, 378–97.

Sen, K.C. (1993), 'The use of initial fees and royalties in business-format franchising', *Managerial and Decision Economics*, **24**, 58–77.

Sharkey, W. (1982), *The Theory of Natural Monopoly*, London: Cambridge University Press.

Shaw, S., D. Nisbet and J. Dawson (1989), 'Economies of scale in UK supermarkets: some preliminary findings, *International Journal of Retailing*, **4**, 12–26.

Shepard, A. (1993), 'Contractual form, retail price, and asset characteristics in gasoline retailing', *Rand Journal of Economics*, **24**, 58–77.

Simon, H. (1989), *Price Management*, Amsterdam: Elsevier Science Publishers (North-Holland).

Smith, A. and D. Hitchens (1985), *Productivity in the Distributive Trades*, London: Cambridge University Press.

Smith, M. and E. Brynjolsson (2001) 'Customer decision making at an internet shopbot: brand still matters, *Journal of Industrial Economics*, **49**, 541–58.

Smith, R. (1982), 'Franchise regulation: an economics analysis of state restrictions on automobile distribution', *Journal of Law and Economics*, **25**, 125–57.

Spence, M. (1976), 'Product selection, fixed costs, and monopolistic competition', *Review of Economic Studies*, **43**, 217–35.

Stern, L.W. and A.J. El-Ansary (1992), *Marketing Channels*, Englewood Cliffs, NJ: Prentice Hall.

Stremersch, S. and G. Tellis (2002), 'Strategic bundling of products and prices: a new synthesis for marketing', *Journal of Marketing*, **66**, 55–72.

Syrquin, M. and H. Chenery (1989), 'Patterns of development: 1950–1985', *World Bank Discussion Paper*, No. 41.

Thompson, S. (1994), 'The franchise life cycle: a contractual solution to the Penrose effect', *Journal of Economic Behavior and Organization*, **24**, 207–18.

Thurik, A. R. (1981), 'Transaction size per customer in retailing: theoretical and empirical aspects concerning French supermarkets, Research Paper 8106, Research Institute for Small and Medium Sized Business in the Netherlands.

Thurik, A. R. (1994), 'Comments', in G. Lillien, L. Gilles and B. Pras (eds), *Research Traditions in Marketing*, New York: Kluwer Academic Publishers, pp. 197–200.

Tirole, J. (1988), *The Theory of Industrial Organization*, Cambridge, MA: The MIT Press.

US Bureau of the Census (1991, 1998, 1999, 2000, 2001), *Statistical Abstract of the United States*, Washington, DC: Department of Commerce.

Vance, S.S. and R.V. Scott (1994), *Wal-Mart: A History of Sam Walton's Retail Phenomenon*, New York: Twayne Publishers and Toronto: Maxwell Macmillan Canada.

Varian, H. (1984), *Microeconomic Analysis,* New York: W.W. Norton & Company.

Walden, M. A. (1988), 'Why unit prices of supermarket products vary', *The Journal of Consumer Affairs*, **22**, 74–84.

Waldfogel, J. and L. Chen (2003), 'Does information undermine brand?: Information intermediary usage and preference for branded web retailers', mimeo, The Wharton School, University of Pennsylvania.

Warner, E. J. and R. B. Barsky (1995), 'The timing and magnitude of retail store markdowns: evidence from weekends and holiday', *Quarterly Journal of Economics*, **110**, 321–52.

Wernerfelt, B. (1994), 'An efficiency criterion for marketing design', *Journal of Marketing Research*, **31**, 462–70.

West, D.S. (1992), 'An empirical analysis of retail chains and shopping center similarity', *Journal of Industrial Economics*, **40**, 201–21.

West, D.S. (2000), 'Double marginalization and privatization in liquor retailing', *Review of Industrial Organization*, **16**, 395–415.

Whitin, T.M. (1952), 'Inventory control in theory and practice', *Quarterly Journal of Economics*, **67**, 505–21.

Wibe, S. (1993), *The Distribution System in Sweden*, Paris: OECD.

Wierenga, B. and G. van Bruggen (2000), *Marketing Management Support Systems: Principles, Tools and Implementation*, Norwell, MA and Dordrecht, the Netherlands: Kluwer Academic Publishers.

Williamson, O. (1985), *The Economic Institutions of Capitalism*, New York: Free Press.

Winter, R. (1993), 'Vertical control and price versus non-price competition', *Quarterly Journal of Economics*, **108**, 61–76.

Zeithaml, V.A. and M.J. Bitner (1996), *Services Marketing*, London and New York: McGraw-Hill.

Index